Just Out of Reach:

My Challenges & Triumphs
with Co-Dependence and ADHD

By: Kathleen O'Brien Iverson

(NKJV) New King James Version Scripture taken from the New King James Version®. Copyright © 1982 by Thomas Nelson. Used by permission. All rights reserved.

(NLT) Holy Bible, New Living Translation, copyright © 1996, 2004, 2015 by Tyndale House Foundation. Used by permission of Tyndale House Publishers, Inc., Carol Stream, Illinois 60188. All rights reserved.

(GNT) Good News Translation® (Today's English Version, Second Edition) © 1992 American Bible Society. All rights reserved.

(KJ) King James Bible, Text courtesy of BibleProtector.com, © 2012, Used by Permission

(WEB) World English Bible, public domain.

ISBN: #9798575546153

Testimonials

"Kathleen O'Brien Iverson's *Just Out of Reach: My Challenges and Triumphs with Co-Dependence and ADHD* is an apt title for her story with the challenges she faced. She shares her stories of life's ups and downs, triumphs and painful losses, from the later perspective of the role they played in frustrating her heart's intentions. I recommend this book for others struggling to overcome the limitations of ADHD and co-dependence for those who love to read how others have reflected on their lives."
- Dr. Clark Barshinger, Psychologist

"Kathleen created a truly honest, transparent, authentic account of a life that has always found a way to rise above challenging situations and be better. This piece of art demonstrates all of life's intersections and the unlimited potential for success when you stay determined! This is for men and women but if you are a woman reading this story you will be empowered to stay on the path of your vision and never again believe you cannot reach your goals! Embracing your strengths and weakness is a pathway to opportunity."
– Connie Catalano

"Kathleen's memoir was very interesting to me personally. We went to high school together and Kathleen's experiences paralleled mine over the same time. I was impressed with the scope of Kathleen's accomplishments in her personal life and in her career. Joining the Navy and leaving home after college was a brave decision. I really appreciated how Kathleen was able to manage her attention deficit disorder while also benefiting from, growing and ultimately excelling in the Navy environment. A very enjoyable journey!"
- Terry McCarthy Alsterda

"It has been a huge learning experience working with Kathleen Iverson, on her first book, *Just Out of Reach: My Challenges & Triumphs with Co-Dependence and ADHD*. It is not until we read deeply into the lives of others—through their highs, their lows and everything else under heaven—do we really come to know, understand and love them regardless of how they are wired. The author has done an impeccable job sharing her struggles with ADHD, her career in the Navy, and her search for the love of her life."
– Barbara Alpert, Author of *Arise My Daughter*

Dedication

To my lovely daughter, Christina Marie Pepperz. I would not have even thought I could actually write a book, if not for my drive to let you know more about my life. I am so proud of you and love you more than you could ever know. Teeny, I hope this answers all your questions!

To my Aunt Nancy Hodges, who passed away in April, 2020 at 87 years old. She was always there to listen and give advice. She cleaned up after me when I was little, joked with me to cheer me up, and loved me when I was hurting.

To my cousins Pat and Rosalie O'Brien for being at the hospital for me when my brother, Michael was dying and for giving me insight into our family history. Pat passed away in July, 2017 and I miss him a lot.

This book is also dedicated to all who suffer from Attention Deficit Hyperactivity Disorder (ADHD) and their families and friends. I hope that my transparent story is of help to you.

To those suffering from an addiction and/or co-dependence and those that love you, I pray this book will give insight and hope for the future.

To my fellow enlisted, officers and retired members of the U.S. Navy, thank you for your dedication and service. I am so proud to be part of this professional military organization, whether on shore, at sea or retired.

Acknowledgments

I am grateful to my beloved husband, Bill Iverson, for putting up with me while writing this book, causing us not being able to enjoy our retirement together. I love you with all my heart, soul and spirit. Let the good times begin, baby!

Of course, I also want to thank my mentor, Barbara Alpert, author of *Arise My Daughter: A Journey from Darkness to Light* and several other Christian books, who inspired me to write my story and kept encouraging me to keep at it. Not only that, but she spent countless hours by my side giving me advice and helping me along the way to get this book published.

Big thank-you to my close friends, Karen Foster (formerly Karen Perry) and Connie Catalano, for reading this manuscript, giving me suggestions and encouraging me all the way. I love you both.

In addition, I am grateful to my friends Lois Burke, Carole Stephens, Valerie Beebe, Terry McCarthy Alsterda, Lorraine Amideo Brown, Jean Bertoldi Miazga and Skip Amideo for reading all or parts of this manuscript. Your participation encouraged me to become the author I always dreamed of being.

Thanks to Lawrence Russell, Valerie Beebe, Lorraine Amideo Brown, Karen O'Brien; Cousins: Mike, Jack and Dennis O'Brien for providing photos.

Sincere thanks to Dr. Clark Barshinger, Psychologist, for his encouragement, wisdom, ideas, and patience during the writing process of my book. I will be forever grateful.

Posthumous thanks to Bill Amideo Sr. for the early pictures in our Glenview neighborhood, which are included in this book.

TABLE OF CONTENTS

TABLE OF CONTENTS

(Made with emoji me)

Like me, many of my friends in the Navy are very patriotic, so I created an emoji to show how I feel about serving the USA.
- Kathleen Iverson

Prologue: *The Blue Sweater*

*Too many of us are not living our dreams
because we are living our fears.*

— *Les Brown*[1]

I saw it in the window across the street while sitting at an outdoor café drinking a latte with my boyfriend. I could not take my eyes off of this beautiful, cornflower-blue cashmere sweater with white pearls at the neckline and cuffs. It looked way out of my league. Ian was talking about something, but I was not listening because the sweater was mesmerizing and it tapped into my longing for things I could never have. After all, it looked very expensive and out of reach, having just paid my divorce lawyer all the savings I had, eleven thousand dollars, a princely sum in 1991.

Suddenly, Ian stopped talking and directed his gaze to what I was staring at across the street, "Kathleen, do you want to go looking in that store after I pay for our lattes?"

Still staring at the sweater, I replied, "No. That shop seems too expensive."

Ian smiled that Cheshire grin of his that I found so attractive and said, "I told you that I wanted to buy you something today, so why not go there to look? You know I have the money and would really like to get you something nice." As he said it, tears stung my eyes and I could not speak. Ian could read me so well, even though we had been dating only a few months. I knew not to get involved with someone so soon after my divorce, but I really liked being with him. Cocking his head to the side, he said, "What? Don't you think you deserve to have something expensive?"

My feelings of hesitation were compounded by the worry that I might be on the rebound and that if I accepted something that nice from Ian and our relationship did not work out, I would feel guilty. A career woman in my late thirties, I was used to taking care of myself and did not want to lean on anyone for financial support.

1

As I considered Ian's poignant question, my mind reeled back to the first time I felt that I didn't deserve something which translated to, "Everyone else might deserve things, but for some reason I do not, maybe because I am not good enough for what other people seem to have."

This is a drawing that Kathleen sketched depicting the blue sweater she saw in the store window.

Chapter 1: *The Cookie*

It is easier to build strong children than to repair broken men.

— *Frederick Douglass*[2]

Like any normal five-year-old, I liked playing with my neighborhood friends, even though I was not sure I fit in. That unsure feeling started when my best friend Kathy Manero started calling me, "Lucky Ducky" because my parents appeared to be more well-off than most of my friends. From that day on, I felt different.

One day, I went outside to look for my friends so we could play, but no one was around. Being a beautiful summer night in the Midwest, I was surprised to find our street so quiet, so I decided to walk down and look in everyone's windows to see if I could find the other kids. Everyone's door on Keating Avenue was open, with only the screen doors separating their living rooms from the front stairs outside. As I approached Susie Walker's house, I heard kids' voices and found the living room from where the noise erupted. Standing on the steps of that house, I peered into the screen door and saw a group of my friends sitting on the floor playing a fun game. The aroma of freshly baked cookies assaulted my senses and catalyzed my hunger for both food and companionship, so I eagerly knocked on the door, hoping to join the fun.

The door was answered by a smiling Mrs. Walker, who was wearing an apron tied around a summer dress, carrying a tray of newly baked cookies. My mom cooked, but did not bake goodies often because she was worried about her figure, so eating home-baked goods was a real treat for me. Most of our moms stayed home as housewives because that was the norm in the 1950s. We did not have computers, cell phones, video games then, so we played physical and board games and ate homemade cookies for our leisure activities. Television was fairly new, so not everyone had one to entertain them as another possibility for recreation. All we had was our imaginations and each other to enjoy.

Looking up at Mrs. Walker, I asked if I could come in to join the group. A frown crossed her brow as she looked at the crowd of kids playing on her living room floor. I am sure she meant well with her next words and actions, but more than sixty-years later, I still feel the reverberations of those actions in a negative way. Trying to be kind, gesturing to the other kids who were now quiet and staring at me, she said, "We'd love to include you, but as you can see there are too many kids here as it is."

I must have looked disappointed, so she opened the door and stuck a tray of cookies out, indicating with a tilt of her head that I should take one. When I just stood there immobile, she said quietly, "Have a cookie; it will make you feel better." Even then, at five-years- old, I knew that a cookie wasn't going to make everything okay, but I took the cookie anyway. As I turned to hide my tears, I thanked her and ran down the steps, down Keating Avenue toward home. That was the first time I remember feeling left out or unwanted by my peers.

The encounter with Mrs. Walker that day, started a love-hate relationship with food, particularly those that are sweet. I learned then, as I ate my cookie that although a cookie did not take the pain away, it made me feel better for the moment and that seemed better than nothing; however, there are consequences to using food as comfort in one's sorrow, including weight gain and physical and mental health issues, which I have struggled with all my life. That event also gave me my first life lesson: people are sometimes cruel when they do not really mean to be. This established a seed in my mind that maybe I am different and don't deserve to be included.

When starting to write this book, I had planned to do a whole chapter devoted to the underlying illness which seems to cause many of my relationship and group problems that I will outline in this book. When writing it, however, I realized that since this underlying problem affects everything in my life, it seems to be more pertinent to bring it up as the situation arises instead of through a single chapter. The "cookie incident" triggered a life-long battle with food, which was compounded by my impulsiveness, caused by an underlying problem. If the impulsiveness did not show up early through food, it would have been something else.

The "cookie incident" in the story above was just the first event I remember that caused me to turn to food for comfort from uncomfortable feelings or anxiety. Unhealthy coping behaviors, like using food to calm down or forget pain, can develop into an impulsive bad habit. My own impulsiveness has also been made worse by an underlying mental illness called ADHD, which we will examine throughout this book (See p. 311 for resources about ADHD),

This root problem in my life called Attention Deficit Hyperactivity Disorder (ADHD)* talking excessively, lack of attention to detail or being able to pay attention in conversations, which in turn causes difficulty in relationships at work or at home. One can learn to reel in the worst behaviors like talking too much or making rash decisions, but it takes awareness and practice, which I have mostly learned to do, but it will never be controlled one-hundred percent, even with medication and therapy.

When I am tired or emotional, it is harder to control the negative behaviors, but with much work it can be doable. ADHD crops up in most of the painful situations depicted in this book, so I have decided to explain it as I go along, as it pertains to the subject at hand. I suspect that after the first few chapters, the reader will see how it manifests itself in my life without me having to explain everything in full again; therefore, I just plan to mention it where appropriate and explain as new manifestations of this illness raise their ugly heads as they so often do in my story.

The next chapter, "Chatty Cathy" clearly shows how ADHD showed up in my early life at almost six-years old when I went in for surgery, not too long after the "cookie incident." In each chapter, you will notice how by-products of ADHD seem to compound themselves like a train taking on new baggage at each new stop and how this condition seems to have prevented me from having a worry-free childhood and beyond before I got the proper help.

Moreover, it's important to note I didn't get a diagnosis and subsequent treatment until I was forty-three years old. Even before my ADHD diagnosis, I was still able to manage the condition the best I could, particularly in the Navy because of the structure. This caused the first doctor who diagnosed me years later to exclaim, "I can't believe you have come so far in your life and career without proper treatment!"

I do want to point out that during most of my adult years before my ADHD diagnosis, I had a hunger for two things that gave all the evidence of being out of reach. One was a desire for a deep spiritual connection with God and the other was a hunger to grow as a person. Those desires spurred me on to seek counseling, therapy, and education about alcoholism, personal growth and family dynamics. I was studying those concepts starting in my late twenties and through my thirties. So, by the time I came in for an ADHD diagnosis in my early forties, I was primed to learn about my own illness and kind of relieved that many of my difficulties were not about lack of character, but because of an illness caused by something outside of myself. It was through divine intervention that I learned about ADHD just as I was retiring from the military. Another Naval Officer, who had recently retired, had just been diagnosed with it and explained it to me. I saw myself in her description of her ADHD, which I will expound on in the upcoming chapters.

People with ADHD seem to be attracted, like I was, to the built-in structure of a military career. Fortunately for me, my Higher Power seemed to have intervened just at the right time. I wasn't diagnosed with the problem until I retired from the Navy. Had I been diagnosed before retirement by a Navy doctor, while I was still on active duty, I would have been immediately separated from the service due to the requirement to take controlled drugs to mitigate my ADHD symptoms. One cannot take controlled drugs regularly and stay in the service; therefore, I am glad I didn't find out until later. More about how ADHD affected my career in later chapters.

(Above Left) Kathleen, 1 ½ years old; Michael, 6 months. old and Mom, Elaine, 23 years old

(Above Right) Michael, 1 year old and Kathleen, 3 years old

Kathleen, 1 ½ years old   Kathleen, 5 years old

* sometimes called Attention Deficit Disorder (ADD)

Chapter 2: *Chatty Cathy*

Be patient and tough; someday this pain will be useful to you.

— Ovid[3]

Right before we moved to our newly-built house in the Chicago suburbs, I had to undergo a tonsillectomy at the end of kindergarten. During that time, if you had a lot of sore throats, they would take your tonsils out as the standard remedy. Being that I was a hyper kid at five years old, I was not able to be calm before the tonsillectomy surgery and it showed. In the hospital, while they were preparing me for the procedure, I was all over the place, talking a mile a minute and moving a lot on the gurney on the way down to the operating room. The staff in the operating room started calling me: "Chatty Cathy" the name of a popular doll at the time. I was definitely a girl who loved dolls and Chatty Cathy was cool because you pulled a string and she talked. Barbie had not yet come on the scene; her debut would be later, in 1959 when I'd be seven years old, so Chatty Cathy was the "It" doll for little girls in 1957.

The staff in the operating room must have dealt with hyper kids like me a lot because they did something to calm me down so they could stick the anesthesia needle in my right arm. They called my name so I had to turn my head to the left, thereby distracting me from what was going to happen on my right. When I glanced left, a doll was sitting on the gurney with me and I was fascinated with it. I do not know if it was a Chatty Cathy doll, but it did the trick; the medication took hold and I was out like a light.

After that experience, I picked up the nickname "Chatty Cathy" because everyone said I was hyper and talked too much. I was put in the corner every day of Mrs. Hester's first-grade classroom because of my verbosity with classmates, instead of paying attention to the teacher. I did not just talk too much; I rattled on so much, it was not normal, but I didn't know that then. This behavior would have a profoundly negative impact for most of my life until my ADHD diagnosis. The "talking too much" was just a symptom of ADHD. The condition was not really recognized then, as applicable to me, because it was thought to be mostly a boy's disorder,

7

characterized by hyper boys running around the classroom, disrupting the lessons and making noise. Experts did not realize then that talking too much was the way ADHD was expressed in many girls. All I know was that the nuns told my parents that I had a high IQ and they could not understand why academically, I wasn't living up to my potential. What they did not know was that I just could not pay attention and I talked as a way of coping with the tremendous anxiety ADHD brings. Ironically, it was a relief to let all those words spill out and unfortunately, it was another thing that set me apart from my peers and contributed to my not being consistently in sync with others.

Since I did not do well in school most of the time, I had average to below average grades, I started to think that I was not capable, so I did not deserve good grades. It did not help that during the fifties with "Baby Boomers" crowding the schools, there were forty-nine other students in my classroom, making it difficult to get the personal attention that I needed. Oftentimes, I was left out of classroom discussions as a way of shutting me down from not dominating the conversation; I was left out of group play because I had a hard time listening to others (a form of problems with taking turns) and appeared self-centered because of it.

But really, I could not stop myself because the part of my brain that holds me back from being impulsive was not working and eventually what medication later did was to stimulate that part of my brain to work correctly. Put simply, the medication keeps me from being impulsive, and unfocused, although it is not always one-hundred percent effective; I had over thirty years of behavioral therapy to round out the treatment. Group therapy was particularly painful, but surprisingly helpful, in breaking me of using many of my unhealthy coping skills.

Still, I had low self-esteem and truly believed that I did not deserve the good things other people seemed to acquire easily. It appeared that my fervent desires were always just out of reach. Basically, as young as five or-six years old, I had only two obvious coping skills to deal with my feelings of unworthiness and being left out: food and talking too much; however, these coping skills were damaging. There were more unhealthy ones to come, as the years went by, to add to that baggage.

Chapter 3: *The Chicago Tribune*

If your compassion does not include yourself, it is incomplete.

— Jack Kornfield[(4)]

Most people did not see that anything was wrong with me because I was cute, precocious and smart. When we moved to Glenview, IL in 1958, I thought I was normal. What I did not know was that it was not normal to have such feelings of unworthiness when I had hardly lived one-eighth of my life yet; the pattern was building instead of dissipating, because the underlying problem was not addressed.

Since I did not know or understand the issue (ADHD) or why kids stopped playing with me and left me out at times, I concluded what a lot of kids conclude; that it must be intrinsic in me. There was something in me that was bad and that was just the way it was. I am sure my parents hoped I would grow out of what they thought was just immature behavior, because a kid who talks too much can be irritating to adults, as well as to peers. What they did not know was that one of the criteria for diagnosing ADHD was that the disorder has an onset before age seven; I was showing the first signs.

My family teased me relentlessly about my talking a mile a minute, non-stop, like a runaway train. My father affectionately used to call me "The Chicago Tribune" after our city paper, founded over one-hundred-fifty-years ago by Colonel Robert McCormick. It put out lots of news every day and my dad used to chuckle as he told guests not to tell me anything they didn't want the world to know, because I was like reporters at the Chicago Tribune; I could not keep a secret. Not really knowing what was the big deal, I was confused because I was not able to read the cues on other people's faces to understand their feedback. Inside myself, I thought everyone had such anxiety and that they all talked just as much and could not keep a secret.

My problem with talking never really registered with me that I was the only one in a large class of fifty kids, who was sent to the corner every day. Later when I was older, my friends would say things like, "Chill out" or "Calm down" or "Why are you so nervous?" When they said those things, I honestly thought they were nuts and would reply that I felt fine, not feeling hyper and wondered

9

what their problem was. I was so used to living high-strung with anxiety, I had to be overly anxious to even notice it. Only after I was on medication in my forties, did I experience what it is like to not feel hyper every day of my life. It was a revelation! I just could not see what my friends were talking about back then and as a result, I did not alter my behavior. In hindsight, being hyper and anxious presented as talking too much or being impulsive, as a way of coping with these uncomfortable feelings.

Accordingly, these destructive patterns continued and I felt myself not clicking with certain people or irritating them right off the bat. My few real friends somehow got past my initial impulsiveness and it seemed the more I felt the support of a friend, the more I calmed down naturally because I knew they accepted me, even with my faults. It helped me to not be friendless, but often I did not understand when I was left out of something or they got mad at me at times because I could not control the impulsivity one-hundred percent. They may have been able to cope with my being hyper by talking incessantly, but it only complicated my social interactions in a negative way. This behavior, caused by impulsivity created what I call: **Unhealthy Coping Skill One** - *Talking Too Much.* Sadly, I could not change what I did not understand. I have always maintained that one cannot give insight to someone who does not have insight. A person must experience it him/herself to really get it. That which I did not understand led me to stay in a cycle of unworthiness and it was another thirty-five years before I started to climb out of that mind rollercoaster

In order to cope: **Unhealthy Coping Skill Two** - *Ignorance* was born. I ignored the problem and consequently, the awful feelings that went along with it. Being oblivious can be bliss, but it eventually hurt me when I later saw the light. If I had been able to see then, the negative impact my behavior had on others caused by my lack of impulse control, I would have been mortified. At the time, ignorance kept me from being depressed when I needed to stay chipper; however, it did not help me cope with the effects of impulsivity on my friendships.

By the time I was in high school, however, I established **Unhealthy Coping Skill Three** - *Letting Others Mistreat Me.* When my steady boyfriend was late picking me up (sometimes one to two hours), I would wait patiently. My dad would look at me and just shake his head that I would put up with this. But like me, he excused it because he loved Keith as much as I did. What Irish Catholic father like mine would not like a clean-cut, smart, Irish Catholic boyfriend like Keith? Keith was a football player at our local all-boys Catholic high school, had good grades and was accepted to an Ivy League college. After all, I went to the all-girls Catholic sister school near Keith's all-boys school, so we had common friends and interests.

Keith and I met through combined activities of the two schools. I know now that my parents should have had a talk with me the first time Keith was so late picking me up and should have explained that Keith's lateness was not acceptable and that I should say so. I think I was afraid to confront Keith about it because he was really the first mainstream boyfriend that I had who was popular with the other students at our respective schools on the North Shore. It was the first time I had felt accepted by the girls in my high school and became popular by association with Keith's large family from Wilmette, Illinois.

Most of the girls at my high school, Regina Dominican, knew Keith through going to the same grade schools, as did the seven kids in Keith's big family. I had attended a public sixth grade class and junior high school, so I only knew the other kids from my neighborhood in Glenview and those who went to the public schools with me. Located in Niles and Des Plaines, and they were on the other side of town from both of our high schools. This meant that my neighborhood friends that I had known all my life and my new high school friends were in separate spheres, which caused problems for me being able to fit into either group.

As the reader shall see later, those conditions sometimes reverberate to this day. The runaway train was collecting more baggage and I was still only a teenager. Healthy self-esteem appeared to be just out of my reach and traveling farther away from me as time marched on. I had one good friend who saved me from not knowing the pleasures of a good friendship and deep trust in another person; her name was Valerie.

Keith & Kathleen going to a
High School dance, Fall, 1969

Kathleen, 14 years. old as a Freshman
at Regina Dominican High School,
Fall, 1966

Kathleen with Keith on a date for her
18th birthday at the Huddle Cafe,
Evanston, IL., August, 1970

Kathleen and Keith dressed for
Keith's High School Senior Prom,
Loyola Academy, Spring, 1970

12

Chapter 4: *And Then There Was Val*

The friend is the man who knows all about you, and still likes you.

— Elbert Hubbard[5]

In 1958, Glenview, Illinois was considered to be a far-out northern suburb, located twenty-five miles from Chicago or "Chi-town" (pronounced shy-town) city proper. There were horse farms all the way down from Central Road to Golf Road and it seemed like we were still out in the country because of all the trees and greenery. Moreover, remnants remained of the typical Midwest prairies so often written in stories about wagon trains and the westward movement of our ancestors.

Many of the local farms were cleared to allow for building new homes after World War II. There is only one working farm left in Glenview, the Wagner Farm, which was bought and worked by the local park district (and still is today). After the last living descendant of the farm, Rose Wagner, died in 1997, a group of citizens asked for it to be taken over by the Glenview Park District. Today, the property has been restored and chickens and farm animals have been brought back. In addition, the Park District established a museum there in 2006, to describe the history of the 18.6-acre remnant that was left of a larger farm started in 1850 by the German immigrant Wagners. All this was catalyzed by the nostalgic Glenview citizens because nobody could stand to part with something that typified the roots of the community so well.

I met Valerie Beebe (Val for short) in 1958 when my family moved to a newly-built, mid-century-modern suburban house in Glenview. The development was so new that we didn't even have streets in yet and we had to walk on wooden planks instead of sidewalks to stay out of the mud after it rained. Shortly after moving into our new house on Virginia Lane, I went for a walk in the next cul-de-sac and saw two blonde girls about my age (five years old) playing on a pile of discarded bathroom tiles. As I joined the two sisters to play, the back door of their house opened and Mrs. Beebe came outside and asked me my name. I said, "My name is Kathy

13

O'Brien and we just moved in down the street." She then asked if my parents were Elaine and Tom O'Brien. At the time I did not realize what a coincidence this was because in Irish-American, Mayor Daley's Chicago, everyone knows someone named O'Brien. In addition, close to three million people inhabited the city and that total number didn't even count the suburbs like Glenview.

When I answered Mrs. Beebe's question in the affirmative, she told me that she knew my parents because she had lived a few years earlier in the same building in Chicago as my godparents, the Burns family. The Beebes had met me several times, when my family visited their building. And most astounding was that I had already met Valerie before, when we were both only one-year-old. Surprisingly, we had played together during those visits to the Burns family's apartment building, starting in 1953.

During that pivotal day, while playing together on the discarded tile pile in 1958, Valerie and I became best friends. What did we have in common besides our ages (Val turned six three months before I did), having met before as young toddlers and living down the street from each other on Virginia Lane? Plenty. Not only did we go to the same Catholic school together for grades one through five, we both loved hot fudge sundaes at Woolworths, savoring Rice Krispie Treats, climbing out of my bedroom window at 3:00 a.m. to explore our neighborhood, camping outside in the backyard, reading our diaries to each other, playing our ukuleles and of course, we both loved God and the Beatles.

Val and I are still in touch today in our sixties, even though we both have traveled around a lot and now live in different states. Val's positive, consistent and life-affirming impact on my life can't be underestimated. Our friendship balanced out my anxiety-ridden unhealthy behaviors. In fact, much of those destructive behaviors were curtailed because I knew my BFF always had my back and really loved me regardless of my faults. Knowing that calmed me down. With her, I did not talk too much (until later, which is another story).

There was only one problem I had during that time: I started to compare myself with her. It became an issue between fifth and eighth grade, when Valerie transformed. She had been an awkward, gangly, pimply, bucktoothed, four-eyed girl and became a beautiful, popular, petite, blonde, shapely teen who attracted the boys like geese

14

to breadcrumbs. Thus, she got the affectionate nickname, "Ugh" (short for Ugly) from me for obvious reasons. Still, I started to wonder if I measured up.

Val went to the public high school and became very popular there. Although she remained the humble, down-to-earth Val I had always known, her blossoming beauty fostered a bad habit I picked up: *comparing myself to others*. Through teenage eyes, when I compared myself to Val, I usually took second place or worse, especially in the boy department. I coped by eating, which did not help me be as slim as Valerie: she was a 1960s size seven, which was just out of reach for me most of the time (I wavered between size eight and nine). It never occurred to me that having bigger breasts and not needing contacts or braces, as Val did, might have helped me come out ahead.

I was instead obsessed with being thinner. Remember, this was the era of very thin supermodels, Twiggy and Jeanne Shrimpton. The perfect body I craved had all the evidence of being out of reach for me with my slow metabolism and family history of having to battle with extra weight. Around fifteen years old, I started a lifelong struggle with trying to control my weight and yo-yo dieting. This was a problem waiting to happen ever since I wrestled with the "cookie incident", described in Chapter One.

Before age fifteen weight was not an issue, because my metabolism was so strong that I never put on pounds. I have wrestled with my weight off and on ever since then and it has affected my confidence level, whether it was an extra ten pounds or later thirty pounds after having my daughter. Those pounds seemed to define what I thought of myself, as well as, affected my unhealthy relationship with food. It seems obvious to me now that it all started with a cookie to soothe my hurt feelings and angst as a five-year-old who was not allowed to play in a group and felt left out.

Kathleen's Mid-Century Modern childhood home, built in 1958 on Virginia Lane in Glenview, IL.

(Above) Diplomat Hotel, Miami, FL., Valerie, Tom, Elaine and Kathleen, 1960s

(Above) Val & Kathleen on Virgina Lane 1968-1969

(Above) Tom and Elaine O'Brien, 1960s

(Left) Val at one of our group picnics, 1967-1968

(Right) Kathleen's Graduation Picture 1970

16

Chapter 5: *Stop Playing With Fire*

*In the absence of feedback, people will fill in
the blanks with a negative. They will assume
you don't care about them or don't like them.*

— *Pat Summitt*[6]

Val's backyard in summer was large, dark in the corners, private and a perfect place to make-out with our boyfriends. What we did there under the stars was so tame by today's standards. We never took off our clothes, just did some heavy necking with our boyfriends: my boyfriend and I in one dark corner and Valerie and hers in the other.

One evening, Val's dad must have seen us because we heard a booming male voice say, "Val and Kathy, get in here right now!" We jumped up and our boyfriends snuck out of the yard as we ran to the house. Tall, slim and carrying himself with grace and confidence, Ray Beebe had a commanding presence and he treated me like a second daughter. Consequently, he would correct my behavior, just as he corrected Val's. We came in and immediately found ourselves standing against a wall, scared and holding hands, with Mr. Beebe standing erect in front of us, like a drill sergeant with a couple of wayward recruits.

His index finger was pointing at our red, embarrassed faces and yelling at us, "Don't you know that you two are playing with fire when you make-out with boys on top of you, even if you have all your clothes on? It's very hard to stop and you might get into trouble. At some point, the boys will expect more!" We were humiliated, but like the kind gentleman he was, he made his point and moved on. I was staying overnight, so I had to face him again in the morning at breakfast, where it was not mentioned again.

After Val and I had gone to bed, I lay awake thinking about the time in fifth grade when Val approached me smiling, telling me that she had a secret. Of course, I wanted her to spill the beans but she said that her mom warned her not to tell me. When pressed, she gave me the hint that it was about how babies were made. "Why don't you tell me? After all, I am your best friend and we have always told each other everything," I begged. She told me I had to find out these things

17

from my mother and that I should ask her to tell me. That is when I started to drive Mom crazy with questions every time we were alone together.

I would ask her questions like, "How does the baby get inside your tummy?" or, "Val said the husband is involved and it happens when you sleep together, is that right?" I usually questioned Mom at the most inconvenient times, when she was pressed for time. I already knew about menstruation and I had already asked Mom if my dad knew about "all that icky stuff?" These new questions were taking it to a new level and my mom seemed embarrassed every time I brought it up, so she stalled.

In the end, Val broke down and told me how babies were made when we were pondering the idea of the "man going to the washroom" inside the woman, a tale I was told by another classmate. I could just see Val's diary saying, "Today I had to tell Kathy how babies are made because she thought that the man goes to the washroom inside the woman." Since we both still have our diaries from that period, I will have to give Val a call one of these days to see what she recorded in her diary about that day. I tell this story to point out how my own family did not communicate well about uncomfortable subjects and instilled in me shame about sexual things like it was something to be hidden. Valerie was the only one for a long time with whom I could talk about it.

As I grew toward adulthood, love and sex were the same things in my mind and for a girl of the sixties who was supposed to be liberated and free, this contradiction to some of my peer group's perception caused problems. In my early teens, the Catholic girl's school influence on me was a very conservative one like many of my peers. But as we went on to college into the seventies, the "free love" idea took hold and I was caught up in that before many of my friends while at the same time being less mature in male-female interactions.

A hallmark of my ADHD symptoms was impulsivity, which caused me to act before I thought something out, thus negatively affecting my ability to have solid relationships. Early sex in a relationship or before marriage was just one way my symptoms of ADHD played out. Only later did I come to understand that love and sex *should* be the same, but only with the *right* person during marriage. It sounds like an old-fashioned idea, but really it is practical, preventing us from giving ourselves away to the wrong

18

person, unwanted pregnancy or getting married because of guilt over having sex before marriage. I thought I could separate the sex and love in keeping with the free love philosophy of the day, but I could not.

As a result of not being able to separate sex from love, my behavior caused me a pierced heart many times. The more my heart was broken, the more my pattern of shame and unworthiness increased, which complicated any changes I wanted to make. Continuing to do the same things that cause the same results is called the "Definition of Insanity" according to the Twelve-Step Programs I have attended.

As was customary in the nineteen-fifties, when my parents were married, my mom was a virgin still at twenty-one when she walked down the aisle in a white dress. Again, my self-esteem plunged, when I realized I fell short of the ideal standard my mom demonstrated and Catholic all-girls school guilt reigned supreme. I was not yet married when I lost my virginity at twenty years old, so I felt that I would never measure up. After all, if I wanted a man as wonderful as my dad, in my mind, I had now disqualified myself from having someone like him.

Unconsciously, I started looking for men that were much more flawed than my father (albeit unconsciously), because I felt not worthy of someone like Dad. At that time, I unwittingly and unconsciously decided to not even bother finding an ideal mate, in fact I thought a wonderful mate was out of my league. Twenty-to-thirty years later in therapy, I unwrapped a lot of this psychological pathology, as well as the influence of ADHD on my developing personality, with a lot of pain and humility; however, during the early years, I had no clue why my relationships were not very successful. I wondered if true happiness and love would be just out of reach for me in the future.

Even though I had learned to rely on God during my Catholic upbringing, I did not know why I struggled connecting in relationships. Again, I concluded that God must not have been happy with me, so I must not deserve what most people seemed to get naturally. Starting around twenty years old, I went looking for love in all the wrong places, carrying a bag of all the poor relationship skills I had acquired through low self-confidence and a maturity barometer that was missing in action when I needed it most. Fortunately, God had not given up on me, but I still had a lot of pain to deal with in the future. I heard the loud train whistle blowing as I laid myself on the tracks for the inevitable crash coming my way and not for the last time.

Kathleen and Valerie at 15 years old on a family vacation in Florida

Val's parents, Ray and Lorraine Beebe

Kathleen with Valerie right before her wedding to Mark, August, 1974

Lorraine Amideo and Kathleen's First Communion in May, 1960

Chapter 6: *Building Train Tracks of Low Self-Esteem*

A man cannot be comfortable without his own approval.

— *Mark Twain*[7]

You can see where this is going, can't you? And it's not pretty. When Valerie and I walked every day toward our parochial school, we talked about becoming pious nuns like our teacher Sister Valeria, who had recently died or become a lay teacher like Mrs. Hester (who put me in the corner every day in first grade for talking to my neighbor during class). At ten-or-eleven years old, we had not yet seen evidence of our sexual beings. In those days we started puberty much later, around twelve to thirteen years old. The sex talk I had with my mom, already mentioned, did not occur until I was about eleven or twelve, unthinkably late when compared to today's norms. For example, later, when I was teaching fifth and sixth graders, one of the other teachers joked that the only reason these girls were not pregnant was because they didn't have their periods yet. There was a grain of truth to that, a truth that became more evident as we went forward into the seventies and beyond.

Living one block over from each other on Virginia Lane was convenient and safe for Val and me. If we wanted to go to the mall, we would have to walk through a scary field in which, rumor had it, a girl was murdered. Whenever we were afraid, we would break out the rosaries, hold hands and pray all of the "Hail Mary" and "Our Father" prayers out loud and in unison for protection, especially when traipsing through that field. Despite being Catholics, our families couldn't be more different from each other and therein lay the differences in our self-confidence levels and our evolution as sexual beings.

Val's parents were more practical and conservative, living life as homebodies. I am sure having five children kept them both busy and they probably wanted to relax at home during their free time. Being the opposite, my parents were the ultimate sixties "Rat Pack" couple, always going to or throwing lavish parties. My dad, Thomas J. O'Brien, owned his own business and my mom, Elaine was eleven years younger, gorgeous and a talented hostess.

21

Dad would lavish furs, cars, expensive trips and lingerie on my mom and they seemed happy. All in all, it was a good childhood until I was in junior high, when the cracks started to show, in particular, in my relationship with my mom. Until that time, I had never compared myself to Mom as far as looks and assets go. I just wanted to be like her.

Around this period, I was looking forward to going to the local public high school with my best bud, Valerie, and my neighborhood friends. These friendships had been enhanced during sixth, seventh and eighth grades when I was allowed to go to public school. Unfortunately, my parents informed me that I would be going to the all-girls Catholic high school. This was a problem, because most of my close friends, like Val, were going to the public high school. I would be going to the Catholic school with only a few girls I was not close to from the neighborhood. I was devastated and tried everything to get my parents to change their minds, like starving myself or locking myself in my room, but nothing worked.

The impact of my parents' decision to send me to the all-girls school was profound and affected me throughout my life. You're probably thinking, *how*? Here is a kid who goes to private schools, who pretty much knows nothing about real big life problems like poverty or lack of education. So what? If not sending me to the public school with my neighborhood friends was the only cause for problems later in a good life gone wayward, you would be right. But I was already on shaky ground with poor family dynamics, overeating, parental alcoholism, my brother's drug and alcohol addiction, my ADHD, poor coping skills and low self-esteem.

My parents' decision to take me out of my comfort zone, where I finally felt I belonged with my neighborhood group, really hurt my confidence and increased my everyday anxiety ten-fold. Sixth grade and junior high seems to me to be the worst time a kid should be forced to change schools, due to it being such a delicate time in one's development as a teenager. My neighborhood friends (except Val and another friend, Debbie, who attended parochial school through eighth grade), had all gone with me to sixth grade and junior high in the public schools like my friend and next-door neighbor, Lorraine.

I had started first grade in the Catholic grammar school with Val and Debbie, but after fifth grade, I was transferred to the public school. Believe it or not, my parents transferred me to the public school because there were fewer kids in each class, like thirty students instead of fifty in my parochial school. They also said that because of my younger sibling, Michael's on-going learning problems, they needed to transfer him to a school with smaller classes. Since, they did not want him to go there alone, I was elected to transfer too. Changing schools would have been okay, if I knew I could stay in the public schools for sixth grade through high school, which would have stabilized my rapidly changing confidence levels.

Unfortunately, after my public junior high school experience, my dad was adamant: I was to go to the all-girls Catholic High School, Regina Dominican in Wilmette, IL. Well, that messed me up again because even Val was now transferring to the public high school where Lorraine and most of the other kids from the neighborhood were going too. I truly believe to this day that my parents made a terrible decision for me about transferring to a same sex Catholic high school after three years in a co-ed public school, even though they had good intentions doing it. Many parents have several good reasons to send kids to same sex schools. For instance, the idea that girls need a same sex education to excel in math and science, or boys would be more serious academically if girls were not a distraction.

But for me, I did not fit those parents' good reasons for same sex education. Actually, I did better in my worst subject, math in the public co-ed school and much worse in math in the single sex parochial high school. In the end, I believe that kids sent to same sex schools lose out on the most important element of that time in their lives: proper socialization with the other sex. Not just for attending events like sports and dances, but because each sex will be interacting with each other soon in the real world and need to be able to see each other as intellectual human beings, as well as social ones.

When I went to college, I was in class with men for the first time in a long while. St. Norbert College in De Pere, Wisconsin was a co-ed Catholic school. Most of my classmates there came from co-ed parochial high schools in Wisconsin and Michigan. Their co-ed experience seemed to make them be better-rounded and more comfortable around the opposite sex in a mature way, than I ever felt. At first, because boys were present at St. Norbert, I felt like a deer in the headlights trying to hold serious conversations or asking hard questions in the classroom. Socially, all I knew about boy-girl interactions was to flirt or have superfluous conversations, certainly not intellectual ones. This disadvantage set me on the wrong path for future vigorous relationships and did nothing for my self-confidence.

Since I did not know then that I had ADHD or was from a dysfunctional alcoholic family (also called a "co-dependent" family), my anxiety was off the charts, showing up in talking too much or making bad relationship decisions because of impulsivity (classic ADHD symptom). In addition, I had a new problem, making it much worse; I was afflicted with big acne boils on my face and back that nearly destroyed my self-esteem and amplified my anxiety. After about a year, I got the acne under control by going to a doctor, but before then, I was humiliated and it stopped any new growth and maturity in social and intellectual interactions, which I had already needed to be in step with my peers. Again, because of these events, I appeared to be behind others my age in wisdom and experience, which further decreased my self-confidence.

Valerie and I went to two different colleges, so when we talked on the phone, I was anxious and dominated the conversation. This surprised her because around our neighborhood group, I had been much more relaxed. However, since Valerie had always been my go-to person for feeling cared about and understood, I was desperately seeking her validation and friendship long distance. Hence, I was prone to having anxiety and talking too much on the phone. This behavior of not letting anyone else get in a word edge-wise is characteristic of impulsivity. Eventually, Val told me that I was just talking too much about myself and that it appeared that I didn't seem to care about what she had to say.

That is the first time I realized, just a little, how my anxious behavior was manifesting itself as a mile-a-minute speaker and a person who seemed arrogant. I was devastated that even Val was put off by it for a while. But because she was my BFF and she truly cared about me, I could hear her feedback and would try to change it. I still did not know why I would get like that at times, but at least she was the first one that made me more aware of it as a problem.

After the first year of college, I became less anxious about the way our new status as college girls would change our best friend relationship, so I was less talkative on the phone and could listen to what was going on more with Val. It would be many years later in

24

therapy that I became aware of how ADHD affected all my relationships, mostly in a negative way. For example, I often have a hard time paying attention (ADHD symptom), especially when other things are happening around me or I am nervous. This causes me to miss important non-verbal (non-verb) cues, which is 85% of all communication. Non-verbs like: facial expression, body position and tone of voice are what most people pick up before they even register the words that are being said. These issues hindered most of my relationships until I learned to read these cues years later.

Val's honest feedback about my talking too much was the first time I became aware that this could come across as self-centered. That was news to me because I equated self-centeredness with being arrogant and I was anything but. This new behavioral information gave me a glimpse as to how I came across to others. Thankfully, our relationship became more give-and-take, like it had been before, especially because of her concerned honesty, which develops trust, the main ingredient of close relationships.

After that, why I was so anxious or why I still did not usually pick up on other people's body language or facial expressions was not yet understood by me. But this period was when I started to see that most of the time, I did not get other people's motivations or behavior. My peers seemed to pick up the nuances which clued-in the majority of people as to when their own behavior needed to be tempered. That memo was lost to me because I could not distinguish the noises and distractions competing in my brain (ADHD symptoms) due to the loud roar of the train, as I barreled down the tracks without a brake system.

Do not get me wrong, I met some wonderful people at St. Norbert College, but I really did not greatly improve my interaction with the opposite sex. I had twenty-three boy cousins and with all those boys around me, including my two brothers, one would think that I would get plenty of experience interacting with boys. Unfortunately, it was not the kind of experience one gets from meeting new boys in school, becoming friends and dating them, which is what I really needed.

Although my dad's only brother, Ray (ten years his senior) and his wife, Anne O'Brien had had ten children (all boys), we saw them only a few times a year and they were not potential dates or people I had to work with. I could get advice the handful of times a year that I saw them, but it did not give me any experience with intellectual or dating-type conversations. If anything, it worsened the reality of my boy problems, since they had their own issues learning how to relate to girls due to not having any sisters to teach them.

The other problem this created: I developed crushes on a few of them and most of them treated me as very special, because I was the only girl cousin for a long time at our family parties. Those cousins were handsome men and more than a third of them were much older than me, so I got minimal peer boy-girl learning for my own future dating situations from them. Unable to interact appropriately with the opposite sex, I was still clueless in male-female interactions.

It took me a long time to feel comfortable working with men and not looking at them as someone to flirt with. That was probably why I later went into the Navy (albeit unconsciously) because I had a need to know how to be around men in a healthy way. Even after I joined the Navy, it took me a long time to learn how to interact with men normally.

One thing that was helpful was that when I became a Commissioned Officer a few years into my military service, I had mostly men working with and for me. On the other hand, many were either married or I could not date them because they were subordinate to me and it would be in violation of the military fraternization rules. Eventually, my Navy career helped me learn to properly relate to men in a healthy way, even though it took many years.

At least in the Navy, I could hide behind my uniform to get the respect my knowledge and education and my love of people deserved. We used to say, "Respect the rank and the uniform and the rest will follow." I acted as if I deserved their respect because of my rank and the rest *did* follow. I had no time to dither on important decisions and the more I made good ones, the more confidence I had in myself and the more confident my subordinates were in my leadership. In all my Navy assignments, most of my bosses, my colleagues and my subordinates were men. It all worked well together to help me build my interaction skills because the people who worked for and with me could see I was honest and sincere. They knew I would ask for help with new endeavors and I always showed my respect for their advice and experience.

Both my subordinates and superiors recognized that my rank and training may not have equipped me for the technical parts of a particular job; however, I was told to lead it anyway, a common situation for junior officers at the start of their careers. The upper echelon officers figure that in the Navy culture, a junior officer might be on a ship some day without anyone above to directly tell them what to do. Those superior officers have experienced this themselves; therefore, they get it that junior officers must jump in and take charge anyway and get the job done. As time went on, I in fact became quite comfortable interacting with all types of men at all levels and improved my social interactions with them.

When I entered the Navy, there were few women role-models to follow, until later when more women entered the service and were allowed in additional combat positions. Until then, we looked to the female civil servants and the few women senior officers we encountered for guidance. In my experience, the Army, Air Force and Marines have different mindsets in their cultures. Usually, the land-based services are not sitting out at sea with radio silence and no way to communicate with their superiors. Those in the Navy are often under those "silent" conditions at sea, so Naval Officers are encouraged to act now and ask questions later, a mindset I did not see as much in the other military services.

One of my heroes was Admiral Grace Hopper. She was still in the Navy when I joined. Hopper was a computer pioneer, who helped shape the use of computers in the military, for which she was dearly respected. President Reagan promoted her to Admiral in the 1980s. Many hold her as the person who really championed user-friendly computer platforms. She felt computers were for everyone and not just for high-level mathematicians like she was. This belief was reflected in her development of the computer language, COBOL, as well as spurring on Navy innovation in that realm. The Admiral's mindset regarding how to operate effectively with all levels in the Navy, informed my own leadership study and it is something by which I have lived also.

Grace Hopper respected her subordinates and their abilities, regardless of rank, showing the best kind of leadership. Her leadership style is summed up by this well-known quote from Admiral Hopper: "It is easier to ask for forgiveness than to ask for permission."[8] I heard this expression many times during my time in

27

the Navy and most people really followed it. I am not sure if this was said before her time, but it was attributed to her, especially while I was still in the Navy. And military people took it to heart at all levels.

It appeared that we would not get into trouble for trying something new without permission, if it was within our own purview. Our bosses respected us *less* if we played it safe and colored within the lines only. They wanted us to take reasonable risks and would congratulate us on our inventiveness. Even if what we did was a mistake, we were often counseled that it was a good calculated risk; we win some, we lose some. But we would also be counseled in more detail about why it probably did not work and what we could do differently in the future; however, before they told us why it probably did not work, the good bosses would ask us first why *we* didn't think it worked well and how we would approach it differently or if at all the next time.

The outcome of this thoughtful kind of leadership, resulted in most people learning how to implement new things well. So, as we got more senior in rank, our growing ability to critically think from these kinds of discussions with our leaders created a more mature decision-maker and therefore, a better sailor. In this way, we would be able to take calculated risks that enhanced the running of our departments, as well as improve Navy procedures and processes.

These scenarios, with thoughtful bosses like Grace Hopper or other great officers I have worked for were NOT exceptions to the Navy mindset, but were integral to our daily operations. We were being prepared as if we would have our own ship someday, unable to get a hold of our leaders due to radio silence or because of the idiosyncrasies of ships in a war zone. The quote from Grace Hopper above really typifies the Naval Officer's ingrained way of thinking, encouraging us to think and act for ourselves. According to Admiral Hopper, there were two ways of ensuring we would be successful in our Navy careers, "You manage things, you lead people,"[9] I always knew the difference between managing (organizing and overseeing) and leading (inspiring others to better performance) and it greatly informed how I conducted business.

When there are tensions in other areas of the world that are important to America's interests, the Navy usually is the first service moved to be on scene to show a presence or take action because they can be sent quickly without congressional approval, especially in an emergency. The whole Navy is run as if we were on the brink of an emergency situation, which many times we are. This is not only because many of our jobs require working with dangerous equipment, but we are also in dangerous situations, even on shore duty and when we are training for deployment.

My ADHD did not always show up negatively in crisis situations because I was used to drama from growing up in an alcoholic home. That is the reason I seem to become calm in a real crisis. In addition, the great structure in the military allowed me to follow procedures easily. There was a lot more flexibility in the military than the average person thinks because I had a wonderful framework in which to weave in and out during my Naval service. This allowed me to be creative in my solutions, but also to have solid procedures to fall back on. ADHD people usually need variety, but also need structure to be productive, and in the Navy, I had both.

Thank God for a career I could be successful in without the problems I would encounter on a regular job. The variety I needed came from transferring to different jobs every three years and the structure came from regulations, manuals and leadership principles that were similar and standard wherever I went for duty. I suspect many people with ADHD are attracted to the military (even if they do not know why) and I was just such a person. For many years, it gave me almost everything I needed.

Earlier on in my Navy career, I realized that I needed to keep people in my life who were working on similar issues in a healthy way and going out to Twelve-Step meetings like Al-Anon in the civilian population was one way to do it. Most Commissioned Officers don't seek help within the Navy system for drug and alcohol or psychiatric problems because that could be career-ending. Seeking Navy help can hurt enlisted sailors as well, but not initially be career-ending, as long as they haven't admitted to lying on their enlistment forms about past drug use.

In fact, when I was still working with drug and alcohol cases in San Diego, I was increasingly frustrated by the way the Navy manual on substance abuse counseling was written because the explanation for confidentiality was very confusing. This was a problem because a sailor could say something that the counselor would have to report, like lying about past use to the recruiter. If that got out, it would undermine the trust between the counselor and the sailor. We had to be sure that all the people we were counseling knew the risk of admitting prior drug use or other issues like homosexuality, (then still banned in the services) to the counselors.

One day, I boldly called up the office for the Navy Drug and Alcohol program in Washington, D.C. (where the manual had been produced) and told them my problem about how the manual was written. They said simply, "Why don't YOU rewrite it to be more understandable to both the counselors and the people being counseled, so they know what they can disclose without the counselors having to report it up the chain of command?" Accordingly, I rewrote it very succinctly and they put my writing, almost verbatim, in the next Navy-wide manual as reference for Substance Abuse Counselors.

At that time, counselors in this field were not medical professionals or Chaplains. Chaplains were the only ones who were exempt from reporting what they heard to higher authority, which could get the client in question into trouble and possibly cause the client to be separated from the Navy. That is why our clients needed to know what they should keep to themselves during sessions with certified Substance Abuse Counselors, unless the client wanted to be kicked out of the service.

We para-professional counselors protected the records of our clients as best we could within Navy regulations, but technically the client's Commanding Officer (CO) could find out what the sailor told us if he/she forced the issue. A minimal summary evaluation, without details was what was usually given to the client's command.

Most COs sent their sailors over to get help because we were the "good guys." A court martial was a legal process, separate from the counseling mission, so we did not share that information with Naval Criminal Investigative Service (NCIS) or other law enforcement agencies on the base. If they needed detailed information about the client in question, they would have to gather the evidence separately, not from us.

We didn't want it to appear to our clients that we were "telling on them" to law enforcement. If that happened, no client would tell us anything and their chances of getting real help for their substance abuse problems would be nil. That is why I was pleased that my writing in the manual explaining the limitations of confidentiality was used by the whole Navy as a reference. Sometimes it pays to have nuns teaching you English for all four years of high school and this is one instance when what I learned from the all-girls Catholic High School paid off handsomely. The other time it has obviously paid off in a big way is in writing this book.

Of course, I was on my own in the personal relationship department and therein lies the problem. To top it off, I could not see that there were many elephants in the room because I did not know anything about the issues I found in my family until about twenty-nine years old when I went to the Navy's Drug and Alcohol Counseling School (NDACS) in San Diego, California in 1982. At this school, I learned, not only about the different kinds of drugs and their effects, but also, how to counsel and evaluate the sailors whose sobriety was in question. I was required to go to NDACS in preparation for taking over a drug and alcohol counseling and evaluation center called a Counseling and Assistance Center (CAAC) at Naval Air Station, Miramar, CA. This was the same duty station depicted in the first "Top Gun." Movie.

It was at that point in time that I recognized the patterns present in my own immediate and extended family. Before then, I had not given myself permission to name the main problem in our family – addiction and all the denial, broken promises, manipulation and relationship issues that were caused by this beast. I was probably unconsciously drawn to the school and job that followed because I needed answers, even if it was painful to face the extent it created havoc in my own life.

At NDACS, I was required to be a member of a student small group, with a counselor guiding us to look at our own problems and then confronting us with our issues. We students used to joke that we were not going to finish and graduate from counseling school unless we cried in there, at least once, to show that we were dealing with our own problems. We were going to have to ask our client sailors to go deep to get well and recover from their addiction; therefore, we needed to deal with our own issues to be effective and to better understand what they were going through. It was not pretty and for an officer Lieutenant like me, it was downright brutal.

Commissioned Officers are taught to be strong and not to show weakness to the troops. The reason for this is because the troops need to have confidence in us to lead them in the right direction, so it was hard to break us officers down. In typical fashion, I was one of the only officers in my group because as manager-candidates, preparing to run a CAAC, they felt we too needed to understand how to counsel and evaluate like our enlisted subordinate counselors. Thus, we were put in group counseling with enlisted members to experience what it was like to have to open ourselves up to others.

A perfect storm was created through the convergence of all the factors I have related above, like my ADHD, coming from an alcoholic family, lack of proper interaction with the opposite sex, relationship issues and low-self-confidence. It is easy to see why I was not healthy. Other dynamics played into my lack of self-esteem. "….Shame is the feeling of being flawed and worthless. It demands that we hide and live in secret. Shame-based people guard against unguarded moments. In an instant of unguardedness, you could be exposed and that would be too painful to bear…"[10] *Bradshaw on the Family: A New Way of Creating Solid Self-Esteem — John Bradshaw* What I learned while reading various books about these issues is that I won't be healed from "adult child" hurts unless I deal with the root source, which is toxic shame from childhood. Unless my toxic shame is dealt with, healing will be out of reach for me.

Ray & Anne O'Brien's 10 Boys – 1970's

Chapter 7: *Shame plus Low Self-Esteem Equals*

a Train Wreck

"As children we were loved for our achievements and our performance, rather than for ourselves. Our true authentic selves were abandoned." [11]
Healing the Shame that Binds You — John Bradshaw

When my parents were dressing up for a formal party, I would sit and watch my mom get dressed and put her make-up on. She was so beautiful and glamorous, with a great figure and wonderful taste. She'd fix her coal-black hair into a French roll or a Beehive and put on a striking gown that was reminiscent of Jackie Kennedy's formal attire for soirées at the White House. Mom had a whole trunk of elegant ball gowns that I would go through, try on and pretend I was her. She would take my dapper tux-clad father's arm and off they would go on their adventure. I never even thought of comparing myself to Mom until I was about thirteen, when Val and I were starting to mature ourselves.

Before puberty, I felt that I looked good and besides, I mostly felt beautiful inside and out because that was how Dad treated me. He was always building me up with regard to my character and abilities. I always felt special and loved by my father as his firstborn, and the only girl in my generation on his side of the family. He was very demonstrative with everyone and I never wanted for his loving attention and his sage advice.

Never failing to tell me he loved me as a person both inside and out, Dad's love and encouragement sustained me. I became puzzled by my mom's behavior after Dad would spend time alone with me. She suddenly seemed judgmental of my dress and the choices I made. I thought our discordance was related to my becoming a teenager and some of that was true, but for reasons much deeper and darker than I could really fathom in my young mind. Only later, after much therapy, did I realize that she was jealous of me as a person and especially, as an attractive woman. I saw myself as the girl next-door type, who liked sportier, or more conservative things than Mom.

Because we were the same size, Mom would let me borrow some of her outfits if I was going to a dress-up party or some other special event in high school. I enjoyed being a little more glamorous once in a while by borrowing her clothes, but overall, it wasn't really me. When I did not like or want to wear something she liked, she'd say that I had no taste; however, that wasn't the worst of it, something I didn't find out until later during much self-reflection and soul-searching when my life became a train wreck in matters of the heart. The "worst of it" could be seen in several events I recalled, as I reflected on my past as to how it related to my low self-esteem in adulthood.

First, the most vivid event in my mind was when I was about fifteen and my mom was about thirty-seven years old. My dad and she were going to some big event and she came downstairs dressed to the nines in a shocking pink, short, pleated, knit dress (it was the sixties after all) with an empire waist and a very low neckline, showing ample cleavage. She wore pink, pointy, spiked heels and lipstick to match. I thought she looked beautiful, but that wasn't the problem. It just so happens, my boyfriend, Ed, was there to take me out and when he saw her, his eyes popped out of his head. She seemed to play up her sexiness, even more, when he loudly said to me, "I think instead of you, I'd like to take your mother out." I didn't really recognize the sickness in her initial sexy comportment while in Ed's presence, nor her self-satisfied reaction to his compliment. It did not compute; no wonder I had difficulty as an adult discerning appropriate relationship interaction from inappropriate.

Second, there were several times in my life when upon meeting a new beau of mine, Mom would comment in his presence something like, "If I was twenty years younger, I'd take him myself." Even into her sixties, she said the same thing about my future husband, Bill while he was standing there. It was only later that I realized that this was inappropriate.

Third, her favorite sister, my Aunt Nancy, later told me that when Mom, who was then a widow, was visiting and Nancy was out of the room, my mom made an unsuccessful play for Nancy's husband! In Mom's defense it was around the time she started to show symptoms of the dreaded Alzheimer's disease, killing her fourteen years later. Hard to say if Alzheimer's or her heavy drinking could have exacerbated that unseemly behavior toward her brother-in-law.

Fourth, there were the arguments. My parents would argue

about decisions they made concerning me or differences of opinion regarding my behavior and what, if anything, to do about it. I must admit that unconsciously, I was in collusion with my dad against my mom, and secretly supported his side of arguments most of the time. Not only was I the subject of their arguments, but more insidious were their arguments regarding my mother's lack of character or her self-centeredness. Dad was always trying to make Mom into a better person than she was in both our eyes.

If you thought of the ultimate example of a co-dependent, there was no better one than my father, who also wrestled with his own alcohol demons from time to time. My two brothers and I later concluded that our mother must have been Dad's trophy wife because he was always trying to make her more sensitive and compassionate toward others and that did not always fit her. In our immediate family, we usually assumed that she was motivated by her own interests first. She seemed mostly to worry about her appearance and that everything was just so, even to the detriment of others.

When I got married, one of my bridesmaids was very overweight and my mom was embarrassed to show the pictures to others because of it. When acne struck me in the teen years, my mother, whose complexion was perfect said to me, "I just cannot understand it. I never had a pimple, why do you?" My dad tried to explain her behavior away as issues my mom had had in her own life with always feeling less than the other kids in her school. The other kids at school had money and wore expensive cashmere sweaters and her parents did not have the money for those things.

My mother, though, had her good qualities. She cooked and kept a nice house and did a good job taking care of us, but mostly those good times happened before I became a teenager. She loved us in her own way, even though her mother toolbox was limited in the character department at times.

The saddest thing about Mom's life that I learned when I was an adult from her older sister, Lois was that their older brother had molested my mom when they were kids. That could account for Elaine's skewed sense of appropriate response, which eventually affected my own response and self-esteem. Her shame became my shame and the worst part was unconsciously, I did not think I was good enough for someone like my dad, Thomas O'Brien, who was handsome, successful, kind, compassionate and an honorable man;

35

however, his own drinking and co-dependency got in the way of his happiness.

According to John Bradshaw, in his book, *Healing the Shame that Binds You,* "What is important to note is that we can't know what we don't know. Denial, idealization, repression and disassociation are unconscious survival mechanisms. Because they are unconscious, we lose touch with the shame, hurt and pain they cover up. We cannot heal what we cannot feel. So, without recovery, our toxic shame gets carried for generations."[12]

I did not realize then that I had already begun to compare myself unfavorably to my mom, Elaine and thought no man of Dad's caliber would want me. After all, my dad, Tom picked a stunning trophy wife for a mate. So, I guess I thought that since Dad picked one, it must be the standard I would have to live up to in order to marry a good guy like Tom O'Brien. Of course, life is always more complicated than that.

It appeared to me that Tom married Elaine assuming that he could change her character and Elaine married Tom thinking her only worth was her beautiful looks. Mom was smart, sharp with numbers, a good writer, creative and much more, even without graduating from high school. A pity she never seemed to know those things about herself. It worked in a lot of ways early in their marriage; however, when Mom turned forty, everything started to change.

Even though Mom was getting older, she was still uncommonly stunning. The men of my parent's couple friends often came up to me at soirées at our house and asked me if I knew how beautiful my mother was. Seems like a rhetorical question to me now, but at the time I felt proud that people admired Mom for her beauty, like maybe it would rub off on me when I got older. It did not occur to me that it was kind of an inappropriate question to ask a child.

Mom was a competent and beautiful hostess for my father's social and business-related events. My parents, had pool parties twice a year, where a lot of Dad's business clients showed up. In fact, the get-togethers were arranged for business purposes, given that my dad was in sales and smack in the middle of the sixties, when the two-martini lunch program was "de rigueur" then. These pool parties extended the time Dad spent with clients to a whole day of drinking, as the guests frolicked in the pool, ate catered food and danced to the piped-in music on the patio from early afternoon until late in the evening. I remember going to sleep to those sounds, as my room was just above the pool and we didn't have air conditioning (Due to its high cost, it wasn't common in residential homes then). Therefore, the windows had to stay wide open in the summer.

Most of my dad's large Irish family are in sales and parties with lots of booze were common. In fact, at our family Christmas Eve celebrations, I first saw the adults and my older cousins getting alcohol from a three-foot stationary vodka bottle with a pump on top, which had to sit on the floor because it was too heavy to lift for pouring. I thought pumping vodka into your glass (as often as you wanted) was normal.

My first memory of being scared or puzzled with my parents' behavior was when we were driving home from one of these Christmas Eve parties when I was about ten, Michael was eight and my baby brother, Terry was a newborn in a bassinet. The car started swerving and my dad seemed to lose control of it, running off the curb into the snow. Mom started screaming and saying, "Tom, slow down, the baby is in the back seat!"

My scare-meter escalated when I saw Mom drinking more and more after she turned forty. Dad always drank a lot at parties and usually started singing Irish songs and got sloppy, but that was only periodically. Mom's increase in drinking, however, eventually became a daily practice to maintain her "new normal." Elaine's "new normal" meant going out to bridge parties where copious amounts of alcohol were being consumed. The ladies eventually threw out the bridge games and just went to lunch and drank all day. My parents started arguing a lot about that turn of events.

More disagreements took place when Elaine hit her mid-forties and she started going through menopause. My parents argued a lot about her denial of that stage in life; she felt she was too young to be in menopause and threw away the symptom-arresting medication that the doctor had prescribed for her. This pattern of drinking, arguing and drinking some more started around this time for both my parents. The results were different for my mom, than for my dad, Tom. While drinking daily, Mom became ungracious and mean-spirited. Dad still drank large amounts, but usually only periodically, mostly becoming jovial and then melancholy as the evening wore on.

Later, my friends and I would call their problem the "Irish Virus" jokingly, but it really wasn't funny. In fact, only a few years ago, I got together with my close friend and childhood next-door neighbor, Lorraine. Her astute observations about my family (Remember, we had to keep all the windows open due to no air conditioning) revealed that my own perceptions were very sobering (No pun intended). In addition, Lorraine was part of my neighborhood "gang" of friends including Val.

What Lorraine said many years after the fact stunned me: she told me that she and her family could hear my mom screaming at me all the time. I was mortified, even sixty years later. One thing that conversation with Lorraine did was to help break down the "Alcoholism: A Merry-Go-Round of Denial," the title of an Al-Anon Family Group's (a recovery group for families and friends of alcoholics) pamphlet in 1969/2003[13] to explain alcoholism's effects on the family. I had been deluded in most of my younger years, thinking that my childhood was normal. But it wasn't.

As the first child, living in a chaotic alcoholic home prevented me from developing healthy self-esteem. "Because of the expectation and pressure caused by parental youth and over-coercion ("first child jitters"), first children often have trouble developing high self-esteem." —John Bradshaw, *Bradshaw on the Family: A New Way of Creating Solid Self-Esteem*[14]

Until I was in puberty, my childhood was mostly typical, but some of the signs of family pathology were starting to come through. "These symptoms of the family disease of alcoholism or other dysfunction made us co-victims, those who take on the characteristics of the disease without necessarily ever taking a drink. We learned to keep our feelings down as children and kept them buried as adults. As a result of this conditioning, we confused love with pity, tending to love those we could rescue. Even more self-defeating, we became addicted to excitement in all our affairs, preferring constant upset to workable relationships." Adult Children of Alcoholics World Service Organization (ACOA) *https://adultchildren.org/literature/problem/*[15]

During one of our mother-daughter conversations, my mom told me to be careful and not to ever get drunk on a date. She said she vomited on one of her first dates because she overindulged, which did not impress the boy she was with. I believed that counsel was appropriate until I was seventeen, when I actually saw her intoxicated for the first time. Then, her advice became contradictory, hypocritical and confusing. My parents still were very functional at home and at work most of the time, so I did not really get that alcohol was the problem. But it was really a hidden problem for me as their child, which I did not recognize as such until I got into recovery.

My parents were able to complete all their obligations and remained sober often, so I still thought our family was normal (The merry-go-round had started picking up speed). I did not understand that it could only get worse and that a normal family was becoming totally out of reach, just in time for me to start college. Since it was not apparent to me that alcohol was the problem, somehow, I thought it was *me*. The shame I felt and the related train-wreck of my life was just beginning to take shape.

Tom and Elaine O'Brien at a National Business Forms Assoc. ball, 1960s.

Kathleen with her brothers sitting on the diving board of their pool, 1968

Kathleen's dad in white at his pool party for customers

Lorraine and her son Nathan, 1980s, when she verified for Kathleen how dysfunctional my family was

(Above) Lorraine and Kathleen at Easter, 1960-61

(Below) Terry at 5 years old with Kathleen, 15, on vacation

(Left) Aunt Nancy and niece, Kathleen, 1980s

(Below) Kathleen (11 yrs.) with her mom (33 yrs.) and brothers Michael (9 yrs.) and Terry (6 mos. in lower right)

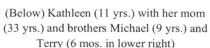

(Below) Mike S. and Kathleen going to their first high school dance, 1967

Chapter 8: *Mike's Venom Sauce*

*"Accept yourself, love yourself, and keep moving forward. If you want to
fly, you have to give up what weighs you down."*

— Roy T. Bennett, The Light in the Heart [16]

Even though there was a real condiment named "Mike's Venom
Sauce," this chapter isn't actually about the sauce, even though it has
some role in the story. The sauce was created by my brother Michael,
who was an Executive Chef and only twenty months younger than
me. He's the real story and I used the title of his sauce to imply a
revenge motive here: mine, not Mike's.

This chapter is in revenge for all the people who made fun of
him behind his back because he was different. Mike walked funny, on
his toes with a bounce, often destroyed everything in his path, was
clumsy at sports, and was hard of hearing. In addition, he replied to
others with either no answers or incomprehensible ones due to his
always tuning out, especially in class. These tendencies made him
look like he was slow-witted and perhaps unintelligent. I do not know
for sure, but he was likely a kid, who was picked last for a team.

And while pointing the finger at others who knew him, I need
to point the finger directly at myself too, his only sister. I thought

badly of him also, even though it didn't occur to me to make fun of him. I was just exasperated by him because he was always interfering with my plans and causing trouble. For example, one day when we were very young, I went into my room to have a tea party with my dolls and found that he had sawed off all the legs of my prized tea table.

I was such an uncaring sister that, when we were coloring, I only allowed him to use my orange crayons because I did not like the color orange. He got all my leftovers, and yet he took it in stride, with a smile on his face and kindness in his heart because that is who he was, not a mean bone in his body. When I was a pre-teen, I caught Michael trying to see me naked by way of the mirror near the slightly open door in my room.

When I was twelve, just about to get my period, Michael became interested in all things about puberty. After all, he was on the cusp of the inevitable hormone havoc himself at ten years old. Curious about everything, Mike was exploring under my bed where I had hidden the Kotex box (sanitary napkins) in preparation for my impending "transition to womanhood." He just thought the box contained huge cool bandages (We were all so delightfully naïve in those days at the cusp of puberty, not like today). Michael had a cut on his leg, so he wrapped the Kotex pad around the affected limb and started walking down the street to find his friends. Just then, Mom looked out the window, saw Mike's "bandage" and started running down the road after him.

Years later, we found out that he wasn't slow-witted at all. He did poorly in school until the powers that be found out he could not hear well due to an eraser stuck way into his ear. Moreover, his learning was further complicated because he could not see the board in school; he desperately needed glasses. To make matters worse, Mike never mentioned these issues to the teacher and they were not discovered until he transferred to public grammar school, where he was automatically tested for vision and hearing.

Michael was just a curious little boy and would inadvertently destroy things because he took everything apart that interested him to figure out how those items worked. He just wanted to understand what their purpose was. Any item in the universe would do, especially, MY prized possessions, but not only those. One time, Mike even took apart the telephone with my grandmother still on the other end of the line. My mother, who was talking to her mother on the phone had stepped away to get something and when she came back, she could hear my grandma talking, even though the whole earpiece was disassembled. Problem was, Michael seemed never to be able to put things back together again so that they worked well, at least not until he was much older.

Another time, Mom tried to open the back door and it was stuck. Upon further examination, she found out that it was nailed shut with a board across it on the other side. Michael had gone down to see "the workers," as he referred to the carpenters, who were building the house next door, and obtained a piece of scrap wood and nails from them. He then proceeded to practice being like a carpenter by nailing the door shut. That was not the only instance when Mike took something from "the workers" next door. Little did I know, this would become the house of my future good friend, Lorraine.

One day, some carpenters came over from the construction site to tell my mom that a lot of their tools were missing and they thought maybe the missing tools could be located at our house. Lo and behold they were found in our home! Michael was still very young, about four years old, and did not understand that those tools weren't for the taking. He just thought he was another carpenter doing his job alongside the other fellas.

Because he was a businessman who grew up in an apartment in Chicago, without learning how to work with his hands, Dad was no help in putting items back together or fixing things. His talents were in sales, with an ability to relate well to all sorts of people. At times when my parents needed something built or repaired around our house, they had to hire out.

Indeed, it was Mom who tried to fix or put back together the items that Mike got his little hands on. It only occurs to me now that my mom was dealing with a comedy of errors during Michael's younger years and we should have given her a lot of credit for her ingenuity and sense of humor during his early childhood. When Michael was a grown man, he learned to fix cars and other items as a hobby, but he wreaked havoc until then.

So, how are these stories related to the revenge I seek for my sweet brother? Well, as time went on, Mike showed others that he was a creative and intelligent human being with a talent for cooking and his ultimate masterpiece was his "Venom Sauce." The connoisseurs of very hot sauces raved about it and were his steady customers. Michael even patented it and worked with a canning company to start producing it, still hand-picking the tomatoes for his sauce until the end of his life. Regrettably, he died before he realized his dream of being set for life with the proceeds, but that is another part of this story in which his perseverance and integrity finally won out before he went to his Maker.

You see, Michael was an alcoholic and a druggie. Alcoholism was inevitable in our family with its history of hard drinking and smiling Irish eyes, while they drank themselves silly. Both my parents and many of my aunts, uncles and cousins indulged often in the "drink." Michael's sensitive side and inability to handle his pain from life's ignoble events, ensured his eventual succumbing to the "virus." His behavior was just one of the first symptoms of our family dysfunction. And sadly, Mike was the scapegoat for all our family problems during the drug culture of the 1960s and 1970s.

In what sociologists call "Family Systems Theory, everyone in the family usually takes on roles, when they interact with each other. Michael was the poster child for the role he took on called a "Scapegoat." According to the theory, at least one person in the family system takes on this function: "The Scapegoat is the 'problem child' or the 'trouble maker.' This family member always seems defiant, hostile and angry. The Scapegoat is the truth teller of the family and will often verbalize or act out the 'problem' which the family is attempting to cover up or deny." — *www.outofthestorm.website*[17]

My parents tried everything they knew of to help him. When Mike was fourteen years old, they sent him to a military boarding school to straighten him out academically and behaviorally. Michael told me later that he just felt like he was "sent away" and it was a sign to him that they either did not want him or didn't love him.

As a result, during his inaugural year of high school at St. Thomas Academy in Minnesota, he experimented for the first time with drugs and continued with that even when he was sent home after his freshman year to attend the local public high school. My parents didn't know any other way to make it better for Mike; however, they had good intentions, but no insight into what was needed to really help him thrive.

While away in college at St. Norbert in De Pere, Wisconsin, I would get frantic calls from my parents telling me that Michael stole money from Mom's purse to feed his habit or that he was arrested for drug use. There is usually another significant person in the addict's life, who enables the substance devotee's use of alcohol or drugs, cleans up their messes, denies there is a problem and perhaps doesn't even drink at all. All the people in our immediate family played the role of an enabler, but Dad was the most representative.

The person who plays this role in the system feels like it is their responsibility to save their loved one from themselves and in doing this, becomes just as sick as the drug or alcohol dependent family member. Our immediate family certainly became sick trying to maintain the status quo with an uncontrollable elephant in the room. In classic Alcoholics Anonymous lingo, the enabler is called the "co-dependent." Children, friends or a spouse can play this role too.

Although my dad had his own alcohol demons, being the strong co-dependent that he was, he saw to it that legally, Mike got off with a slap on the wrist for his behavior, when he was caught using marijuana. Co-dependents are known for always saving alcoholics from the consequences of their actions. This enabling only hurts substance abusers because it keeps them from feeling the pain of their addiction, something that is needed for the addict to finally decide to get sober.

In order to make sure that Michael would graduate from high school, Dad drove him there every day until the day Mike finished his secondary education. My parents were worried about Michael's choice of friends and activities too. But he was too old for my parents to try to curb his behavior. When they did, Michael just went to live with his friends in the City, where he had no restrictions.

Why should someone like Mike, who is an addict feel the repercussions of his unhealthy choices, if we, the rest of the family enable him to carry on drinking and drugging without him feeling the ramifications of his actions? Really, I felt helpless so far away at college and I even resented Michael for "ruining our family." Co-dependents are addicted to rescuing addicts close to them from their substance abuse and/or the consequences of it. Moreover, the addict is addicted to being saved by the enablers in his family. Meanwhile, the whole family is getting sicker by the minute and they do not know why. I was one of those getting sicker and my understanding of Mike's problem appeared to be just out of reach until I later got the education to grasp the concept of alcoholism as a disease and other types of substance abuse.

Case in point to my last sentence above: I am ashamed to admit that one summer home from college, I beat Michael up by pushing, shoving, punching and berating him (Mike was close to six-feet tall and much bigger than my 5'3 ½ inch frame, so I didn't inflict a lot of damage). Frustrated as the oldest and acting out what is called the "Hero"[17] role in Family Systems Theory, I just wanted it (the chaos caused by his addiction) to stop!

Usually, the oldest child like me takes on the "Hero" role, trying to keep the family from falling apart. Did I ever put my "Hero Complex" in Mike's face by blaming him for all the family problems! I later understood that it must have been devastating for my brother to feel like the troublemaker in the family, not getting the regular praise and accolades from our parents that I took for granted.

Today, feeling so remorseful for how I treated Michael, and my inexcusable actions, I would give anything to be able to ask for his forgiveness for my pernicious behavior toward him when we were young. I would even give him all my other crayon colors to use, not just the ones I didn't like. It never occurred to me during frantic calls from my parents in my college years that Dad and Mom should not have put this burden on me; they should have gone to counseling themselves to deal with Michael's problems with alcohol and drugs, instead of turning to me to be their confidant and counselor.

All these unhealthy behaviors of ours that I already described, illustrate how the disease of alcoholism destroys families from within, especially a prideful Irish family like mine, where appearances were everything and looking good at all costs was vitally important. My parents were never embarrassed by their own behavior when they drank, but God help you if you wore the wrong thing to a family event. I saw this happen one time when Mom practically chopped off my sibling, Terry's head because he was wearing shorts to a casual party hosted by my father's business friends, in honor of my dad after he died.

Of course, at that business party, Mom had been drinking and I remember her sister-in-law, Anne was looking at her sideways because she had never seen my mom act like that. Too bad that her own children had seen her act like that quite often during their lifetimes, but we were made to feel that what was really happening in our home was just a figment of our imaginations, so it was hard for me to figure out until I was older and got counseling.

My kind, non-violent and sensitive father even acted out negatively by throwing my brother across the room one time, where Mike accidentally went through the plate glass window. I know my dad felt a lot of guilt about that because he had caved into his anger to hurt his own child. It was so atypical of Dad's normal behavior; he was not cruel in any way and I had never seen him strike anyone, certainly not anyone in the family. Instead, I saw him hit the wall a few times, punching a hole. No one said a thing and Mom just put a picture over the damage, as if this was normal. Usually, Dad displayed kindness, tolerance, and compassion for others, so I am sure his uncharacteristic physical action towards Mike is one of the things he drank over himself.

Michael was indubitably the scapegoat for all our problems, but it was just the beginning of more heartache in the family. A few years later, Mike stopped coming around altogether. In the meantime, my middle brother was using all kinds of drugs and drinking himself into oblivion. God knows what he got into. We heard he was living somewhere in the city of Chicago near all the prostitutes and other questionable people.

After not having seen Mike for a couple of years, I was in the pharmacy near my parent's house in the suburbs when I unexpectedly ran into him. He looked dirty, disheveled and frankly: mangy. I asked him what he was doing way out in Glenview, when he was living in the City (Chicago). He told me he had just picked up a prescription. My suspicion radar went up and as soon as Mike walked away, I went to the pharmacist and yelled at him. I said, "Did you know HE (pointing Mike out as he was walking out the door) is a DRUG ADDICT?"

I grilled the poor pharmacist about why he had given Mike drugs. (Do you see raging co-dependence by me here anyone?) The pharmacist apologized, saying he was just filling a legitimate prescription and did not know. You see, a lot of addicts get prescriptions from many different doctors to deter investigation of their drug use and I suspected that my brother, who lived in the City, was way out in Glenview to pick up a prescription where his scheme would be less likely to be detected. I did not understand the problem then, therefore; I was acting like the big sister co-dependent that I was.

Not long after seeing my brother at the Glenview pharmacy, my dad found Mike passed out in his car at the end of our driveway and it was then that my distraught, weeping brother asked my dad for help. Michael went to treatment three times and the third time was a charm. He gave up alcohol and drugs and eventually all tobacco and started going to A.A. meetings. Later, he touchingly gave me his ninety-day-sober chip as a memento of his sobriety. Still residing in my jewelry box, I cherish it, and think about how hard he had had to work to stay sober.

A creative man, Michael liked to cook and to play around with mechanical things as his major interests. At first, turning Michael's mechanical tinkering into a great skill took many years of constant effort. He never gave up and just kept practicing on anything he could get his hands on. Mostly, the puttering relaxed Mike and was more like a hobby. Cooking, however, became a profession, and he was great at it. He went to two years of college to learn how to be a Chef.

Mike was very different from our younger brother, Terry, who was more interested in sports and business, taking after our dad. I see Terry's family role as the "Mascot" in the system. "In family therapy dialogue the mascot is the family member, who deflects tension and conflict with humor or distraction ... Many comedians once played this role in their families ..." *https://www.edmondfamily.org/efc-articles/family-roles*.[18]

Terry could always see the humor in things. I could see it in his actions and his little kid drawings like his creation, "Terry's Terrible Toothpaste." Even at two years old, he made us laugh with his witticisms and ingenuity. His sense of humor helped him later to be a very successful salesman and his creativity shows up in his job to this very day. Later, when I talk about some of Terry's antics as a toddler, the reader will see his ingenuity bear out, even at such a young age. Again, when Michael and I left the house for school and work, Terry was only about thirteen years old and he was left alone to bear the brunt of Mom and Dad's drinking.

Like most of the O'Brien men, Dad was hopeless when it came to mechanical things and always hired out to get things done around the house. Dad passed on the qualities of compassion and people skills to both of his sons, needed in the future to be successful in both of the O'Brien boys' chosen careers, time well spent in my opinion. Terry went into sales and Michael got into cooking.

If Mike wasn't into drugs and alcohol, I think he would have moved up to a Chef position more quickly, or at least found work in places where he could have made a lot more money, maybe even have been a celebrity Chef. The only thing about being a Chef was having to work the grueling 80-hour weeks, which tired him out and didn't help his drinking problem.

Handling all those orders at the same time required close to acrobatic skills, but he did it well. Once or twice when I came home from college, and needed to make money, Mike and I worked at the same restaurants: me, as a waitress and Michael as a cook or a Chef. Two of these restaurants were Glenview Country House and Hackney's on Lake, both in our hometown of Glenview, IL.

Vividly, I remember an instance when I was picking up an order in the kitchen near where my brother was cooking. One of the managers came in and started making sexually harassing comments to me, as I waited for my order to come up. This guy actually reached over to me and tweaked my breast on top of my thin uniform material. The scene in the kitchen became even more awkward because the manager did not realize that Mike and I were siblings, and was taken aback when he noticed Michael watching him suspiciously after he had the nerve to touch my breast right in front of everyone.

That crude and grabby manager was really flabbergasted when Mike spoke up to him in a harsh voice, "Hey, that's my sister!" The man immediately stopped niggling me and quickly left the kitchen. If my brother had not been there, I am sure that that entitled manager would have bothered me every night until I went back to school at the end of the summer. Today, with strong laws to back us up, the strides women have since made in our ability to stop sexual harassment and assault (because that incident would surely be considered assault today) have been warranted and remarkable.

At Hackney's, Michael learned to make my two favorite dishes on the menu: strawberry cheesecake and a large loaf of onion rings that were to die for. If you ever go to Glenview, stop in Hackney's on Lake to try their onion rings, which are famous in the local area. Our family loved it when Michael would cook the Hackney onion rings and cheesecake for us at home, but it was not often because he worked so many hours. If mom was cooking when Mike was home, all he wanted to eat was her meat loaf or her spaghetti, just our customary family fare. He rarely ever wanted to eat anything fancy himself.

In the late seventies, Mike met the love of his life, Karen Funke, at a restaurant they were both working at in Chicago. The two of them were a very committed couple because no matter how much my brother drank and used drugs, they were able to stay together, due to Karen's abundant patience and love. Getting married on November 2, 1979, they eventually left Chicago to get away from the bad influences of some of Mike's friends. This geographical relocation tactic usually does not work without other forms of help. Nevertheless, they moved to Indianapolis, Karen's hometown.

They lived by the racetrack where the "Indianapolis 500" was held every year. In fact, for a few years, Mike made extra money by parking cars of the race goers on his lawn. After several years of sobriety, he became the Executive Chef for Howard Johnson's Restaurant, right next to the "Indianapolis 500" racetrack.

By trusting my brother with cooking for the racetrack V.I.P.'s, the owners let Michael order and outfit a brand new very expensive trailer with all the bells and whistles, which they acquired as their on-site kitchen to cook for the well-to-do racetrack guests at the mother of all race car events. I was truly proud of him, but it was a stressful life of eighty-hour work weeks for him. Happily, he spent his off-time fishing and working on mechanical things, hoping one day to change his career from cooking to repairing cars and such, but he never got the chance.

During the eighties, when Mike's sobriety was not yet a foregone conclusion, his weight fluctuated and he would balloon up quite a bit. Smoking was another habit he indulged in quite regularly. He later told me that smoking and overeating were the hardest for him to give up. After abstaining from drugs and alcohol for good, he started to work on his other addictions.

Although he stayed clean and sober from alcohol and drug abuse for the last eleven years of his life, he still had the smoking and overeating issues to tackle. Smoking was the next vice to go, which he successfully gave up. While he was working on overeating and caffeine abuse as his last hurdles, an old illness appeared that he had probably contracted in the seventies as a result of his drug use.

Michael had known for years that he had contracted Hepatitis C, but the disease had laid dormant for most of his life. It only reared its ugly head around the year 2000, when his liver had trouble processing the medicine he was prescribed for a nasty cold. At the time, there was no cure for Hepatitis C, but the symptoms could be mitigated for a long time with the proper unique combination of medicines; however, his time started to run out because his liver started failing.

He was only forty-seven years old in May of 2001, when his doctors performed liver transplant surgery. Mike knew several people who had received a transplant and then lived a full life after that for many years, albeit having to take anti-rejection drugs for the rest of their lives. Mike fully expected it would happen that way for him.

As he was waiting in the anteroom of the operating theatre, I went in to see him. The Hepatitis C had taken a toll on his body, especially on his skin, which had turned very yellow. In addition, his eyes now had a yellow cast and he had lost a lot of weight, which would have been good under any other circumstances. He seemed calm and ready to tackle this fifty-thousand-dollar major surgery with tranquility and serenity, learned from almost eleven years in twelve-step recovery programs like A.A. To help Mike gain that inner calmness, he often said a prayer he learned in A.A., like so many other alcoholics trying to recover:

The Serenity Prayer
https://en.wikipedia.org/wiki/Serenity_Prayer[19]
(Section 9 Part 2)

God grant me the serenity,
To accept the things I cannot change,
Courage to change the things I can,
And the wisdom to know the difference.

— Reinhold Niebuhr

AA 90-day sobriety chip like the one Mike earned and gave to Kathleen as a keepsake. (from the author's personal collection)

Michael had eleven years of sobriety before his body succumbed to years of abuse. Unfortunately, a long life was out of reach for him as he died at only forty-seven due to Hepatitis C and a liver transplant that didn't take. But he died at peace with his Maker and with his family and all those he had helped stay sober for the last eleven years of his life—a time of contentment and sobriety for Michael. This is not the end of Mike's story or his influence on my life as you shall see in coming installments.

The story of Michael's life with sobriety is inspirational and bittersweet, especially, how his life unfolded after so many years of abusing his body. I thought my brother would keep drinking until he died in his thirties and that sobriety was out of reach for him. Fortunately, I was wrong about that last part; let the rest of Mike's addiction/recovery story unfold later in this book. It is such a profound tale, which needs its own chapter to give justice to his transformation.

Mike at 14 years old in St. Thomas Academy, Minnesota, 1972

(Above) Mike at 16 years old, in the midst of his drug addiction, two years after the St. Thomas picture was taken (Right)

(Left) Kathleen in Theta Phi Sorority Pledge Class of 1972 (Second from left, first row) at the White Rose Ball, St. Norbert College, De Pere, WI

Chapter 9: *Shame Does Not Discriminate*

Nice to meet you, my name is Shame.
My soul is broken and I'm full of blame.
It's about who I am, not what I've done.
You'd better be careful, I'll give you some.

My Name is Shame — Kathleen Iverson, Verse 2, 1996

You don't have to be an addict to feel shame. Guilt is normal when you know you did something wrong. Shame is different and is not usually a constructive nor a rational emotion. Toxic shame occurs because the ones who experience it feel like they ARE the something wrong or are mistakes in and of themselves; therefore, it comes from somewhere deeper. This is due to earlier destructive experiences from incidents that are not usually perpetrated by the person in question, but by others.

John Bradshaw, an expert in understanding family dysfunction says in his book, *Healing the Shame that Binds You,* "…We are taught to be nice and polite. We are taught that these behaviors (most often lies) are better than telling the truth. Our churches, schools, and politics are rampant with teaching dishonesty (saying things we do not mean and pretending to feel ways we don't feel). We smile when we feel sad; laugh nervously when dealing with grief; laugh at jokes we don't think are funny; tell people things to be polite that we surely don't mean…"[21]

My brother Mike's addiction was the first visible sign of a family falling apart. We had a beautiful picture taken when I was nineteen years old (see page 57). Later, I knew better that it was a fantasy, which kept me wondering when the picture in my heart would match the picture of my family in that photo. Instead, it never lived up to what I hoped for. I had just started to realize that there were cracks in our façade. It was a family colored by a lurking disease of addiction, characterized by shame. In reality, that photo had been a gift from me to my parents. It was a letdown that the appointment for the photo session was early in the morning on the weekend and my parents grumbled all the way to the studio that I was making them do this.

Of course, my parents were out the night before, which meant they probably drank a lot and were in no mood to get up. I don't think they ever liked that picture or any other ones taken when Elaine was older than forty years old. I knew this because years later I sketched a composite of those pictures for my mom as a birthday gift after my dad died and she never put it up on the wall, nor did she ever put up the original photo. Mom made it clear she did not like the part of the photo (see page 57) or the subsequent drawing I made that included her. My dad also looks a little hung over, but looking at it, the average person would not know that. To most people though, the photo looks like a gorgeous family of two parents and three children. I was hurt and ashamed of their reaction to my gift and later Mom's less than excited reaction to my drawing based on the photo.

Shame was involved because I thought there was something wrong with me instead of seeing their reaction as being inappropriate to the situation. I concluded that I was not worthy of receiving a show of warmth and thanks from them for my thoughtful present because my parents had to get up early on the weekend to obtain them. Shame is like that: insidious, working its way into your psyche with every scenario where the outcome is similar: me feeling like I was a failure or less than and not worthy of their praise. They never considered the expense I incurred for the photo when I was only a poor nineteen-year-old college student.

After Dad died, Mom never acknowledged the time and effort I put into drawing her a picture based partly on that photo. The reality was, they had made unwise decisions the night before the photo shoot about drinking that caused hangovers, which was their responsibility, not mine. Even at nineteen years old, that bit of wisdom about who was responsible for what in life gave me the impression of being out of my reach. It wouldn't be obtained for a long time to come, after much therapy and work on myself helped me to understand the impact their drinking had on our family.

My reaction to that whole episode demonstrated how I unwittingly took on the shame my mom harbored within herself. Again, it shows how shame can get passed down within the family and my mom's stemmed from her childhood when she was molested by her older brother. As gorgeous as she was, she did not have confidence in herself, which could explain her flirting with my boyfriends and wearing low-cut outfits to make herself feel better.

Inappropriate behavior begets inappropriate behavior. It was all very confusing for me and contributed to my own low self-esteem and shame. I knew right from wrong but was not sure how to behave in a lot of situations. And my trust-meter was broken. How could it not be with the mixed messages I received from both my parents?

Even though I loved my parents, faults and all, I couldn't understand what was going on in our house. My youngest brother, Terry thinks Mom was a "narcissist" and after studying it, I spotted many of those traits in her. But with ten years longer as part of this family than Terry, at times I also saw in my mother some love and caring for others. Terry, being much younger than me, did not really experience the healthy times with my parents because the drinking was already well underway, when he was six to seven years old and I was about to leave for college. During my high school years, I noticed that when she imbibed, Mom's drinking made her kind of mean. Terry lived with this behavior, when my parent's change in drinking was much worse, until he himself left for college.

Because of her drinking and how her personality changed as time went on, Terry was ashamed to bring people home which is something I only started to experience for the last years of high school, before I left home for college. Terry allowed his anger toward her to be his overwhelming emotion as a way of coping with her behavior. I used to feel the same way, but lots of therapy helped me really forgive Mom and appreciate her good qualities, which gave me a more balanced picture of her. To do that, I tried to think of some great things she did during my childhood, like she always ensured we were properly fed, clothed, and sheltered. More than that, I remember her going out of her way to make me the best costume for Halloween, giving me her costume jewelry and letting me use her fur stole as part of my get-up. Until my teen years, when Mom's drinking became more obvious, I remember being secure and happy.

Around her fortieth birthday, she started drinking a lot more as she was getting older, but I only figured that out years later. Is it no wonder that I was confused about people, especially relationships? Now, as mentioned earlier, I see that she was jealous of me and how close I was to my dad. Jealousy from my mother was the last thing I thought of when I pondered our arguments that took place during my teen years. It always seemed she wanted me to be glamorous like her.

Almost everyone I knew would exclaim how beautiful she was upon meeting her. I really did not have a sense of how pretty I was, but I always knew I could never be in her league; her beauty was comparable to Ms. Elizabeth Taylor, who was almost the same age as Elaine and they looked alike. Like Elizabeth, Mom was very exotic looking with dark hair, a flawless complexion, high cheekbones. and almond-shaped "cat eyes;" however, their eye colors were different. Ms. Taylor's eye color was violet, and my mother's was yellowish-brown. I used to call myself the "girl next door," whereas I called my mom, "Elizabeth Taylor beautiful."

At the time, I could never imagine jealousy toward me coming from my glamorous, beautiful, elegant mom. My parents were very popular in their social circles and went dressed to the nines to a myriad of events like conventions, balls, and trips for my dad's business. I used to watch Elaine put on her make-up, jewelry, and a gorgeous ball gown and wanted to be just like her. After all, she had my dad, Thomas Joseph O'Brien, the handsome son of Johanna Spillane of County Kerry, Ireland and John Joseph O'Brien of Chicago, Illinois. When my parents went out, people used to remark that they looked like the ultimate power couple at the time, Richard Burton and Elizabeth Taylor.

For Elaine, what was there to be jealous about regarding her only daughter? My question should have been, "What was wrong with this picture?" It is not normal for a mother to be jealous of her only daughter, especially since my dad gave her a lot of attention, compliments, romantic gifts, and love. They spent a lot of time together and my dad was always home for 5:00 p.m. dinner or out to dinner with her. He treated her like a queen and made sure to always point up her good points to the children so, I suspect, to help us to love her more than we did.

However, Dad must have known some of her feelings towards me were not appropriate because I recall an episode, when I had lost a lot of weight while being away in the Navy. Upon coming home to visit in uniform looking healthy and slim, Dad later told me that when he picked me up from the airport and I looked so thin and beautiful in my summer white uniform, that he was afraid of Elaine's reaction to my new look. His fear was not unfounded, as seen by how she reacted. Saying sarcastically to my friend who had come over to see me, "What do you think of my THIN, beautiful daughter?" That trip home, she picked on me a lot and was very critical.

Another time, Mom told me it was MY fault that Dad had had a heart attack because he had to take out loans to send me to college. Dad told me later that it was not true because he, in veritably, took out loans to take Mom on vacations. Elaine had also told me that since I came along only ten months into their marriage, that it was MY fault that she never had much alone time with my father before I was born. At the time, I did not see how shaming her words were, causing me to feel like *I was* a mistake. When I wrote the poem/song seen under the title at the beginning of this chapter, I really had experience with that debilitating emotion called shame, which contributed directly to too many of the poor decisions I made later as an adult. Healthy relationships still seemed out of reach for me for many years of my life to follow.

(Right) O'Brien family picture that Kathleen gave to her parents for a present. Upper row: Michael (17) and Kathleen (19) Front row: Elaine (41), Terry (9), Thomas (52)

(Above) Kathleen looking slim in her light blues, about 1979

(Right) Kathleen home on leave with Tom, Elaine and Terry 1980s

Ensign Kathleen O'Brien & Recruiting District
Captain in Orlando, FL., 1980

(Above) Kathleen is being promoted by
the NTC Admiral (left) and the Chief of
Staff (right), 1981.

(Above) Kathleen and Christina, 1989

(Left) Elaine's 60th Birthday Party, 1990

Kathleen (middle Right) next to friend wearing
the first Navy pregnancy uniform, early 1980s

(Above) Elaine and Kathleen, 1990

Chapter 10: *The Trouble with Friends and Groups*

In order to develop good group dynamics,
you must first develop good relationships.

— https://en.m.wikibooks.org › wiki › Group Dynamics [22]

I think I always felt like I did not fit in, except for a few grand periods of my life. I truly did not know why I was different. I remember thinking when I was in college that people seemed to really like me when we first met, but as they got to know me a little bit, somehow, they distanced themselves from me. In hindsight, I wonder if this was a result of my undiagnosed ADHD symptoms. However, if we really got to know each other, they liked my honesty and sincerity. But that only happened if we spent a lot of time together, like being college roommates or sorority sisters or by growing up in the same neighborhood.

Years later, I started to get a clue about why the process of friendship was not an easy one for me. It also never occurred to me that someone could be jealous of me because I thought I was just an average person, nothing special. Since I could not find any reasons for people to be jealous of me, I underestimated some people's intense dislike of me and therefore, did not see pain approaching when it raised its ugly head, one made of betrayal, exclusion and with no regard for others. Not naturally skeptical of people's motives, it seemed to me that sometimes folks could be cruel out of the blue and I had not seen it coming.

An example of this behavior toward me took place in college, walking down the middle of the campus square during class-changing time with plenty of other students within listening distance. Two boys I thought were my friends yelled to me from the tower, loudly shouting down to me, "Hey, Motor Mouth, what's happening?" I was mortified and embarrassed and tried to laugh at it, but it hurt that people saw me that way.

Other examples of unkindness happened when I introduced friends from one of my circles to acquaintances of my other circles. I introduced my college roommate to someone and they became friends and began to leave me out of social situations or not include me when they drove home for Christmas break to the Chicago area, where we all lived. Countless other times I introduced people who shortly became friends and proceeded to leave me out of their plans. It has even happened into my sixties, so that I have become skittish about introducing people that I know who have a lot in common with each other because I didn't want the inevitable to happen. I do not mean that they just left me out of adventures they did together, but they stopped talking to me as a close friend or did not enjoy my company alone, as they had done before.

When I was stationed in California in the nineteen-nineties, I had a best friend named Bonnie F. Luckily, I am still friends with her to this day. But it got a little shaky when I introduced her to a girl I met with (unfortunately) my same name, "Kathleen O'Brien." The two met when they were both invited to my fortieth birthday celebration. They hit it off and became close friends. Since I was in the Navy and would be transferred the following year, they became even closer friends after I left the area.

In fact, when Kathleen got married, Bonnie was her Maid-of-Honor. Bonnie had been my Maid-of-Honor earlier that same year, but all the above was not the reason I felt uncomfortable. It was because I felt replaced by someone who had my exact name, spelled the same way. When I called Bonnie one time she asked, "Which Kathleen O'Brien is this?" I also heard others in Bonnie's family say to her, "Which Kathleen are you talking about?" I wanted to shout, "*I am the ONLY Kathleen!*" because Bonnie was MY best friend. Even though I liked Kathleen a lot too, it brought up *my own* insecurities.

To this day we are still close friends and Bonnie has proven many times that I am special to her, but that was a time I wondered. Bonnie does not trust people that easily and I have seen that she trusts me with everything she has and that goes a long way. She accepts me, even with my faults and is not afraid to tell me when she is irritated with something I do and then we move on and I know we are okay. She allows me to tell her truth with love too and it grows our relationship. It was just kind of weird, given that Kathleen has my exact first and last name, spelled the same way. In a childish way, I thought, "*Can't I have my OWN best friend? Is that out of reach for me too?*"

Another time, I had a close friend that I met through church named Katie Anderson. She and I did everything together in the singles ministry. She was a little more mature spiritually than I was because she had been a serious Christian a lot longer than I had been. At first, she was kind of a mentor and one time she was a singles-ministry coach to me when I was leading my first church small group, so I looked up to her. We both wanted to be married, but for a long time, it was not meant to be. Six or seven years later, however, we both got our wish. I met Bill Iverson, my now husband of twenty-three years first and she met Dan Tyler soon after I married Bill.

Bill and I had been part of a wonderful church couple's small group for a few years that had four great leaders (two couples who took turns leading). About ten to fifteen years older than we were, they were wonderful marriage mentors to us and many others. We will call the older lead couple, James and Mary Thomson and the slightly younger co-lead couple, Joe and Patty Walter. Katie often remarked about how she wished that she and Dan could be in our couple's group, but we already had ten people and that was the max. The four co-leaders of our group felt that if the group got too large, it would be too hard to manage to ensure everyone would get a chance to share during our meetings. So, I told Katie that our leaders had decided that we had too many people and that there was not enough room for another couple.

One New Year's Eve, Bill and I put together an impromptu gathering and invited the Walters and Tylers to come over for snacks and games. That night, our two couple friends met each other for the first time. After that get-together, unbeknownst to me, Katie started to contact Patty on her own and asked Patty if Katie and Dan Tyler could be part of the small group. Patty said she wanted to talk to her husband and co-leader, Joe, as well as James and Mary Thomson, the other the co-leaders and then discuss it with Bill and me to see how we all felt about it. A lot of problems could ensue because the addition of a new couple would require our larger group to split into two smaller separate groups to ensure intimacy and productive engagement for each member.

However, before those talks even happened, Katie talked to me, saying she had discussed it already with Patty and that Patty said it was OK for Katie and Dan to join the small group, if *I* said it was OK. Later, I found out that Katie told Patty that I had already said it was OK, even though I had not even agreed to that yet. In other words, Katie lied to manipulate the situation. I only agreed to the Tylers joining our group when Katie told me that our leaders, the Walters and Thomsons already said it was fine, even though I felt a foreboding with this decision. Patty only agreed because she thought I had already told Katie that I was OK with it. The re-forming of our group was now based on false assumptions.

After it was decided that the Tylers could join the group, the other co-leaders made the decision to split and take half of us to form another group, which is something I had worried about up front and did not want at all; however, I had already agreed to the Tylers' joining the larger group, hoping we would not need to split. My worry about breaking up our great group came true. When the group split (also called "birthing") we would now be in a new group with Patty and Joe, Katie and Dan and another couple, the Nelsons.

Before we had our first meeting as a birthed group, I had a long talk with Katie about my sensitivity to the situation. I told her that in the past, I had introduced people to each other and that they later became good friends and would leave me out. She assured me that that would never happen with us. After all, we had been close friends for seven years, who confided almost everything to each other. I did not want to seem selfish, so I swallowed my reservations and went with it.

Not long afterwards, I started regretting my ascent. Suddenly, Katie was harder to get a hold of and distanced herself from me, no longer talking on the phone with me as often as we usually did. During small group meetings, Katie would cut me off, when it was my turn to speak or appeared to be competing with me during small group discussions. I started to feel that I did not have a voice in the group anymore.

After about a year of this, fortunately, Dan and Katie got involved in another ministry and decided that they could not do both, so they made the decision to leave ours. I was secretly relieved. Katie told me she was afraid we would not see each other a lot in the future due to their leaving our group. I assured her that we would still be friends, which I sincerely meant because our friendship with the them had worked well before Katie and Dan joined our group, so I thought it would go back to how it was before.

Even though I was secretly glad they were leaving our group because the dynamics there had become weird, I really thought if we were not in the same group anymore, our relationship would be better. Our small group took our regular summer break, planning to start up again in September sans Dan and Katie.

Another couple was invited to take their place, Jack and Juliet Cole, but the night before we started our meetings with the new couple, Joe and Patty called an emergency meeting of the original members because Katie had reconsidered and was asking to come back into the group. Joe and Patty asked us what we thought. With only the original group members present, I finally came clean and told the two other couples that if Dan and Katie came back, I could not remain.

I then proceeded to tell the Walters and the Nelsons what had transpired during the year that Katie and Dan were part of our group. I explained everything and told them that during that year, Katie had stopped confiding in me and there were many important things she had never told me about. She had started telling Patty those things instead, leaving me out of confidences I had always been a part of as her best friend.

The Nelsons said, "If the Iverson's leave, we will leave," explaining to us that they had noticed and did not like the way Katie was behaving in the group and especially did not like how I was being treated during meetings by my so-called best friend, Katie. I was surprised; I had not realized that it was so noticeable. During the discussion that followed, our leader, Patty and I realized that Katie had duped us; Katie told each of us separately that the other had already said it was OK for the Tylers to join the group and that was not really true; however, both Patty and I had eventually said yes because we thought the other one had said yes first.

Basically, we were manipulated by Katie, so she could ensure Dan and she would be let into the group. Not only that, by Dan and Katie joining our original small group of ten members, it forced us to split up into two small groups, changing the dynamics and pretty much destroying the original group that Katie had coveted.

When Patty and Joe told Katie and Dan that the group said, "No" to letting them back in, Katie went crazy and called poor Patty every name in the book. Later, she also accused me of being the one to not let them back in and kept screaming at me on the phone. I finally said that she had ruined the group for me, even after she had promised that she would be sensitive to my past experiences with introducing my friends to each other from different spheres in my life. I felt betrayed.

In therapy, my counselor helped me understand how toxic my relationship with Katie was and that I should let it go, which I eventually did, even though it was excruciating to do so. I truly did not want to let go of that formerly close relationship we had built up for seven years. Katie tried to apologize by sending me letters and I forgave her, but had to explain to her that even though I forgave her, I would never trust her again, so we could not be close friends. There had been a few other lesser betrayals by Katie before this, which I had forgiven, but this was the last straw. After that, it seemed for a long time that I was skittish entering into a close relationship with someone at church. One thing I had to remember to get over this was that churches are made up of people and people make mistakes. No church is perfect, but the honesty and integrity of our four leaders helped so that the problems in our group were ultimately handled with integrity and sensitivity.

Also, thank God for my two close friends from California, Bonnie and Karen. They are still good friends, whom I have trusted for all the thirty-plus years that I have known them. If it wasn't for those two, I would have thought that healthy close friendships were out of my reach because it took me a long time to trust new people that I had met at church at a deep level like I thought I had shared with Katie for seven years. Tearing myself away from Katie was agonizing, but I knew that for my own mental health, I had to do it.

Knowing Bonnie and Karen, whom I trusted implicitly for so long eventually, made me ready to try to form close relationships again at church, but it took a while. I also remembered my long-term friendships with Val and Lorraine, which began in my neighborhood growing up, giving me hope for forming good new relationships.

In the meantime, it seemed like having a best friend close by, as I had had with Val, was never going to happen again. I trusted my old friend Valerie because I knew her from the neighborhood in Glenview since we were five years old. Now we live in different states. How do you make friends like Val, when you do not grow up with them, which entails spending many years nearby? That was my new conundrum. Should I have just accepted that I would never have a close friend like Valerie again, approximate to where my career and life had led me?

However, I again remembered I did have another good friend from the neighborhood in Glenview, who had lived next door to our house, the very house my brother Michael stole the wood from the "workers" on Virginia Lane. Lorraine Amideo was someone who always seemed wiser than me. Where I was impulsive and hyper, she was calm and collected. Her influence had a great impact on me during the growing up years until we went to college and to my surprise, an even greater one as we matured, even though we also lived in different states by then.

Lorraine and I have kept up our visits and correspondence, albeit sporadically, but it has never seemed awkward when we do come together and through our later talks, I have gained insight into my family dynamics and about people on Virginia Lane. For example, Lorraine told me about how her family had heard a lot of the commotion happening at my house because they lived so close to us.

Plus, we loved playing together with the first Barbie dolls, which came out in 1959, when we were seven years old. As young girls, we acted out life for hours with Barbie, Ken, Midge and Skipper in our elaborate doll houses, built from cardboard and other found objects.

Our families used rectangular milk metal delivery boxes with hinged lids, (Yes, milk was still delivered to our houses in the fifties and sixties) so, we used them to make garages for our Barbie and Ken cars. The cars fit perfectly and if the milk delivery boxes were laid on their side, with the hinged door swinging up; they, in effect, simulated an actual garage door, like on our real life-sized houses.

Our make-believe houses included elaborate stone walkways made of pebbles we found on the street. Some of us even had the Barbie House and Barbie Fashion Store to set up as part of our pretend neighborhood. Moreover, Barbie cases stood in for the closets that we used to store our gorgeous designer-like doll clothes and we packed them up each day when we finished playing, to again be brought out for the next day's session.

I bring all this up about our doll-playing because of one sweet thing that happened when we were in our thirties having to do with these precious dolls so representative of our go-to activities from our time in the sixties. In the early eighties, Lorraine told me that she had something to give me during a visit to her house in Georgia. I was so surprised when she brought out her old Barbie doll case. She opened it and inside was my Midge doll (Barbie's best friend) still dressed in a red velvet and white sateen strapless cocktail dress.

Lorraine told me I must have left the Midge doll at her house in Glenview, the last time we played Barbie at about twelve years old. She had kept this doll all these years, which touched me greatly, especially since without asking me, my mom had given away my whole collection of Barbie dolls and paraphernalia when I went away to college, to include: the fashion store, car, house, clothes and other items. Lorraine had surmised correctly that I would cherish our memories through having one of my most precious dolls in my hands again from that era.

And for you all, who hate the idea of Barbie dolls because of their seemingly unnatural big bosoms and impossibly small waists (which have since been redesigned to be of more normal proportions for today's kids) I think you have the wrong idea about how Barbie affected us, well, in particular, me. Barbie was so over the top in her shape and style, not one of us took her seriously as our "ideal" role model. She was just a fantasy to most of us to make believe, conversing about life and creating new scenarios and new spaces of which we had total control and of which no one could change or alter, but us. We used Barbie for play-acting out our lives as adults, like we saw our parents living or Rob and Laura Petrie on the Dick Van Dyke Show behaving. Just because Laura was thin and beautiful didn't mean we saw all our mothers that way, or even cared if they were.

We knew the difference between the reality of our mother's situation and Laura Petrie's. She was a young mother on T.V. and our mothers were real, loving ladies in our homes, even if they all were not that young, thin or beautiful. I compared myself to my friends and people I knew, not to what was "make-believe" on T.V. As a result of these experiences, I do not subscribe to the idea of not letting your child play with Barbie because she is glamorous or of an unattainable shape. Are boys kept away from Spiderman figurines because their fathers are afraid the kids will feel damaged because they do not meet the look or criteria of being an action figure? I think not.

Most of the girls I knew had many other dolls besides Barbie, like Chatty Cathy, Betsy Wetsy, or Patty Play Pal for different periods in our lives. The worst influence (if you could call it that) on me by playing with Barbie dolls would be that I loved beautiful clothes later in life, whether I bought them or made them myself. Learning how to mix and match the clothes and styles while playing with Barbie, positively influenced my color coordination, taste and flair for dressing well, even on a budget.

Knowing that I probably would never be a model was reality, but Barbie let me feel like I was one, through play-acting with her. Dolls never let me feel "less than;" only other people did. Mostly those I knew personally and only because my foundation of self-esteem was low, the further I got into puberty and adulthood. The other factors I have already described, like ADHD, family dynamics, and alcoholism were the real culprits in my life before puberty and it was rare to start puberty before twelve or thirteen years old then. Playing Barbie with my friends were the happiest and most rewarding times of my younger childhood. Back then it seemed that a good life was available for me to embrace and nothing was out of reach.

Kathleen & Valerie in the 1990s

Bonnie F. with date — Navy Ball, 1992

(Left) Second Couples Group at Willow Creek Church

67

(Left) Carol Koski and Kathleen on their way to see "Solid Gold" show in LA, CA.

(Right) Kathleen in 1991, when "Glamour Shots" were all the rage.

(Left) Our First Couples Group at Willow Creek Church in early 2000s

(Right) My First Women's Group at Willow Creek Church in late 90s

(Left) Willow Creek Couples Small Group Reunion in 2019 Kathleen is in front middle and Bill is behind her.

Chapter 11: *Celebrity Encounters of the Third Kind*

*"You only live once,
but if you do it right,
once is enough."*

— Mae West [23]

Obviously, the title of this section is a play on words referring to the very popular seventies film called "Close Encounters of the Third Kind"[24] directed by Steven Spielberg about a man played by Richard Dreyfuss in his first major role as the lead actor in a movie. It also marked the return of science fiction as a popular genre among the public. The idea for this movie was inspired by the writings of J. Allen Hynek who outlined three types of encounters humans could have with aliens in his book first published in 1972 called *The UFO Experience: A Scientific Inquiry*.[25] The three types of encounters are as follows:

- Close Encounters of the First Kind: an unidentified flying object is seen close enough to see some detail.
- Close Encounters of the Second Kind: an unidentified flying object is seen close enough to experience physical ramifications, like lights flashing or objects spontaneously acting out.
- Close Encounters of the Third Kind: an unidentified flying object is seen close enough that animate objects or people are also encountered and communicated with.

The movie, named after the third type of encounter is pertinent to this chapter for several reasons. First, it was released near the time I was coming into my own as an adult after finishing college and working at my first teaching job. Moreover, I joined the Navy and started experiencing things and people that were previously thought to be out of my reach and a lot of those new encounters had to do with celebrities.

69

Second, it starred Richard Dreyfuss, a brilliant actor who always seemed to play a regular guy. He happened upon unbelievable circumstances that somehow changed his life in good ways by bringing out his courageous spirit and calling for him to stretch himself farther than he ever imagined that he could go. Some of my encounters during this time stretched me as far as I could go too in my twenties.

Third, Dreyfuss made another movie around this time called *The Goodbye Girl*[26] for which he won an Academy Award about a man not always understood or liked at first encounter because of his unusual ways, relationship failures and laser focus on making a success of his career as an actor above all else. Like me, the character Dreyfuss played, felt misunderstood a lot because of his awkwardness and unusual ways, so I identified a lot with him.

All the quirks and reactions demonstrated by Richard Dreyfuss in these movies, as well as the themes expressed, seem tailor-made for explaining my own encounters with new situations and relationships in the seventies and beyond. As a byproduct, I was made stronger and wiser. Along the way, I have had some unbelievable experiences to share, mostly encounters of the *Third Kind*.

As I have thought about the following story from my life, I started to wonder if it was something I made up. After all, it occurred forty-plus years ago, and I even had to ask a classmate at my high school reunion, who was with me at the time of this encounter, if it really happened. She verified that it did, just as I'll describe below.

In 1970, Nancy was one of my roommates on the Regina Dominican (all girls) High School Senior Class trip to Washington, D.C., Boston and New York. When we arrived in New York, we were thrilled to see the tall modern building that was to be our hotel there: the Americana Hotel. It was so exciting to finally be in the "Big Apple" after first traveling to Washington, D.C., and Boston.

We unpacked and were preparing to go out exploring as we listened to the radio. A popular song called "Aquarius" was playing and we were all singing it. Just so happens, I was in the chorus at school and we had recently sung the song for a concert, so I knew the lyrics well. The tune was performed by a popular band called the Fifth Dimension. At that time, most of us did not know the individual members of these large bands, except for the Beach Boys or the

Beatles, but we certainly knew the lyrics to their popular songs played every day on the radio.

That evening, we put on our white lipstick, bell bottoms, bangles and mini-skirts and got on the elevator to do the town. Our rooms were located on the upper floors and so we were looking forward to a long ride down to the lobby as we got on the nearly packed elevator, still singing "Aquarius." I turned around once and noticed the people behind me were smiling as my friends and I were still singing. When we reached the lobby, the doors opened and we all got out. Starting to be on our way, I was stopped by someone who had been on the elevator with us.

He asked us, "Don't you know who was on that elevator with us?"

We replied, "No, why do you ask?" The man laughed as he pointed at a poster in the lobby. We looked at the poster, and it was an advertisement saying, "Playing here tonight at the Americana Hotel, the Fifth Dimension." On it, were pictures of the band, including Marilyn McCoo and Billy Davis, who were the people standing behind us and smiling on the elevator as we sang their song "Aquarius." They were probably smiling because they thought we were knowingly singing it to them on purpose. I was so embarrassed because just as I thought I was being a grown-up in the big city, they probably thought we were just teenagers goofing off.

Truly clueless about who sang what songs in those days; I just knew the lyrics to songs I liked that played on the radio a lot. If I knew all the band members like my husband, Bill does from that era, perhaps encounters like what happened above would not have happened to me. It just goes to show how oblivious we were when it came to recognizing the movers and shakers of the hip music scene, even though we listened to their music every day on stations like WLS in Chicago. We did not have cell phones, iPads, personal computers or any other gadgets to keep us aware of who the people were that entertained us. It was a much simpler time.

My next-door neighbor, Lorraine's older brother Skip used to babysit for my two brothers and me during his high school years in the sixties. He dated our summer Mother's Helper one year and was a die-hard New York Yankees fan. Often, when Skip came over to babysit, he would have boisterous debates with my dad about who was the best major league baseball team in the American League: the

Yankees or my dad's own favorite, the Chicago White Sox, being that my dad grew up on Chicago's southwest side where the White Sox held court in Comiskey Park. During summer, when the neighborhood was out and about and we could smell barbecue and swim in our pool, were especially happy memories.

Lorraine and Skip Amideo were a special part of those memories for me, and during that time, I started to become aware of great musical acts and sixties folk music and rock and roll and it was through Skip that that seed was inadvertently planted. In high school, he was friends with the late singer/songwriter Steve Goodman, whose younger brother Dave hung out with the kids who were closer to our age in our Virginia Lane neighborhood. I believe I went to a party at the Goodman's house when I was in junior high school and therefore, probably met Steve at some point.

Furthermore, I knew of Steve from the Amideo family and being in junior high classes with his younger brother, Dave, but didn't really follow Steve's music until much later, even though it was on the radio a lot in the sixties and seventies. Forty years later, I was visiting the Atlanta area, where Lorraine and Skip both lived and we all went to dinner together. At the restaurant, Skip reminded me of a neat episode in the mid-60s, when he and Steve Goodman found themselves on the train going from Chicago to the University of Illinois in Champaign, to attend college.

On the way down to Champaign, they discussed Steve's desire to be a musician and songwriter and how he was going to accomplish all this. Finally, after about three hours, the train stopped at their station in Champaign and Skip got up to get off; however, Steve was still seated. When Skip looked at him, Steve waved him away saying that he (Steve) was not getting off the train. He had decided that he was not sure that he was going to college after all, and planned to ride the train to its endpoint in New Orleans to think it over. Steve told Skip that *this may be* the right time to start his music career; therefore, the aspiring singer/songwriter would stay on the train until it got to its last stop in New Orleans, Louisiana and then make the decision as to what would happen with his budding career.

Eventually, the country was blessed with songwriter Steve Goodman's big hit: "The City of New Orleans," which was also the name of the train that the two friends were riding on when Steve decided not to get off in Champaign, Illinois that fateful day in 1966 or1967. It was not until 1971 that Skip first heard Steve's song on the radio sung by Arlo Guthrie, who had asked Goodman if he could record it right after Steve had first played it for him. It is a good thing that Steve started his wonderful singer/songwriter career at an earlier age because he did not live a very long life, including never being able to see his beloved Chicago Cubs win a World Series.

A life-long Cub's fan, Steve had written a current song about the team, still sung by the crowd at Wrigley Field each time the Cubs win the game, called: "Go, Cubs, Go." As I have been writing this in the summer of 2019, the Cubs have been winning a lot and in fact won the game just last night and so, according to tradition, the fans stood and sang Goodman's song. Moreover, short life or not, Steve's legacy continues to live on and I was thrilled to be an extraneous part of it.

My little brother, Terry was born in 1962, ten years after me and eight years after Michael, the middle brother I talked about earlier. For all intents and purposes, Terry was like my own baby because he was born when I was ten years old and so, I was responsible for babysitting him a lot. Since Michael of "Venom Sauce" fame was, shall we say "adventurous" as a child, my parents did not trust him to babysit Terry, even though Michael was eight years older than our little brother.

Because Mike was always curious and taking things apart to see how they worked, my parents used to say they were wary of letting him babysit because they were afraid that he would, "blow up the house" when they were gone; therefore, unfairly, they relied too much on me to babysit, even though this was when I was busy with my own junior high and high school activities.

Mike knew that he was getting away without having to babysit and why. I knew this because whenever my parents left to go out and I was to stay home and babysit, the same thing happened every time. As soon as they would leave the house, Michael would literally say to me, "Ha, ha! You must stay home and babysit while I get to go out with my friends!" Mike was a smart cookie and figured out if he played middle brother terrorist occasionally, my parents would never give him the responsibility of babysitting Terry. And he was exactly right.

In later years, Terry just happened to become good friends with the Ron Santo family, who lived in our neighborhood. Ron

Santo, the third base powerhouse for the Cubs, lived in a big home on the lake in Valley Lo Country Club in Glenview. My family also lived in Valley Lo, albeit in the townhouses. Ron had two sons named Ronny J. and Jeff that were close to Terry's age, so he palled around with them, becoming good friends of the two boys and their sister Laura.

At the time they all met, Ron Sr. was in his thirties and still playing with the Cubs. Because he was still young and an excellent athlete, Ron Santo Sr. would play all sports with the boys whether it be hockey on Valley Lo Lake, baseball, golf or whatever. Terry has always said how good Ron Sr. was at every sport and my littlest brother was enthralled when he got to go to spring training with the Santo family and the Cubs team in Arizona. Then and during the regular season, Terry often sat in the dugout and talked about meeting other players like Glen Beckert, Billy Williams and Ernie Banks. Our brother Michael's eyes would get as big as saucers because he could not believe the people that Terry was able to meet through his association with the Santo boys. To this day, Terry keeps in touch with the family and even went to Ron Senior's memorial service in December of 2010.

What I vividly remember about the graciousness of Mr. Santo took place one night in the late sixties. My parents answered the doorbell when Terry was still a small kid, maybe seven or eight years old and voilà, it was Mr. Santo carrying a horizontal Terry in his arms. Santo and the boys had been playing hockey on the lake and by accident Terry received a black eye. My poor dad could only wish he could play with his son and the other boys like that; however, Dad was twenty years older than Ron Sr., who apologized for giving Terry the black eye.

The next day, Terry went to school and told everyone that Ron Santo, the great Cubs third baseman, gave him his eye shiner! Michael could only shake his head that his little brother got to have these amazing experiences at such a young age. I wonder if Michael had babysat for Terry more often like I did, how much closer they would have been as brothers? Mike, perhaps, would have been able to meet some more of the great ball players of that time due to the connections of his little brother.

During high school (1966-70), the only celebrities I encountered would fit under the First or Second Close Encounter

Kind, but considered big nevertheless, to a lowly high school kid like me. Besides "The Fifth Dimension", the Goodman and Santo stories, there was one other celebrity who touched me indirectly in a First or Second Close Encounter way. During the 1968 Winter Olympics in Grenoble, France, the girls in my high school were closely following the Women's Speed Skating portion of the games because one of our own was competing: Diane Holum, who won a silver medal there. I used to sit next to her younger sister, Patty Holum during that year in one of our sophomore classes.

The whole school was excited for Diane's accomplishments, and because of the buzz, I vividly remember an incident one day when Diane's first Olympic race was to begin. During the intercom announcements at my high school that day, delivered by upperclassmen in Diane's class, the announcer said, "Good Luck, Diane. BEAT THEIR BUNS OFF!"

Today, those words would only produce a chuckle or maybe an emphatic fist bump, but in 1968 in an all-girl's Catholic high school like Regina Dominican, it produced a crisis! The nuns were appalled and we heard later that the announcement team got a severe reprimand for including such "foul" words in their cheering on of our schoolmate, who not only won silver and bronze medals for speed skating in 1968 at Grenoble, France, but also took home the gold and silver medals in 1972 for speed skating in Sapporo, Japan. She is also well-known for excelling at coaching male speed skater Eric Heiden to win five gold medals at the 1980 Winter Olympic Games.

To reiterate how times were different, e.g., more shocking for teens in the sixties, if taboo subjects like sex, drugs or rock-and-roll were raised, and even more so in Catholic schools, another incident illustrates how prudish we were compared to today. Note: people talk about the free sex and love and drugs of the sixties and that was certainly true; however, most of that behavior happened in certain places like San Francisco or progressive universities with older teens or young adults or with rock bands like the Rolling Stones or the Beatles.

Free sex and love and common expletives were not usually seen outwardly in an all-girls parochial school in 1968. Even for the public-at-large, shocking behavior like big gatherings, displaying open use of drugs, public sex and prolific nudity were not yet commonly seen by the average person until after the Woodstock,

New York music festival in August of 1969, just before my senior year at Regina started.

One thing that helped me to fit in, was joining a sorority in college, even if this new club environment was all girls again. During those days, Theta Phi Sorority, which I pledged in 1971, worked on service projects and I did get practice working with men, even celebrities. For some reason, our sorority was assigned to escort entertainers, who came to campus to perform. One of these was Barry Williams, the oldest brother, Greg of "Brady Bunch" fame. We discovered that he was not too friendly, in fact, he seemed a little standoffish, perhaps because he was uncomfortable with so many girls his own age staring at him.

Another time, we chaperoned the singer-songwriter, John Denver, whom we talked to back stage. I was able to tell him how much I liked his music, especially "Annie's Song" and he seemed more normal and even appreciative of compliments. Interactions like these helped me to become more comfortable around men in general, but I still had some learning to do as time went on. Even my much-respected art professor, Mr. Bohné, only twenty-nine then, teased me about liking artists like John Denver because John was considered so mainstream instead of what we called hard or "Acid Rock" from musicians, like Black Sabbath and Alice Cooper, who were leaning toward heavy guitar solos and almost un-danceable melodies. For those kinds of bands, most of the crowd sat down on the dance floor and smoked dope instead of dancing, which disappointed me greatly. It was not my scene; I was bored with the music and the lack of dancing at those events and I did not like drugs.

Growing up in my Midwestern world, most of us only dreamed of seeing our favorite bands, celebrities, or heroes and if it happened, it usually fell under Encounters of the First or Second Kind. In other words, celebrities were seen in person through concerts, plays or by chance at a distance. In addition to the Close Encounters of The Third Kind already described earlier, there actually are more memorable times like these I shall describe.

Upon graduation, I looked for a teaching job, but could not find one, which I will depict in a later chapter. What is important here, is that I had to take a waitress position for a year-and-a-half, before getting my desired teaching job. Because of that, I had some interesting and valuable experiences that I would not have had otherwise. By working with people who had been waitressing for their main job for twenty years, I realized that without a college education at that time, there were not a lot of employment choices. I saw that I was so lucky to have spent four years in college, which would prepare me for the future. These hard-working wait staff were making the best of their own "futures" by working diligently with the limited education they had obtained already. My colleagues at Hackney's on Lake Restaurant in Glenview, were great at what they did and took their jobs seriously, so I was able to learn about having a good work ethic, no matter the circumstances.

Anyway, at Hackney's I frequently waited on a nice couple, who owned Snodgress Travel in Glenview. During Christmas 1975, their daughter, Carrie was visiting with her disabled son Zeke and she was introduced to us wait staff, people closer to her own age. Many of the younger staff had a New Year's Eve Party at someone's house and Carrie Snodgress[27] was invited, so we all had a great time together. She was very down-to-earth. Around that time, someone told us that she was the actress who was nominated for an Academy Award for the film *Diary of a Mad Housewife*[28] in 1970 and later appeared in many other films, stage plays and T.V.

Zeke's father was Neil Young, the famous singer-songwriter, whom she had been living with for five years. Sometime later, Hackney's hosted the funeral reception for Carrie's mom and Neil Young attended. The wait staff, including me, were all mesmerized, when during the reception, the much-revered musician, Neil, broke out his guitar and proceeded to perform his big hits. I became a waitress at Hackneys, while waiting to find a teaching position because of job shortages. Waiting a year and a half out of college for a teaching job was absolutely worth it because of that chance to see Neil perform at a small private venue.

In the summer of 1975, my dad's secretary, we will call Diane, (I cannot remember her name and everyone I could ask has passed away, so Diane will do.) called me and asked me to go with her out on the town, since we were about the same age, and had common interests. She told me that some very good friends of hers that she grew up with were in town and asked if I would like to meet them. I was up for this, so I said, "Sure!" in reply and she proceeded to tell me to meet her in downtown Chicago at the Whitehall Hotel where her friends were staying. I drove down there and knocked on the door of the hotel room that she had told me to come to. She answered the door and behind her I saw a dimly lit room with at least eight or nine guys sitting on the floor and in the available seats.

Diane proceeded to say that these were the guys she had grown up with from her neighborhood and proceeded to introduce me to each one, using only their first names. Good thing too because I would never have remembered them all anyway. Many of them were cute with long hair and fashionably dressed in tee shirts and bell-bottomed jeans. Later, Diane told me who they were and I almost fell over. They were the very popular and famous band Chicago, who were in town to play a three-night run.

The band Chicago's[29] songs: "Beginnings," "Saturday in the Park," "Color My World" and "25 or 6 to 4" and many other original songs were on the radio day and night. They were so popular because their sound was unique, incorporating a horn section into a rock band, along with drums, keyboard and electric guitars. Many of their voices were soulful and used baritone and tenor harmony to round out the beautiful songs. A few years older than me, this band would become iconic and very representative of the creative juices seen in the "Baby Boomer" generation.

Needless to say, I was ecstatic when Diane invited me to come to their show each night and sit backstage. I was invited to bring a friend because Diane was not able to be there each night of the concert. The most amazing thing was that I was getting the music of two great bands for the price of one on the "Summer of 75"[30] tour, Chicago was performing with an older band, who was becoming popular again after fifteen years of already huge successes, starting in the early sixties.

The older band was called The Beach Boys, still featuring the original members sans Brian Wilson, who at the time was dealing with mental illness and could not tour anymore. Of course, no one could do what Brian's high and versatile singing voice could do, but his brothers Carl, Dennis and cousin Mike Love, as well as original member, Al Jardine, could still recreate the iconic beach sounds and the fans loved it. In addition, Billy Hinsche of Dino, Desi and Billy fame and replacement singer, Bruce Johnston, rounded out the band, all still sounding very good.

Since I was allowed to bring a friend, I brought Carole H., a girl I worked with at a few small restaurants that summer, before I landed my first teaching job in the fall. The year before, I had met Carole when we were both contestants in "The Miss North Shore Beauty Pageant," (I am sorry, but that is what we used to call it – not exactly a title that would set a feminist's heart on fire). In fact, neither of us won the pageant, but we met great people and honed our talents (I played guitar and sang a song in French).

Because we were a Miss America preliminary pageant, we were taught how to walk, smile, wear a swimsuit, (I hated that part!) and be poised in an interview. Carole and I still keep in touch to this day, forty-plus years later. As if I was not a glutton for punishment, I had already competed in an earlier contest "The Miss Glenview Beauty Pageant" at nineteen years old and did not win anything. Before you question my sanity, I need to say that there was a method to my madness.

During the first contest, Miss Glenview, in 1972, I had just come from two difficult years in college, where my skin, especially my face, was covered with large acne boils no matter what treatment the doctor tried. I had also gained some weight and felt my old low self-confidence, just as I was starting to meet boys in my new coed setting at St. Norbert College. So, I decided that this contest would give me the confidence to try and improve my looks, as well as, to sharpen my singing voice and guitar-playing abilities. Moreover, I lost the fifteen pounds I had gained freshman and sophomore years of college and my skin cleared-up by using the drug tetracycline. I practically kissed my doctor when the medicine worked and my skin looked wonderful.

Throughout high school, people told me that I had a nice singing voice and I had some experience performing in choral concerts, so I decided to try and enter the first pageant. I never perceived that I would win, I just needed to challenge myself, or so I thought. In those days, no one I knew of was going to psychotherapy to get down to the bottom of problems like depression and low self-esteem to correct the source of all that angst. My performance and appearance at the pageant came off well, except during the first few notes when I was so nervous, my voice started to falter; however, after a minute, I then was able to recover and sing the rest of my song in my full, clear soprano voice. I am thankful that my parents were always there to support and encourage my endeavors.

One reason I did not sing and play much after college, was because I was not able to get over my stage-fright, at least at the beginning of a performance. In college, I had played and sung during Sunday Mass, but that was a small crowd and often, others were singing along with me, which helped to mitigate my fear.

After college, I gained weight and decided to try my same method to boost my self-esteem because as I said, I was a glutton for punishment. There was another beauty contest on the horizon for me. I realized later that those types of endeavors only go so far to improve one's self-concept. The fix is located deeper in the psyche. At twenty-three years old, I wasn't aware of how to obtain a lasting solution for my issues, so I enrolled in my second pageant where I met Carole. Neither one of us won the contest, but it helped my confidence and I now had what was to be a lifelong friend in Carole and most of all, we had fun.

Although I didn't really believe I'd win either one of those two pageants, it is clear that I was reaching for a more permanent state of high self-esteem and hoping to lose the depression that had dogged me on and off since my pre-teen years. At that time, I did not know I had ADHD or that anything was really wrong with me because I had had impulsivity and anxiety for so long, they seemed normal. Carole was majoring in acting at the prestigious Northwestern University, so her confidence was much more ingrained in her because of all the shows she was already a part of and because she had won the Junior Miss Pageant as a young teen in her home state of Massachusetts.

I think I always hoped Carole's high self-esteem would somehow rub off on me. Alas, that high confidence struck me as being just out of my reach and just as unlikely for me to obtain as winning those pageants. Anyway, Carole was thrilled to meet fellow performers by being invited to come along with me to sit backstage at those Chicago-Beach Boy combined concerts in 1975. Little did I know that after the concerts one night, we would be invited by the band's entourage to go dancing at a local club (owned by the drummer of Chicago, Danny Seraphine) called Beginnings after their hit song. The roadies from both bands also came out to the club to celebrate the engagement of Mike Love's daughter to Billy Hinsche. So, Carole and I excitedly drove out to the far northwestern Chicago suburb of Schaumburg, where Beginnings was located to go dancing.

I did not know back then that my life would be profoundly affected by what happened that night; however, that is a story for another chapter.

(Above) 1967-1968 Friends in Glenview L-R   Ed, Kathleen, Paula and Don

(Above) Kathleen (seated) as contestant for the Miss Glenview pageant, 1971

Publicity photo of the music group The Fifth Dimension, 1969 From Wiki media Commons [31]

(Above) American Hotel, New York City, 1970, scene of Kathleen's Senior Class Trip, where she met the Fifth Dimension band.

(Right) Old 45 record of "City Of New Orleans" by Steve Goodman (From the personal collection of Author)[33]

(Above) Choral and Guitar group at Regina Dominican High School 1968-70 — Kathleen is sitting on the top step, third from right.

(Right) Carole H. and Kathleen making dinner, 1980

(Left) Kathleen's High School Graduation,

(Right) Regina H.S. choral group 1969-70, Kathleen second from front on left side.

(Above) Pioneer Press ad of Miss North Shore Beauty Pageant contestants [34] (Top Right, Kathleen, bottom Right, Carole H)

Chapter 12: *Children of the Greatest Generation—The Baby Boomers*

"Due to their reluctance to tie themselves down at a young age,

they have the capacity as well as the predisposition to be

their own bosses and following their own dreams."

— Bernard Salt [35]

By the end of the tumultuous decade, the likes of which had not been seen between the younger generation and their parents beginning with the Woodstock, New York music festival in August of 1969, there were big cracks in the stability of American societal norms. I hate to say that this was my generation, the Baby Boomers, who created these loosening mores, probably a reaction to the moral and behavioral restrictions of the fifties. I am not proud of some of my high school peers and the college students of this time, where every evening we watched the real-time violence of the Vietnam War being played out on the 6 p.m. news.

These times were the beginning of the last years where the press just reported the facts and showed us pictures of what was really happening in as unbiased a way as possible in the newspapers and on all the three broadcast stations that everyone watched. We did not know their opinions because they took their jobs as print media journalists and anchors on TV and radio seriously.

During my high school years, looking at all facts was still a cherished hard-won American value in most places in the U.S. Then, it was still taboo for journalists to give us their opinion on air and they took care to give us facts and information from all sides of an issue. Today, most everything is about opinion and causes deep-seated polarization. Civilized comportment and compromise seem to have been lost. What a way to run a world and I feel, my generation of seventy-six million Baby Boomers are the ones who started it all!

Later in life, I read books about some of these journalists and found out their personal opinions after they retired. Although several differed with my ideas, I still respected and was grateful for each and every one of them, especially people like Walter Cronkite, David Brinkley, Diane Sawyer, Jane Pauley, Harry Reasoner and even

Barbara Walters before her "The View" days. Because these journalists only reported the facts, it allowed me to make up my own mind. We thought we were "Children of Destiny" as per the Neil Young song, but it turns out many of us did not fulfill our great potential because drugs and the Vietnam War got in the way.

In reality, the Vietnam War was begun and conducted by our elders, but the younger generation's reaction (excluding peaceful protest) broke down the norms of civilized discourse, without respect for American values and the institutions important to our free way of life. What does doing drugs openly, having public sex with strangers in front of the world, taking off one's clothes and smoking dope at huge multi-day camp-out concerts like Woodstock, have to do with protesting the mistakes made by our government, like getting into the Vietnam War? It only made officials take notice of our immaturity and not of our serious message of stopping the War.

Today we have the Black Lives movement and Antifa, which are the antithesis of "peaceful" when they protest. Their own manifestos encourage looting, rioting, violence, and disorderly conduct. How does that get them what they really want? Yes, they get attention, but this behavior does not garner respect or get them the changes they want. Some of these youth need to spend a few days looking at films of Martin Luther King Jr., to see how it should be done.

Moreover, our Vietnam War veterans were terribly treated upon their return by the so-called young people protesting the War. To me, this was appalling because fighting the Vietnamese was not the military person's own decision. Admirably, they were only doing their duty as promised, whether volunteer or drafted, but returning with broken bodies or death to show for it. Yes, we can and should blame people like President Lyndon Johnson and even President Kennedy before him for getting us into an unwinnable war, but the violent protests and unseemly behavior (open drug use, public nudity and sex) were excuses to act out our own sorry hedonism and entitled attitude.

In hindsight, I see that those self-centered morally suspect behaviors of my generation, disguised as protests and serious societal change measures were not born out of considered thought and research. Nor were they created out of our generational intelligence created by having the most college graduates ever seen to date. Not to mention the mistakes of some of our government leaders, these non-starter actions that corrupted our whole generation had begun from a mind-set of impulsivity and a "Me Generation" attitude.

Due to our parents having had to live through the Depression, they understandably were never going to let their kids experience that same type of hardship, so they made sure we never would by giving us everything. That was where the *entitlement* attitude of my generation was born. At the same time, in addition to the war in Vietnam still raging, we had seen horrendous events with great violence playing out on TV in our living rooms, especially with the assassination of President Kennedy in 1963, when I was eleven years old, on through my high school years (1966-1970). During those years, some of the worst events occurred and were seen live on TV.

The end of my sophomore and into my junior year (1968-69), was unexpectedly, a particularly violent time. It started when the beloved civil rights leader, Dr. Martin Luther King (MLK) Jr. was murdered in April 1968 as he stood on the balcony of his motel in Memphis, Tennessee. Ironically, he had taught his followers never to use violence, but to use boycotting and peaceful protest methods to get the unfair laws changed for the better, regarding the treatment of African-Americans, then more commonly called Negroes. He was much-loved and respected by both black and white races, but due to those who were prejudiced against people of color, Dr. King knew he was taking his life in his hands every-time he stepped out of his house or even gave a high-profile address. Inevitably, his own dark premonitions came true and he was assassinated at the young age of thirty-nine.

Violence in our country continued during the June 1968 presidential primary for the Democrats. One of the most popular candidates, Robert Kennedy (RFK), was killed two months after Dr. King's death. Ironically, RFK was the one who announced MLK's assassination during a speech in Indianapolis.[36] Robert was a younger brother of the 1963-assassinated President John F. Kennedy (JFK), and was gunned down at a California hotel in early June 1968. Robert was leaving the hotel through the basement kitchen after having finished his acceptance speech for his California Primary win for President The new primary winner planned to go to the 1968 Democratic National Convention scheduled for later that summer.

Surrounded by an excited entourage of supporters, Robert was on his way as a Democrat Party front-runner candidate for continued state primary contests, when he was assassinated in the kitchen of the Ambassador Hotel in Los Angeles. This despicable act was horrifyingly caught on TV cameras, with his thirteen-year-old son, David watching it alone in his hotel room. Who knows if RFK hadn't died then, what would have happened at the upcoming convention.

Also, how would David's life have turned out without the trauma of witnessing his father's death alone in a hotel room? A *New York Times* headline by Reginald Stuart, dated April 26, 1984, pronounced: *"ROBERT KENNEDY'S SON DAVID FOUND DEAD IN HOTEL."*(37) David was only twenty eight years old when he died. Unfortunately, his short life was plagued by substance abuse, starting two years after he witnessed his father's death.

The Democrat Party Presidential Convention was held in August of 1968 in my hometown of Chicago, where due to a large showing of anti-Vietnam War protestors in Grant Park, Mayor Richard Daley Sr. felt the need to call out the National Guard in riot gear to break up the huge crowd of protestors in front of the venue. Again, the Baby Boomers and their parents were treated to TV footage of police in protective gear using batons to beat the protestors when they would not leave. In addition, guardsmen were pointing rifles at the students, who were out of control with screaming or standing firm when asked to move along. This type of riot scene had already happened in April, 1968 in Chicago, due in part to Martin Luther King's assassination. At those riots, TV coverage had depicted a similar chaotic scene with batons, attack dogs and fire hoses being used on the protestors in the Windy City.

The responses from Mayor Daley were becoming more common in other cities like Cincinnati, due to unresolved conflict between black and white. Race riots and the 1968 Convention cemented the common view of the Chicago area, where I was born on August 17, 1952, as a violent city again. Those events of the sixties hurt our standing as "Second City" at that time, (second to New York in size and as a commercial epicenter). The bad reputation Chicago was finally getting over as a result of the killing and disruption from Al Capone and his mob in the nineteen-twenties and thirties, erupted anew in 1968 due to politics and the two assassinations of great Americans within months of each other.

As the United States moved into 1970, my high school graduation year, I was preparing to go to college in the fall. But before I could be on my way to higher education, one more disturbing and brutal incident took place in Ohio on May 4, 1970, a month before graduation. It is commonly called "Kent State" or the "Kent State Massacres,"[38] named after the college where it took place. The National Guard was called out in response to a student protest to the U.S. invasion of Cambodia, which some saw as an escalation of the Vietnam War because of those two countries' proximity to each other. It is not clear what exactly happened to cause the soldiers to fire on the protesting students, but they did, causing nine injuries and four deaths of the activists.

Not common then, as it seems to be in present times, this type of atrocity, especially something that started out as a peaceful protest, caused people of my generation to stop trusting government authorities, who were scrambling for answers that never came. On the other hand, there were events at this time that gave me the impression of being the ultimate contradiction to the violent actions of society during this period. Thank God for the positive historical events which helped to give us respite and hope during the despair and confusion of these years.

The uplifting event I remember most was the first moon landing ever in July of 1969. That night, I went to a pool party with my boyfriend, Keith and many of the other teens in my high school world. Someone had set up a black and white portable TV out on the patio in anticipation of one of the greatest events of all time. In awe, we all watched the first landing of astronauts on the moon, where Neil Armstrong's American crew were planting the U.S. flag and collecting scientific specimens.

The young forty-four-year-old President John F. Kennedy, who had symbolized the youth and hope of the nation made a prediction on the twenty-fifth of May, 1961.[39] He forecast that by the end of that decade, we would witness the first safely executed moon landing. Ironically, earlier in that same decade, violence and chaos reigned. JFK was one of the first victims two years later in 1963, when ever-increasing bloodshed was being played out on TV; however, his prediction of success in space exploration and a moon landing came true in 1969. It was a sweet irony for mankind's terrible and wonderful interaction with technology.

87

The contemporary minds that could put a man on the moon, we were shocked to find out, were also capable of using technology to kill a democratically elected president like President Kennedy, who never lived to see his dream realized. Other dreams were dashed and like Kennedy, Dr. Martin Luther King Jr., the beloved civil rights leader, was assassinated. Sadly, King never lived to see his own dream realized either; it was a dream of seeing a man in the future being "… judged by his character instead of by the color of his skin."

As a country, America is not finished fulfilling Martin Luther King Junior's dream yet; however, there are plenty of places where people are now judged by their character instead of their skin color, thanks to Dr. King's work.

Unfortunately, King's untimely death set us back many years in getting his dream fully realized. Then again, I think if Dr. King came back to life in contemporary America, he would be amazed that we elected Barack Obama as the first black President of the United States in 2008 and again in 2012, within only one generation since Dr. King gave his "I Have a Dream" speech.

There is progress, not perfection and had John F. Kennedy lived, he would be gob-smacked that not only did his dream of a moon landing come true, but the civil rights movement he also championed would produce an African-American president within fifty years of JFKs own death.

During college, (1970-74) at a small, private, co-ed, liberal-arts school in the small town of De Pere, near Green Bay, Wisconsin called St. Norbert, I was able to increase my social life experiences and skills, albeit, at a school with a relatively small population of fifteen hundred students. But it was all new to me, given I was on my own for the first time and there were BOYS going there! This was the first time since I was in junior high that I started to work with boys on projects or was part of a mixed-crowd intellectual endeavor, in addition to my now-expanded co-ed social life.

Most of my old neighborhood friends like Val or Lorraine had been encountering the opposite sex in intellectual pursuits for the four years of high school. I had wanted to attend the public co-ed high school with my friends from the neighborhood, but it was not in the cards, due to my parents' wishes of me attending an all-girl's parochial high school, Regina Dominican in Wilmette, IL. This resulted in me being more immature at eighteen years old than those of my friends who had attended a co-ed public high school, as we all went off to our separate colleges.

In what ways was I more immature than others I knew? The answer to that question appeared to be centered mostly in the ways of the mixed-crowd world. I had never seen a boy naked, nor had any sexual experience past second base. That wasn't as rare as the reader might think because I had come directly out of a Catholic all-girls high school which really hadn't seen much of the sex, drugs and rock and roll, as had students at the average secular schools.

Feeling totally ill-equipped to be in class with men in small classrooms of twenty-five students or less, the first weeks and months of college were awkward for me. To top it off, I majored in Art Education, with a minor in French, courses notoriously smaller than the average classes, even at St. Norbert. That meant a more intimate intellectual experience, or shall we say, a "close encounter of the third kind?"

I was either too forward with my male peers or too intimidated. In these situations, I did not know how to behave naturally. Because of my ADHD, (which I had no idea about at that time) I was awkward. To be able to handle the nervousness, I either talked too much, said something stupid or nothing at all. I learned as time went on to deal with the opposite sex more appropriately, but I always felt more behind socially than my other friends who had attended a co-ed setting before college. Since many at St. Norbert had come from small towns, their high schools, even the parochial ones, were co-ed, unlike those of us from bigger cities, whose only choices of parochial schools were all larger single-sex institutions.

Furthermore, as a freshman in college, my first classes were in drawing from a live, almost-nude male model (wearing only a jock-strap to be in code with the Catholic school I assume). At first, this complicated my mixed-crowd learning experience greatly. Case in point: my fellow freshman friends and I were sitting in "Life Drawing" class on the first day, with our heads down and red faces, waiting for the model to come in. Looking down, embarrassed and whispering under our breaths when we heard the model arrive at the classroom, we asked each other nervously whether he was already naked or whether he had something on.

We learned later that the protocol was for the model to come into the class while wearing a robe, go to the raised platform, disrobe, pose and the student sketching would begin. We had clipped 18" X 24" paper to our even larger drawing boards and began sketching. By the end of the semester, we were so comfortable with the lack of dress on the model that we had moved up nearer to the platform to draw from different up-close perspectives of the body.

That first live figure drawing class at least cured me of being awkward around males in a co-ed setting, but it did not suddenly make
me eloquent and mature regarding men. I still felt clueless when it came to discussions or conversations that are the most important factors in developing mature relationships with the opposite sex. Later I realized that a lot of these problems around a mixed crowd came from underlying "boundary" or "limits" issues.

My parents did the best they could, teaching us right from wrong, but I never understood that I could prevent many things going out of control if I had understood HOW to set boundaries in all relationships. In the men-women arena, the main problem was hearing the mixed messages I got at home, on T.V. and in social situations. I could not seem to distinguish when to do what. For instance, I was encouraged to stay a virgin and not be overtly sexy until marriage, yet my mom went out with my dad in sexy low-cut outfits and I was allowed to wear very short mini-skirts that barely covered my buttocks.

We were told not to do drugs and that sex was sacred, yet the 1969 Woodstock festival was shown on T.V., with indications of naked attendees making love and smoking dope out in the open grass at the concert. I was taught to act "...like a lady." Yet my mom and some of her friends would drink all day at the bar in their country club and get sloppy drunk when they were supposed to just be playing a friendly bridge game. Contradictions and hypocrisy were everywhere. The following are some other examples of being surrounded by confusing messages:

Every day, the network news showed graphic depictions of blood and death during the Vietnam War, but our government could give us no good answer as to why young men were dying in a deadly conflict so far away.

When I babysat my younger sibling, Terry, I tried to stick to my parent's rules for the house, but when Terry complained, they loosened them up for him; therefore, basically they were contradicting what I had been trying to enforce, as per their previous instructions to me.

When my high school boyfriend Keith brought me home late one night, my dad yelled at him about how unacceptable this was. Yet when Keith routinely picked me up for a date one half-hour to one hour late, they never counseled him or me about what the expected protocol was for going on dates. I know they really liked Keith, so they let his tardy behavior slide and did not advise me to talk to him about it or at least set boundaries. This is how I learned to accept the unacceptable from people in order to stay in the relationship or to keep the peace.

With all the contradictory messages cited above, how was I supposed to know how to behave in a healthy way, much less how to set boundaries for myself or for the others in my life? Much later, I learned that there are solutions. Some of these answers I found in a book by psychologist and speaker, Dr. Henry Cloud called: *Boundaries: When to Say Yes, How to Say No to Take Control of Your Life.* He says, "...Setting boundaries inevitably involves taking responsibility for your choices. You are the one who makes them. You are the one who must live with their consequences. And you are the one who may be keeping yourself from making the choices you could be happy with."(40)

Since I did not know who Henry Cloud was yet, as I left for college in August of 1970, I was ill-prepared to form healthy relationships or to question authority, when I was not getting what I needed out of my college classes. For example, I would rather have learned traditional art techniques in class like oil painting or watercolors or even more clay sculpture than I was given, but during those periods, acrylic straight-edge painting and making raku pots fired naturally in the woods were the go-to-popular art-activities then.

Realistically, as a traditional co-ed, I didn't always fit in with those newer kinds of activities. I felt that I should learn traditional art techniques first, so I would have a complete art toolbox from which to choose. Even the famous artists like Pablo Picasso and Paul Cézanne were classically trained artists who could draw and paint with the best of them, but as time went on, they were able to explore new avenues in Art like a style called Cubism, which was known for experimentation in abstract perspective and the use of geometric planes to depict subject matter.

My sophomore year, I had joined a sorority called "Theta Phi" and sororities were not considered cool by many in the art world in the early seventies. One of my beloved art professors, Mr. Bohné sometimes was prompted to tease me by calling me and those like me "hot dogs" to emphasize my lack of being so-called "avant-garde" or one who creates unorthodox works through experimental methods. This was the preferred art style at the time.

Also, joining a sorority was considered kind of too establishment in that era of the "God Damn Independent (GDI)." GDIs were what people were called if they did NOT join a fraternity or sorority. It struck me as being the counter-culture's badge of honor, another thing with which I did not feel comfortable. Still, some of the girls I met in my sorority, like my suitemates, Anne F., Joanie C., and Jean B. (nicknamed Bert) became good friends. Another wonderful suitemate, Pat O., joined us sophomore year. I will always cherish the friendships we made and the escapades we had living together.

There were four rooms per suite in Dorm Four our senior year and it was a lot of fun. Our suite was far away from where the house mother lived and on the first floor so, many girls (and sometimes their boyfriends) wanting to get in after-hours, would knock on Joanie and Bert's window and climb in. Sometimes this could cause problems for Joanie and Bert (whomever had their bed directly under the window) due to people stepping on the two girls, as they were sleeping. Later, we took a picture of all the footprints going up the side of the white wall under their window, which I still have.

If I had graduated from high school even five years earlier and then started college, all those activities I dreamed of, like regular prom-like dances and learning to paint realistically with oil paint would have been considered "de rigeur" during the normal art major's college experience. Instead, I was taught how to paint in all straight-edge acrylic abstract ways. I appreciated all types of Art like abstract painters, Pablo Picasso and Henri Matisse; however, I really loved Impressionists, like Monet and Renoir and even some realistic and classical art. But again, I was thrust into conditions where I felt that to complain about what I was learning was not my call, but that of those who seemed to know more than I did about things.

Later, I always wondered how much being part of the first third of the "Baby Boomer" generation set me up for these problems.

Every time I entered a new phase of life, it seemed as if others were doing it before me in a slightly new way or with changed expectations and I couldn't seem to grasp on to it fast enough. For example, there was a teacher shortage in the sixties and so guidance counselors were calling for people to go into teaching. Many of the Baby Boomers went into education as suggested; however, right around the time I graduated from college in 1974, the teaching profession had been flooded with new prospects and there were no more jobs. There were jokes about PhDs having to drive cabs, and it was not so far from reality. Consequently, I had to be a waitress for a while before landing a teaching job.

For many years after that bottleneck of the Baby Boomers trying for a limited number of teaching jobs, the education field was difficult to get into. The first year I applied, I sent out two-hundred-fifty resumes to as many schools and got only one interview and one job. The second year, I put out five resumes (after one year of experience) and was invited in for all five interviews. Of those five, I was lucky to get one job in a higher-paying public school district. Even after I got the job, keeping it was difficult because the guy who lost the job, whom I was replacing, was fighting the school district to get it back, so my tenure there was shaky.

In the end, after finishing that second teaching job, I left to go into the Navy, a much more secure employment opportunity. Surprisingly, being a Baby Boomer and the effects of that fact, followed me throughout my life, even to this day in my sixties. Squeezing seventy-six million people into the same phases of life at the same time has put a tremendous stress on the system every step of the way. In the late seventies, when I was in my twenties, I went to buy my first house and so did everyone else, so the interest rates shot up to between eleven and fourteen percent.

Around the same time, I went to buy a brand-new car and the only interest rate I could get was at seventeen percent. Today, I would buy a used car and pay in cash for it, but I was never counseled in detail about the best way to handle money for big purchases. To be fair, if I had asked my dad, he would have given me advice, but I wanted a new car and wanted to handle things on my own, so I did not ask for much guidance.

In my fifties, as I was searching for a future home to retire in Florida, the places I looked at were overrun with others my age looking for the same thing. It was almost comical to see that all the people crowding into the builder's reception area were in my age group. When I asked the home sales representative if there were any houses available to buy, he said, "I would sure love to sell you one, but I don't have any left in this phase. I should have some available in the next phase, which will not be built for several months." TRANSLATION: "I should have some available to buy in the next phase, but the prices will be higher then." This too seemed out of reach for me. Again, I was only born in 1952, in the first third of the Baby Boomer generation after World War II (1946-1964). The two-thirds of the seventy-six million Boomers who were born after me will have it even worse. Unfortunately, we still have fifty-million, one hundred, sixty thousand to go before the bottlenecking stops.

(Above} Kathleen with her parents at St. Norbert College Graduation, 1974

(Left to Right) Pat O., Kathleen O., and Joanie C. at St. Norbert College, 1973

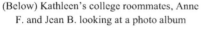

(Below) Kathleen's college roommates, Anne F. and Jean B. looking at a photo album

(Below) Kathleen at her school desk, teaching Art, 1977

94

Chapter 13: *College Years and Oh là là*

Character cannot be developed in ease and quiet. Only through experience of trial and suffering can the soul be strengthened, ambition inspired, and success achieved.

— **Helen Keller**[41]

Even though in prior chapters, I already mentioned some of my college experiences, I would like to talk about additional observations I have gleaned from the valuable four years I went to study at St. Norbert College in De Père, Wisconsin in August of 1970. I had a friend at Regina Dominican High School named Patti Maravic who told me about St. Norbert College because she knew I was looking for a small school and she had already decided to apply there herself. My dad thought that I would do better at a smaller college because of possibly getting more personal consideration from professors.

Patti was an honor student, so she had no problem getting in soon after she applied. I was a different story because my grades were mediocre. I think I had a 2.5 average or maybe below that. The college's student body consisted of roughly fifteen-hundred students and to my relief I was accepted, albeit on "probation." I guess the administrators knew that some students indeed blossom in college and that was what happened to me.

What a concept to study and then get good grades! I really did not know any good study skills, but because we were roommates, I was able to closely observe Patti's study habits and learned a lot. Our dorm room was quiet, so she could do her work and as a result, I had nothing to do but study. I watched when and how long she would study for a test and I tried to copy that process. The other reason I did better my first semester in college, was because I knew it was a financial sacrifice for my parents to send me to university and I did not want to let them down.

In the early seventies, our country had a recession and my dad was having problems meeting his obligations due to customers defaulting on what they owed him. A small business is greatly affected by these issues and I surmise that at first, my father did not have enough cash flow to cover his expenses, while at the same time putting me through an expensive private college. Later on, I found out

95

he ended up tng out bank loans with less favorable terms than could be obtained from my school's Financial Aid Department, being that my father was too embarrassed to disclose his income to the college. Without a lot of training for parents about the financial aid process then, my parents were ashamed their income had gone down quite a bit; therefore, Dad eventually took out his own loans at a much higher-than-the-student-rate to put me through school rather than requesting aid.

Something new that I noticed around this time was that Dad started to complain about how much things cost if we went out to eat or on vacation, but he never talked about his financial condition going south when the kids were around. He was always generous to a fault, especially with those he loved, so I had no idea he was struggling with finances. And of course, it only got worse as my years at St. Norbert went on when it became clear that my university-level courses were very expensive for my dad, especially during a recession.

A lesson I learned from this time in my life was that parents should be honest about what they can and cannot afford with their children. Dad's business had always done well, o, I think my parents thought, "This too shall pass." As a result, they did not say anything to me about their true financial condition. Thus, I went along happily, but when I realized the extent of the problem, I did work two jobs in summers to pay my own small expenses at school. Dad refused to let me work during the school year because he was afraid it would mess up my improving grades. My parents were delighted with my 3.56 out of 4.0 average the first semester and shocked and awed with my 4.0 average for the second semester during my freshman year.

I kept my grades up all through college and ended up graduating with a 3.56 average in 1974. I believe those higher grades were due to a combination of factors: my roommate Patti's good study habits, so I wasn't out on weeknights partying like a lot of the other kids; the worry about my parent's financial condition once I was made aware of it; I liked the subjects I was taking and most of all, I wanted my parents to be proud of me. In addition, graduating was the only way to get a good career in something I was interested in, instead of taking boring jobs because I had no choice. I wanted more choices.

What was astounding to me is that I found out that I loved learning—all kinds of things. This college experience began a life-long love of acquiring new learning and really stepped up my desire to read. I always liked English in high school (the one subject besides Art for which I almost always got an "A") and I read for assignments, but I did not read much for pleasure. In college, I blossomed into becoming a human sponge, constantly wanting to acquire knowledge and read all sorts of books. Hence, now as an adult, I read all the time.

You are probably wondering why I did so well in college if I had ADHD weighing me down. Since I did not know I had it, I coped by studying all night for the tests, writing highly-appraised papers and turning things in on time because I do much better if I have a deadline. I also would ask a lot of questions in class and after school I went to see the professors if I was having trouble. Also, I took copious notes with illustrations in class. The adrenalin rush I got when studying at the last minute or all night acted as a kind of stimulant. This proved to me that I needed some kind of impetus to be able to focus well in lectures and to be able to pay closer attention, while doing homework assignments. Later, I learned that medication, such as Ritalin or Adderall, could take the place of an adrenalin-rush to keep me focused and on task, without the added side effects of hyperactivity and lack of sleep.

Furthermore, at college, I was not being distracted by a noisy roommate, so I could pay attention better. Probably, I would have graduated with straight "A"s, if I had had the proper medication for ADHD then. All those factors, especially happening in my first year of college, ultimately led to making me believe I was smarter than I ever knew. My mom had told me many years ago that I was tested and had a high I.Q. and my teachers knew that, so they were always asking her, "Why Kathleen wasn't living up to her high potential?"

Moreover, I was never told what my IQ score was. I did not put much stock in knowing it because I did not usually feel smart and some of the subjects like math were really hard for me. I remember, I liked my math teachers in public middle school/junior high and seemed to understand the process of algebra, but then my answers were always wrong and I was really puzzled. I just thought that I was intrinsically bad at math, so I just tuned out most of the time in class.

None of my teachers in either public or private school ever mentioned that I could possibly have a learning disorder or even tested me for one. When I switched to public school because of smaller class sizes in sixth grade, I was told to go see a special teacher to help me lose a lisp I had acquired. I worked on that for a couple of years and did improve the lisp, but that was the only problem I had for which I had to see a specialist.

Regarding math, teachers seemed to just give up on me and I gave up on myself. It was only later in my thirties that I caught myself switching around numbers dictated to me on the phone. Then I learned to take each number slowly and that way I could write it down in the correct order. Also, double-checking them for errors really helped. This number-order-switching problem is an actual disability called Dyscalculia. It was such a relief to find out the reason I couldn't seem to get a correct answer in math, when I knew I had followed all the steps correctly, as required in Algebra. And so, I signed up for the first math courses the average person takes in college, when I was in my thirties, and could truly understand math much better because I developed better coping skills, like good note taking and a better listening ability because of lots of practice in the Navy.

Looking back, I find it hard to believe that I only had to take science courses, not math at St. Norbert and that was sufficient to graduate in my major from college at the time. Unfortunately, when I went back to school for math, I found out that the first math courses my fellow college students took to work towards their degrees no longer counted for credit. The bar had been raised and it appeared to be that way at all the schools I enrolled in, as I moved around the country with the Navy.

The good news was that due to my new-found confidence and study skills, I was able to get "A"s in those beginning courses. I didn't get credit, but what it did for my self-esteem was priceless. Moreover, I became more comfortable with math and as a Department Head in the Navy, I did well giving presentations with correct numbers, as well as, writing and staying within a budget.

Later, when I was a teacher, I was able to do my grades in a systematic way and be successful with them because I double-checked everything and a friend of mine suggested a new method. My friend, Georgette M. worked with numbers at her job and she suggested that I base my grades on points using multiples of three. For instance, if sixty points were the max points one could earn for a project (like 100%), an "A" grade, would start at fifty-four points, a "B" would start at forty-eight, and so on. It was so much simpler and made my grading task easier, even though I still had to check things over more carefully, due to fear of number transposing, taking me longer to grade than the average teacher. Thanks, Georgette, you made my life so much better!

It was in college that I also developed a life-long love of languages and culture. I had taken languages in high school, but they were not the ones I signed up for. The nuns had decided that since my grades were mediocre, I did not qualify to take French, which is something I really wanted. They put everyone into Latin for the first two years and then we took Spanish, French, or German for the last two years. I should have gotten into the language class I desired because my English grades were always good. Being good in one language, I later learned, is a precursor to doing well in others. The nuns made me take Spanish instead.

I did alright in Latin because for some reason, language structure made sense to me and we did not have to speak it, since it was a "dead" language. All "Romance" languages are based on Latin, so it was much easier to learn Spanish, French, Italian and Romanian if you had Latin first. Disappointed, I never really studied or enjoyed Spanish class, but I passed it both years. I had to wait for college to take French.

When I signed up for college, I tested well in all the languages I had already taken, but I did not want to continue. I had dreams of being a fashion designer and wanted to go to Paris to study for that in the future. Naturally, I would need to study French. The university powers that be said, "You shouldn't start a new language in college because it goes much faster and covers much more material than the high school level." One college semester equals one year of language study in high school. But, when I have a dream, it is hard to stop me. I knew what I wanted. I studied French for almost every semester in college and I even went for one semester to Paris, where I became fluent from listening and talking to everyone in sight in the target language.

In Paris, during my junior year, I shared an apartment with two other American girls. To this point, they had studied just as much

French as I had, but they refused to go out and buy groceries or talk to people at events. Since no one at that time spoke English in France like many do now, it made getting around difficult if you did not know French. I only became fluent because I loved the language and culture of France and practiced every day I was in Paris.

I became comfortable with speaking the language because my two roommates elected me to go to the Mouffetard Market across the street to do the shopping; they were too afraid to go out and speak French. When we returned to America, of the three roommates, I was the only one who could speak fluently. The lesson I learned here was that if you want to learn how to really speak a language well, force yourself to go out into public and talk to as many native speakers as you can in the target language.

According to the website, "O' Bon Paris", Marché de la rue Mouffetard (Mouffetard Street Market) is listed as one of the top five street markets in Paris.[42] Located in the Fifth Arrondissement (district), kitty-corner and across the street from where I used to live at 10 bis avenue des Gobelins in the Thirteenth Arrondissement. This street market was huge. Thus, I conveniently shopped there every day for food due to having no refrigerator in our apartment. Consequently, in the winter we would put the cold items outside on the windowsill of our fourth-floor walk-up to keep the items fresh.

Practicing French daily with the Parisian Mouffetard Market proprietors in the little separate shops: pastry, dairy, bread, meat, etc., located in the small labyrinth of slate streets, was in fact how I became a fluent speaker of French. Another reason I quickly became fluent was that I had developed a friendship with a French-speaking Parisian named Alixe Regnier and her family.

Alixe had studied in the U.S., but after a few years there, she became homesick and came back to Paris for her final year. I met her at Schiller College, the school I went to for my exchange program in the Seventh Arrondissement. Schiller College was on the American system of credits, which was the same system Alixe had been on when she was going to university in the U.S. Hence, this American college credit plan was necessary for Alixe to be able to finish her degree within four years. If she had tried to start on the French system at this late date, it would have taken her a lot longer.

Knowing Alixe positively accelerated my speaking ability in French. When I was in my French Conversation course, I was intimidated at first because many of the women I knew there already spoke high-level French. This was due to having boyfriends who spoke it well, or because the women had spoken Italian or Spanish fluently before. Naturally, Alixe spoke French beautifully, due to her being a native Parisian. I appeared to be the only one in our French Conversation class who had no experience speaking it fluently.

Suddenly, I shut down in Conversation class because I was intimidated and only received a "C" in the course; however, everywhere else I spoke French more fluently. I spent a lot of time at Alixe's house, where her father declared that we should only speak French there. Again, my speaking ability increased even more by being immersed in a French family home. Additionally, I remember going to a French wedding with the Regniers and having a whole conversation about politics (the Nixon-McGovern Presidential race of 1972) with other guests at our table, spoken only in French.

The first time I remember completely understanding a French conversation was after about two months being immersed in French in Paris. I took "le Métro" (subway) to school every day and one time, I noticed two people talking in French as they sat behind me. To my everlasting delight, I realized that I totally understood the conversation, including the nuances. After that, I would speak to Alixe in the hallways and at school events, exclusively in French.

One day, some haughty people from our Conversation class happened to walk by Alixe and me, as we were conversing in French at top speed in the corner of the school lobby. My judgmental classmates stopped abruptly, looked straight at me and said sarcastically, "We didn't know that YOU could speak French!" Alixe and I just looked at each other and burst out laughing.

One reason I was so welcomed into the Regnier family was explained to me by Mr. Regnier himself when I was staying over there during the Christmas holiday. If they had not invited me to stay with them, I would have had to go to a hotel during the school break because I had already moved out of my apartment. Mr. Regnier told me that he wanted to do anything he could for me while I was in France because he never forgot how kind the American family was that Alixe had stayed with while she was going to school in the U.S. He was grateful for how well Alixe was treated, especially when he could not get money over to her because of the frequent mail strikes in France.

Conversely, sometimes I didn't get money from my family when I needed it because of the continuous mail strikes while I was in Paris; however, the Regnier family was always there to fill in the gap for me, by feeding me or lending me money until the mail strike was over. I have found that French people, although hard to get to know at first, are loyal and kind friends once they make your acquaintance. And when you get to know them in a deep friendship, they will always be your friend for life. I have not seen Alixe or her family since I left Paris in 1973, but I am confident if I could remember where the Regnier family lived and knocked on their door even now, they would open the door with welcome arms.

Unfortunately, it was easier to lose track of people in the seventies because phone calls or travel used to cost an arm and a leg, so we didn't do it as much. I never even talked to my family on the phone once during the whole semester I was there because overseas phone calls were the most cost prohibitive. And of course, the mail strikes were ever present before and after my semester abroad. I retrieved the headline below because I couldn't find one from France about the postal strikes during my time abroad, but this headline shows why I had trouble keeping touch with the Regnier family right after I left Paris and beyond: "Labor Troubles Spread in France" by Clyde H. Farnsworth Special to *The New York Times*, Oct. 30, 1974.[43]

Due to the kindness of the Regniers, I fell more in love with French culture and was determined to remember that people are people, wherever they live and many of those we are afraid to get to know are just as kind as the average American is to newcomers. If somehow Alixe and her family read my memoir, I hope they contact me through the information in this book. What a reunion that would be! I say "Bien sûr!" to that. "Alors," I better brush up on my French, as soon as possible, in case that happens!

Another lesson I learned as a result of my study abroad in Paris was that Americans (sad to say), who complain about the unfriendliness of the French, often bring it upon themselves because they do not know or respect the history of the French people. Americans visiting France, never see how they are viewed by French people, when in their country. I noticed Americans at that time would not even try to speak French, and often would treat the French like servants, who should cater to every American's wish. That is not how I want to be remembered by my French friends.

As a result of France's proximity to stronger countries that want their land, the French haven't appreciated being overrun by other countries during two World Wars and other conflagrations. The French are particularly proud of their nationality, and because of these many conflicts with their neighboring countries, they have low trust levels for the motivations of any foreigners. If the French feel undervalued, they get cranky, like most humans do. Many American tourists pick up on this surly French attitude, without understanding the history behind it, so they do not try to get to know them better; therefore, they miss out on making French friends and understanding their rich culture.

After each setback, the French have picked themselves up and started to rebuild, which I think is very admirable. Think of a world without their rich cultural influences and you will understand why they should be appreciated. Even with all they have withstood, like the Nazi Occupation and the devastation of WWII (in my opinion) they come out on top in the areas of superior wine, scrumptious cuisine, the arts, melodic language and fashion to name a few.

Even if an American tries to speak French and they butcher it, the French are pleasantly surprised by their efforts because they know Americans are not known for speaking other languages well. Just make an effort by treating them with politeness, speaking a few French words, praising their products like food and wine, as well as, their artistic endeavors and you will notice a marked difference in their attitude and behavior towards you.

When I came back from France to St. Norbert, at the start of second semester of my junior year, it was an adjustment because by that time, I felt much more worldly than my fellow college students and even dressed like a European. Alixe and I would spend hours trading fashion tips. I showed her how to wear Yardley make-up like the popular model Twiggy wore. She would show me what most French women of the day liked. We both told each other that we wanted to look like those fashionable people in each other's country, so we helped each other achieve it.

Through Alixe's influence, when I came back to the U.S., I wore the chicest make-up and fashions from France I could afford. This chic new look, as well as my flipped bangs and blow-dried haircut (Think: Farah Fawcett, with a long page boy that went to a point in back) had not yet been seen in the U.S. Our U.S. stylists were still using rollers and having clients sit for long stints under gigantic stationary hair dryers. American hairstylists did not even know how to cut my hair or use a round brush and a blow dryer to create the French style with the flipped bangs yet. As a matter of fact, I was an anomaly when I arrived back on U.S. soil because of that new haircut, stylish dolman sleeves, larger bell-bottoms and unique platform shoes.

These new French styles I had already discovered would not come to the U.S. until six months later, but for a while I was getting tons of compliments on my new "French Look." Things were so expensive then in Paris, I didn't buy a lot of clothes there and ate at cheap restaurants to save money, but the few things I had from Paris made me feel like a queen. Also, I really *was* more mature when I came back because I had had many grown-up experiences. Moreover, I wondered if I had still fit in with my college chums back home or that because of my new overseas experiences, reconnecting would be out of reach for me.

For example, when I began my journey to France in the fall of 1972, I first traveled from Chicago to the "Big Apple" (aka New York City) by plane, where I boarded the luxury ocean liner, the *U.S.S. France* there. During the five-day crossing to Europe, I met some of the other students, who were going to study at Schiller College, like I was going to do. The boat stopped in Le Havre, France, where I caught the "boat-train" to Paris. The "City of Light" looked like a classic postcard night scene when I arrived because of the wet streets after a rain and the reflection of street lights on the Seine River.

Taking about seven days and a multitude of transport vehicles to get to Paris, all on my own, changed me profoundly for the better. Since then, I have not been afraid to go anywhere alone and it gives me a lot of comfort and confidence to know that I can get around myself or meet new people. Incidentally, I was reading a magazine not long after I returned to the U.S., and discovered that one of my favorite comedic stars of the seventies, the late John Ritter, from the T.V. show "Three's Company" had gone to the Schiller College Theatre Program in London the same semester that I was studying Art and French at Schiller in Paris. Who knew he would become so famous only a year or two later as an American T.V. star?

Other interesting experiences occurred when I was there. It was amusing to see how the French responded to lively American performers like Ike and Tina Turner. They either stayed seated or stood quietly during the concert, in contrast to us Americans dancing and singing along with songs like "Proud Mary." Besides seeing the Ike and Tina Turner show in Paris, I had more unique experiences there worth mentioning.

A painting course I took through Schiller was located one day a week at an atelier (artist's studio) of a well-known painter named Hugh Weiss. In his private studio, I painted with him side-by-side, using canvas with some of his old painting sketches on the back, so I could save money by not having to buy and build new canvases.

Mr. Weiss, originally an American, told me to whiten out his old canvases later with gesso, so no one could copy or sell them. I never got around to it and still have paintings I've done that were painted on the back of canvases with Hugh's sketches on the other side. I recently "googled" his name and saw that he lived a long life in Paris with his Swiss-born wife, Sabine Weiss, a world-famous photographer with photos in magazines like *Town and Country*, until his death in 2007.

(Below) American painter, Hugh Weiss (1927-2007), Kathleen's painting teacher in Paris
From: Wikimedia Commons, File: Hugh Weiss (1995).png[44]

(Above) St. Norbert College, De Pere, Wisconsin
From: Wikimedia Commons, File: Old Main Hall St Norbert College.jpg[45]

(Left) Kathleen with French classmates at Schiller College, Paris, 1972

(Above) Kathleen and roommate Patti M. going to their first dance at St. Norbert

(Above) Mary K. and Kathleen, (wearing her dolman sleeve sweater and chic haircut from Paris) looking at pictures of Kathleen's trip to France, 1973

(Left) Kathleen with her new "French Look" and haircut, (Above Right) French Postcard Kathleen sent to parents

(Above Left) The S.S. France that Kathleen sailed from NYC to France in Sept., 1972

Alixe Regnier at Schillet College in Paris, where Kathleen met her.

Chapter 14: Take Me Back To Chicago

"Growing apart doesn't change the fact that for a long time
we grew side by side; our roots will always be tangled.
I'm glad for that."

— *Ally Condie, Matched*[(47)]

Even though during my Navy career, I had been living in mostly California and Florida in the late seventies through the eighties, I still thought of the Chicago area as my home. It is where my father was raised and he had many great stories of being from the "Windy City" which most people think was given the nickname because of the wind off Lake Michigan. The wind off the lake can be fierce at times, but the nickname came from Chicago politics, at least that is one explanation.

Politicians were considered to be "windy" for not only talking too much, but for promising the citizens the world, and delivering nothing substantial, but rather, delivering something more tenuous like the air, whipping through the streets near the lake. There are lesser-known explanations for the nickname that can be found in Wikipedia, but the ones above are the ones I have heard all my life living in the Chicago area.

When I want to feel like a child again and remember where I was grounded as a person, I can go to Chicago either in person like I am now or listen to music of the great band Chicago, named after the hometown of this wonderful group of musicians. As I wrote earlier, I was able to meet the bands Chicago and the Beach Boys during their summer tour together in 1975, which took place in several cities, including Chicago. As I write this, I am looking at Lake Michigan, feeling its breeze and listening to the band's wonderful songs like "Take Me Back to Chicago" and some of their other songs, with references to my beloved city. Being here, while listening to the band's songs is helping me to write this bittersweet chapter in my life à la summer in the year 1975.

In my early twenties and a high school Art and French Teacher at the time, I was electrified that I got tickets to see them. The funny thing was that these two bands, which had been insanely popular for fifteen to twenty years already, had some new songs out that appealed to the high school students I was teaching and created a new generation of fans for their music. These bands, their music, my students and the city of Chicago created a perfect storm for my nostalgic remembrances of the seventies era.

In Chapter Eleven, I ended with my actress-friend, Carole and I being invited backstage to listen up close and to meet the groups and their roadies for the few nights they played at the Chicago Stadium in June of 1975. After the concert the first night, Carole and I got in my car to follow some of the crew we had met backstage to a club called Beginnings, located in Schaumburg, a Chicago suburb.

The band was staying in the City at the Whitehall Hotel on the North Side, so we pulled up to the front and stopped, waiting to follow the other cars going to the club. As we were waiting, we spied a cute dark-haired guy we had met standing in front, but there were so many band members and roadies we had been introduced to that night, we could not remember this particular guy's name. I rolled down my window and asked him if he wanted a ride to the club. He smiled sweetly and said, "No, I have a ride. Thank you, though."

We still did not know who he was when we arrived the next night for the concert, but our eyes grew wide with surprise as he hopped on stage and went to the keyboard. Still, I thought he was an engineer checking out the equipment before the band came on stage to play. A few minutes later, the rest of the band took their places and started to play the opening bars of one of my favorite songs "Saturday in the Park." Carole and I looked at each other when "cute guy" started singing the lyrics of the song. Our cute dark-haired guy was none other than Bobby Lamb, the lead singer and author of this popular song.

Going back to the first night of three concerts, when we arrived at the venue called Beginnings for a late night of dancing after the show, we proceeded to sit at a table with roadies who looked familiar, but whom we had not formally met. One of the guys at the table asked me to dance. He was the Sound Engineer for the Beach Boys and he introduced himself to me as Mike Stahl.

Mike told me he worked for the then well-known sound company called "Clair Brothers Audio" out of Lilitz, Pennsylvania. Twenty-nine years old, he was of medium height, sporting glasses, had longish, light blond straight hair, neatly cut, and he was wearing a

Beach Boy's tee-shirt and jeans. What was striking was his bright smile, with perfect white teeth and crinkly sparkling blue eyes, especially, when he laughed. And it didn't take much to put a big, attractive grin on his face. What intrigued me the most though, was his intelligence, as he seemed to have a keen interest in my teaching career.

He had been a junior high History and Math teacher before getting into sound, so my being a teacher piqued his curiosity and attentiveness. I questioned him about how he got into his sound career and he told me it started because he had had his own band and had loved playing guitar in groups in high school and during college. Also, his mother played as first chair cellist in the National Symphony Orchestra in Washington, D.C. Since the orchestra practiced at Mike's home as he was growing up, he listened closely to each instrument and could hear the nuances the average person may miss, but that are so clear to him, thus a career in sound engineering was destined to be his when he grew up. That night we started a romance that eventually became serious with talks of marriage.

After we met, Mike and I were inseparable whenever he was in town working the controls on the soundboard of concerts for various acts who had hired Clair Brothers Audio Company to rig the sound systems for their large concerts. Because I was seeing Michael, I usually had a backstage pass stuck to my jeans, as was the custom for roadies and authorized guests. Before the concerts, some of my high school students saw me walking backstage with that special pass. That four by five rectangle that stuck to my jeans was a magnet for my students. They were attending the Chicago and the Beach Boys' shows because these iconic sixties bands became popular again with the same generation as my high school students. One time, my students saw me and screamed, "Miss O'Brien, how did you get that pass?" They thought it was so cool!

Another time, I was sitting near Mike at the sound booth during a sound check for the concert later in the day. I was grading test papers of my high school French students, while waiting for Mike to be done. Carl and Dennis Wilson and asked me what I was doing. I told them I was grading papers, so they picked up a few and signed their names. Most of the kids were thrilled except some asked, "Miss O'Brien, why did you let them see my "C" paper?"

I replied, "Well, I guess you should have studied harder for the test."

During our relationship, Michael paid for me to fly on weekends to wherever he was working, so we could see each other. I was deeply in love with a man who had similar values and was compatible intellectually and emotionally with me. Michael was also mature, conscientious, hard-working, and attractive and did not seem like a typical roadie who had a girl in every town. Another factor indicating his maturity was that Mike was six years older than me and had a good career going. What was not to like? I even told my parents we were heading towards marriage.

Even though I was Catholic and Michael was raised Jewish, we both were non-practicing. My family was ecumenical on my mom's side, with each of the three girls of five total siblings choosing spouses of different religions. My mom married a Catholic, so converted and made her First Communion on her wedding day. Her older sister, Lois had married a Jew, converting to her husband, Morrie's religion. In particular, I remember Friday nights when Lois and Morrie's family celebrated Shabat with a Kosher dinner at her house, and if we were there, we partook fully in the ritual and the meal. My other aunt, Mom's youngest sister, Nancy and her husband were Episcopalians, and practiced that Protestant denomination. My mom's two brothers, Jerry and Dewey Robinson, never discussed religion in front of me and my mom never mentioned that they belonged to a denomination, so I don't think they were practicing any religion. If they were, I had never heard about it.

Because of all this exposure to different religions in my family, it never occurred to me that my Sound Engineer boyfriend Mike's and my differing religious upbringings would be a problem in the future, especially because we were both non-practicing. The two of us had so much in common like books, music, guitar playing, teaching backgrounds and liking stimulating intellectual conversation, that I thought we were perfect together, and we would have been, except for one obstacle that became totally glaring about nine months into the relationship. He was married with two young children, which he had neglected to tell me about. If he had told me up front, he knew I would not have dated him.

The way I found out was painful and embarrassing. Michael had given me the phone number to the company that he worked for,

Clair Brothers, in case I had to get a hold of him. We did not have cell phones then and Mike was moving to a new city every day or every few days with the bands for which he was engineering the sound on the road. One day, I called the number at Clair Brothers to get a hold of him and as usual, the friendly office assistant, Cathy answered the phone.

This time that I called, however, she seemed a little cold and business-like. I asked her to get a hold of Mike on the road and to have him call me back when he was free to talk. There was silence and then she blurted out, "You DO KNOW he is married, don't you?"

I replied, "Are we talking about Michael Stahl, MY Michael, the Sound Engineer?

And she said in a self-satisfied way, "Yes, I thought you knew about it." I was crushed and somehow got off the phone without losing it.

As one would expect, someone at Michael's office told him of the gaff right away and he called me back soon after. "I am soooo sorry Kathy! (I was still called "Kathy" then, only asking people to call me by my full name, "Kathleen," when I entered the Navy a few years later). I could tell Michael was mortified and remorseful on the phone, but sorry to say, we broke up. He knew I could not date a married man due to my convictions and integrity and he realized that he could not carry on this charade any longer either. Mike was not a smooth talker or the type to have affairs on the road like many of the roadies and band members did.

As I looked back, I saw that there were definite signs that he was living with intense guilt, but I did not recognize it until later. He had been unhappy in his marriage, but he still had two underage kids at home whom he loved dearly. At that time, he had not decided what to do about it all and so, we decided it was best for him to get his head together and for us to break up in the meantime because we both could not live with this conundrum in our lives. Mike and I agreed, that if it had been at a different time, when we were both free, we would have gotten married. We had been dreaming of marriage to each other before Cathy told me that he was already married on that fateful phone call. Moreover, the two of us admitted that we still loved each other, but that we could not have a relationship under these circumstances.

I had been hurt by men in the past, but this was a huge blow because I thought that he was the "ONE" and I believed I would never find anyone that was so right for me. I even briefly thought of killing myself and went into a deep depression because I could not imagine going on in my life without him. The heartbreak was intense and for several years afterward, I did not trust men in general anymore. I had truly believed that Mike was different and would never hurt me like that.

Later, I wondered if I had really been naïve and whether he had done this before. Was he actually a player like many of the other men I had met on the road with him? Doubting my own perceptions about men became a regular pastime for many years after that. This experience colored my decisions about commitment, relationships and where I belonged in the world for years to come. Contributing to the already heavy baggage I was carrying forward, many of my not so good decisions later were a direct result of being hurt in that relationship.

As an epilogue to this chapter, I did meet up with Mike Stahl again in February of 1982 while I was in San Diego attending Navy Drug and Alcohol Counseling School (NDACS). I was there so I could take over a Counseling and Assistance Center (CAAC) at Naval Air Station Miramar, California, later, a Marine base, as my new Naval duty station. When one goes to this school, one must be a part of group counseling as a way of practicing the new skills we were learning. Not as obvious to us, the NDACS instructors were observing us closely as people, to make sure we did not have any substance abuse problems or mental health issues of our own that hadn't been already addressed.

The NDACS instructors wanted to make sure that we were free to counsel others, without our own issues popping up, muddying up the decisions we were to make when evaluating and counseling others for substance abuse problems at our future CAACs. While at this school, I had been learning about myself, both good and bad and had a much better understanding where I had gone wrong in personal relationships of the past. This included the one I had with Michael Stahl in 1976, where I thought I had lost the love of my life.

Our reunion plans took place because one day in 1982 my dad called to tell me that Mike Stahl was trying to get a hold of me and had called my parent's house, which was the only number he had for me. It had been six years since I had even seen or talked to him and I was curious as to what he could possibly want. I guess Dad told Mike that I was a Lieutenant Junior Grade (LTjg) in the Navy, stationed in San Diego and that he (my dad) would have to ask me if it was OK to give out my number and soon all was arranged. Mike got a hold of me at the barracks where I was living while in the counseling school. I didn't realize at the time that this call and subsequent events would answer the question for me if Mike was the guy that I truly thought he was or if he was indeed a player, like I wondered after we broke up.

During that first phone call in half a dozen years, Michael told me that he had finally gotten divorced. Additionally, he said he had never forgotten me and wanted to see if we could start seeing each other again, as two single people, now that he was free. We began spending hours on the phone and I could feel the old chemistry coming back between us. At that point, Mike was the Sound Engineer for Kenny Rogers and wanted me to come to a concert and spend a few days with him; therefore, we arranged to meet in Las Vegas in February of 1982, a few weeks hence, where the show was being held.

Being together was just like before, but I will say that my new maturity through attending intense group counseling at NDACS, cautioned me not to rush into anything yet. After that long wonderful weekend in Las Vegas, where I met Kenny Rogers and his then-wife Marianne, Mike and I made plans for the following month for him to meet me in Orlando, Florida, where I still owned a house. There I would be on leave for ten days visiting my old roommate, Karen B.

For a long time, I could not remember why Mike and I ended things after a promising second start, but recently, I found some writings I had done around that time which answered that burning question. Turns out, Mike had assumed that we would be committed to each other right away, as if we were never apart. I cautioned him on the phone that we needed to take some time to see each other again a lot more, just to be sure before we made a commitment. Also, five years before this, I had begun my Navy career, which made the situation even more complicated to be able to see each other regularly.

Undoubtedly, my strong feelings for him were still there and if he had contacted me a couple of years earlier, I would have jumped right back into the fire again, consequences be damned. Five years of marching and learning how to take charge of things in the military had matured me quite a bit. It made good sense to take it slowly and I told him so. I waited each day of my vacation for him to call me back and meanwhile my leave time in Orlando was slipping away and I would have to get back to San Diego soon.

Eventually, I found out that Mike Stahl had really wanted me to give a definitive answer about our relationship and since I was not ready to at that time, he decided without explaining it to me, not to continue seeing me. We went on with our lives and I never knew what happened to him or where he lived after that until 2016, when I started to write this book. I typed his name into Google to see if I could find him.

Forty-plus years later, I had forgotten all the whys and wherefores about our relationship and desired to find out what happened to him in case I wanted it to be part of my memoir. His name came up all right as a subject of an article in the magazine *ProSoundWeb* on-line. It was entitled: "Mike Stahl Recalls: Mixing Chicago Live in the 1970s—The engineering approach with a seminal fusion group, along with anecdotes and experiences from a unique time... "[48] *by* Mike Stahl, of July 11, 2014.

It was a nine-page first person account of that precious time in the mid-nineteen-seventies, when I had first met him. It included a picture of him at his soundboard working the controls at a concert when he was about twenty-nine years old during the time that I knew him. There was an editor's note saying that this would be the first article in a series that Mike would write about his exciting career and those big-name bands for which he had engineered their live sound. But sadly, there was another article from *ProSoundWeb (PSW)*[49] magazine that came up underneath the first article on Google. It was written by PSW staff and dated: September 24, 2014.

There was also a more recent picture of him attached and the second article was called: "Pro Audio Veteran Michael Stahl Passes Away At 68."[49] In the two-page article, there was another picture of him and his team working the sound at the Super Bowl. Mike's jaw line had filled in with a few more lines in his face, his blond hair had become a shade darker and his glasses had changed, but remarkably he looked much the same as I had seen him last almost forty years ago. As the President of his own sound company in the Los Angeles area and married thirty-one years since 1983, Mike seemed content and to have done well for himself, and for that I was glad.

Seeing that Michael Stahl had already passed away was bittersweet, for it got me in touch with my own mortality and reminded me that we should make the most out of life, which I believe he did. Mike died at the same age at which my dad passed away and I used to think that that was really old. As I edit this book for publication, I myself am now sixty-eight years old, so I guess I must be really old too.

Reading the articles about Mike's career and then his death at sixty-eight, I reflected upon my life and even felt the sadness of something which had seemed so good, being just out of reach for me, again. However, since then, writing this book and looking at all the wonderful and interesting people like Mike I encountered throughout the years, I realized that through them, my life was enriched beyond measure and these experiences have given me wisdom I may never have received any other way.

(Left) Kathleen at middle right above sign in 1982, San Diego, CA

NAVY DRUG ABUSE COUNSELOR SCHOOL

(Far Left) Kathleen as a Lieutenant Junior Grade (jg)

Kathleen as Director, CAAC and staff,

Mike Stahl, Sound Engineer
for the Beach Boys[50]
1970s Photo from
ProSound Web

Aunt Lois, sister of Elaine and
Nancy in Tallassee. FL.1992

(Left) Kathleen in her
Lieutenant uniform talking
on the phone in Orlando,
FL to Mike Stahl

CHICAGO & THE BEACH BOYS
TOGETHER
BEACHAGO TOUR SUMMER 1975

FRIDAY, JUNE 2, 1975
CHICAGO STADIUM
DOORS OPEN AT 7PM

Summer of '75 Chicago-Beach
Boys "Beachago" Tour [51]

Chapter 15: *Proud Military Service for the U.S.*

*... sacrifices. They married in record numbers and gave birth to
another distinctive generation, the Baby Boomers.
They stayed true to their values of personal
responsibility, duty, honor, and faith.*

—Tom Brokaw, The Greatest Generation[52]

In his 1998 book, *The Greatest Generation*, the journalist, Tom
Brokaw talked about my parents' generation as noted in the opening
quote above.

When I was young, I used to watch TV with my dad, Thomas
J. O'Brien, born in 1919. Dad was from what Tom Brokaw calls "The
Greatest Generation," those who grew up in the twenties and thirties
and served in the military during World War Two (WWII). Having
been in the Army Supply Corps during WWII, my dad was always
interested in reading books or watching documentaries from that era.
What a great era and generation it was! They worked hard and
followed the orders of their superior officers to ensure an Allied
victory. Dad taught me about why WWII was important and instilled
his patriotism into me, of which I am supremely grateful.

In the sixties, many of the shows on TV were written for the
time of the forties during World War II. Having occurred twenty
years before, it had all the evidence of being a popular subject again.
There were comedies like "McHale's Navy" and serious shows like
"Combat." Dad and his only daughter, yours truly, watched those, as
well as, war documentaries faithfully; my two younger brothers were
not interested in those days.

When Terry, my youngest brother, got older, he became
interested in WWII books due to my father's influence, unlike
Michael, the middle brother, twenty months my junior. So, for the
early part of my growing-up years, I was the only child of Tom and
Elaine to enjoy those pastimes. My father explained what the military
was like for him and was proud of it. He never actually went to war,
but he was stationed in Alaska, a key area for staging and operating
with our allies, the Russians, during WWII.

As a Captain in the Army, Tommy O'Brien was in the Supply Officer Corps. As part of his job, he was responsible for providing the Officer's ("O") Club with provisions and I believe he got a hold of some alcohol, when he was stationed in Alaska, which is close to Russia. He had many a rowdy party in the "O" Club with Army Commissioned soldiers and Russian officers, for which he got a wink and a chewing out from his Commanding Officer. Nevertheless, his officer evaluation reports were glowing about his leadership abilities. How do I know this? I have obtained his Fitness Reports from the Army archives and with these records, I will pass down the stellar military legacy of my father to my descendants.

I grew up fascinated by the military and attracted to the organization, discipline and travel carried out by soldiers, sailors, airmen and marines. My father taught me to respect their mission and sacrifice to keep us in America safe; however, my dad never thought his own daughter would actually go into the military!

As a child, we lived near both Chicago O'Hare Airport and Glenview Naval Air Station. Many times, Dad would take us to watch the Navy planes take off and land behind the chain-link fence on Lehigh Avenue, next to the Naval Air Station (NAS). Later, when I was stationed at different Naval Air bases during my military career, I would see the F-14s flying in formation above, executing difficult maneuvers and I would get chills seeing these precision military aircraft. I also got goosebumps watching those planes take off and land at Glenview Naval Air Station in the sixties with my dad. When I did join the Navy in the late seventies, Dad was so proud of me, his little girly-girl-turned-warrior. It was his encouragement that got me through the rough times during my military training.

At the time my battalion passed in review, in 1979, at our graduation from Officer Candidate School (OCS) in Newport, RI, my dad was the last one out of the bleachers after we finished the ceremony. Still seated when everyone else left the field, he appeared to be thinking of how proud he was of me and reliving his own service and patriotism. Dad taught me that when I received a salute from a junior officer or enlisted person, I had better not return a sloppy salute; my father said to take care with my return salute, ensuring that it was always snappy to show respect for the junior person who initiated it.

118

I never forgot my dad's wise saluting advice and always took care that my salutes were well-executed, whether I was the initiator or the receiver, to be worthy of respect for the rank and the uniform in the U.S. Military. Almost ten years later, at my father's funeral, I made sure I wore my dress blue uniform and rendered the snappiest salute I could when the flag-draped casket passed by because I sensed that Dad was "up there" watching with a big Irish smile on his face.

How did I cope well with ADHD in the Navy, the reader might wonder? The interesting thing is that the military was the perfect career for me because the certainty, structure, discipline, written rules and traditions allowed me to be successful without medication. I had unknowingly developed good coping skills in the service for the most part; therefore, I could flourish. I did not mind studying harder than others or working longer hours to get the job completed.

In fact, it was only years later that I realized what helpful procedures for myself that I had put into place to ensure the job got done well. It wasn't perfect, but because of my personal healthy and evolving coping skills (even though some of the bad coping skills still existed) I was able to let the good ones steer me during the Navy years, due to the enduring and repetitive military structure.

Some of the healthy coping mechanisms I developed while in the military are as follows: writing everything down, taking as much time as I could in order to complete a project and making good delegation decisions to the right people really helped. Also, I got my first personal Day-Timer (no gadgets or smart phones were invented yet to assist me much in the late eighties). The Day-Timer certainly helped me keep track of important items. Along the way, I found out I was a good people manager because I responded with respect to those people with whom I worked, no matter their rank. I also improved as a leader, as I went on, which the Navy sees as differentiated from being a manager. Leadership is considered a higher calling than managing. It requires stepping out in front to ensure your subordinates have good direction.

From taking leadership courses, I discovered how important good networking skills are to be successful in an organization, something I was always doing naturally. For example, I could always get my hands on the people and information needed for the task at hand in a timely manner because I already knew most of the players, due to networking on base. In addition, I worked well in a team to ensure that our assignments were completed.

Moreover, my creative background helped me to stand out in the innovative ways I solved problems, impressing my bosses. I knew this because during Fitness Report time (officer evaluations one time per year), I was ranked high against others of my same pay grade. Also, during my Commissioned Officer years, I was ranked Number One out of my peers more than once and consistently received high grades and comments with words like, "outstanding" or phrases like, "ahead of the pack" or "Promote her Now!" about my performance.

One time, when I was ranked Number One, I asked my boss why he ranked me that way because I knew the other Lieutenant Commanders that I was up against were excellent officers too. He told me, "Because Kathleen, I know that whatever job I give you, you will get the right people together and get the job done and on time." Of course, I wasn't perfect, but most of the time I was satisfied with my performance and contributions to the commands where I worked.

Yes, my listening skills needed work, a common problem with having ADHD, due to difficulty paying attention for any length of time; however, because I wrote down detailed notes, I could always find an approach to respond in an appropriate and timely way. I am a visual learner, so having big display boards with what had to be done in a week, a month or longer right in front of my desk really helped.

Some other good indicators of how to fit in to a military structure and be successful were tools inherent in the job. We had uniforms displaying signs and ranks and protocols ingrained in us through training manuals. These were standard from base to base, so I often did not have to read facial cues or body language to understand what was expected of me. Those visual symbols and physical actions like saluting or making an about-face movement, for example, were good coping skills helping me to comprehend the human interaction I encountered among military people. Also, I was often complimented on my writing ability, which helped to propel my promotions. In these ways, I was able to carve out a fairly successful career and serve the country I love.

Due to attention deficits, trouble sorting and weeding through normal people expressions could be difficult for me, especially without medication, which are problems hard to surmount for most

ADHD people. The skills I learned as part of a normal military environment and tools I picked up along the way were essential in my overcoming ADHD deficits and were invaluable in ensuring my success in the Navy. Also, military people operate a lot on adrenaline, which acts like a stimulant to focus on the task at hand.

As I got higher in rank, I usually had a great secretary and/or a departmental senior-level assistant that steered me in the right direction. It is important to note that steering junior officers from below is a time-honored value of the "Chief's Mess" (what we call the group of senior enlisted members E-7 through E-9 pay grades, who are like the foreman positions in a regular civilian enterprise).

The unspoken value is that it would reflect badly on an officer's senior subordinates if those subordinates did not use their "blue collar" wisdom to make the officers they worked for look good. Woe to the young officer that does not understand this value and continues to treat senior enlisted with a lack of respect and does not listen to their seasoned opinions. Their thoughts and sentiments were gained from hard-won experience working with the troops on a day-to-day basis. Ignoring these facts are to the young officer's peril.

Still, I always felt that somehow things attained would not last or were somehow out of reach due to my limitations, even though I was not always aware of what my constraints were. Later in my life, my limitations became a little more apparent after I left the structure and discipline of the Navy and that discovery caused me some heartache before I let God take a greater role in my life and learned to accept that I really had limitations.

One thing that helped me to accept my attention deficit disability, was that I saw this disabled man speak one time after I left the service. He said, "I am not disabled, but I am differently-abled." This statement helped me to remember there are many ways to get a job done and that I am not helpless, just because I have limitations as a result of ADHD. What he said opened my eyes to believing that maybe having a fulfilling career, regardless of ADHD, was in reach for me. There are other people who can help or other avenues I can take if I put my creative thinking cap on and if I ask God to help me—we all need a little divine intervention now and then.

The mental and emotional help through psychotherapy that I received, cost me a pretty penny financially, as my insurance did not cover it because I went for help outside the Navy. I was afraid that if I let the Navy know I had emotional issues, it would reflect negatively on my career; however, I shudder to think where I would be if I had put counseling, education and psychiatric help on the back shelf then, regardless of my career.

Above all, I believe my emphasis on my spiritual life was the number one driver to me getting better. My reliance on a Higher Power made the real difference and pointed me towards obtaining the right assistance I needed, even when I did not yet know what was wrong with me or had not yet encountered the God I know much more deeply today. I now understand that He is always with me, watching over me. When I made another bad decision or a mistake, I pictured my father up there with God and Saint Peter, shaking his head hearing Dad saying to me, "I am so sorry honey that you must go through this type of pain again, but you just aren't listening. We will be here waiting when you decide to change your approach to walk toward something better for you."

(Right) Iver H. Iverson, Army soldier in France, WWII, Kathleen's father-in-law

(Left) Thomas O'Brien, Captain, US Army, WWII

(Right) Ensign Kathleen O'Brien in 1979, OCS

Chapter 16: *Anchor's Away!*

The Navy Hymn
(Eternal Father, Strong to Save),

Eternal Father, strong to save,
Whose arm hath bound the restless wave,
Who bid'st the mighty ocean deep
Its own appointed limits keep;
Oh, hear us when we cry to Thee,
For those in peril on the sea!

— William Whiting, 1860[53]

Never did I have any intention of following my dad's footsteps into the military because most of my life, I planned to be an Art Teacher. Even in college, when I passed by the ROTC displays or went to the military balls as a guest of a prospective Army officer, I never thought I would be in the military. It was too masculine for me to consider for a career. I was a girly-girl then and very much of a right-brain person. Not knowing until later that I had even an ounce of left-brain thinking in my head, I concentrated on activities that were artistic, "avant-garde" or decidedly feminine in nature.

Things totally changed for me in my early twenties, during my first year of teaching art at an all-girl's high school in the Chicago suburbs. One of my students, a talented senior named Linda, wanted to go to college to study Art but had no money. So, I told her about my father always telling me about the education benefits for military veterans through the G.I. Bill. Linda found out about a photography program the Navy had. Little did I know that all those real war pictures inserted into old movies like "In Harm's Way" with John Wayne or "Operation Petticoat" starring Cary Grant were taken by Naval photographers. Even today, the old WWII battleship footage depicted on the History Channel or in documentaries showing authentic film of Navy ships at sea, were mostly taken by Navy Photographer's Mates.

While Linda was deciding whether she should apply to become a Navy Photographer's Mate, I decided I would go with her to the recruiter to see what she was getting herself into. If nothing else, I could use this new information to offer to my art students as either a viable career related to their artistic skills, or a stepping stone to eventually pay for college on the G.I. Bill. When explained by the Navy Recruiter, this program sounded fascinating. I found out that many Photographer's Mates took pictures out of planes and of important visitors or of base events for Public Affairs Office assignments.

In addition, they made maps of aerial views, called "Mosaic Maps" (because the panoramic photos were pieced together like a mosaic). Navy Photo Mates also took pictures of Navy festivities on base like Changes-of-Command or Reenlistment ceremonies. They also worked for the station newspaper as Photojournalists. In addition, Photo Mates climbed into jets or other equipment to take pictures of suspected evidence of sabotaged parts flagged by the Naval Investigative Service (NIS), now known as Naval Criminal Investigative Service (NCIS).

Another exciting job handled by Navy Photographer's Mates was standing watch on air stations and taking pictures of planes landing that were having trouble getting the wheels down or other various mechanical issues. In those cases, the photographer was required to jump in the crash truck, drive to the runway and catch the plane in its descent with a motor-drive camera in case it crashed. Luckily, as "Duty Photographer," I never saw a plane wreck, but there was a lot of excitement during the minutes before the plane landed safely, while we were listening to the chatter between the pilot and the control tower on the intercom and then the radio in the crash truck. It was these kinds of the anticipated adventures and the ability to use my artistic skills that convinced me to join the Navy as a photographer.

Ironically, the substitute teacher who took my place for that last month of the teaching year I had to miss by joining the Navy in May of 1977, was the arrogant former Art Teacher just prior to me being hired that had been let go. He had been fighting to get his job back and he probably would fight for the next year because the union was on his side, despite the objections of the school Principal who fired him in the first place. That situation gave me more incentive to join the military, so at least I would have a job. Linda, the student who inspired me to set on this new career path, never did enlist. I eventually joined the Navy toward the end of the 1977 school year with only one month left.

Being a Navy Photographer's Mate required that I did all of the cool jobs outlined above, except one: I never qualified as an aerial photographer. By the time I got out of photo school, they didn't need a lot of pictures taken by Photo Mates from planes anymore. This was because of new technology; the pilots now controlled an aerial camera themselves by pushing a button already built into the aircraft.

While I was in Boot Camp aka Recruit Training Command (RTC) for men and women recruits in Orlando, Florida, I started to wonder if I had made a mistake by leaving my teaching career for the Navy. We had to get up at an ungodly hour, when it is still dark that we really do call "Zero Dark Thirty" as in the title of the movie about killing Osama bin Laden. Moreover, we endured endless marching drills in formation, did contortionist exercises, ran double-time everywhere, completed muscle-cramping obstacle courses, were shouted at and did impossible tug-o-war contests during the eight weeks of instruction that I completed as my initial training in 1977.

After Boot Camp, I finished ten weeks of Photographer's Mate "A" School training in Pensacola, FL and four more weeks of advanced schooling. Finally, I was considered by my instructors to be ready to embark on my new career as a Navy Photographer's Mate at Naval Air Station, Jacksonville, (NAS JAX) FL.

A few months later, on a rare day of rest in Jacksonville, (usually Sunday), I came across a two-page photo spread and article in "People" magazine that really made me question my new change of career again: there were pictures of MY old art classroom back in Illinois, taken with MY former students, the ones I had just left and their new teacher (the arrogant replacement teacher already mentioned). The article told of an art project my replacement teacher had assigned during the short month I had been gone (I admit the project he assigned was a good one).

The teacher who replaced me assigned the students a project requiring them to draw pictures in the style of the famous artist, Joan Miró (1893-1983), who was still living at the time, albeit an old man at eighty-five years old. My replacement teacher had sent the students' drawings to the Surrealist pioneer and Mr. Miró had responded with a postcard. What made it special was an iconic original drawing done by Miró on the front of his return postcard with a congratulations note on the back signed by him. It would be almost as if an artist like Picasso drew a picture on a postcard and sent it.

A big controversy erupted because my replacement teacher back in Illinois planned to keep the priceless postcard for himself. Fortunately, the School Board put their foot down and determined that it belonged to the students and the school, not to the individual teacher. I cannot remember what happened to the postcard, but I will never forget my homesickness and the hard questioning of this new Navy career choice going on in my head as I read that article.

It was hard enough to deal with all the discipline and changes that Boot Camp and early military training required, but seeing the smiling faces of MY class on the pages of *People* magazine almost caused me a big ABOUT FACE on my new Navy endeavor. *Perhaps I had turned my back on my real calling of Art Education, a vocation I had been preparing for my whole life,* I thought, but only for a nanosecond, when I got the feeling my new Navy goals were going to be out of reach.

Fortunately, I quickly regrouped because I reflected upon letters from the third graders from my school, asking me about Navy life. For example, one letter went like this, "Dear Miss O'Brien, do you live in a tent?" Along with these letters, came drawings of how the third graders imagined my Navy life: me hanging out of a plane, taking pictures as a Navy photographer. At first, getting these packets produced terrible homesickness, but then I realized that I was still fulfilling my old long-term career goals of being creative in the photography field.

During this time, I noticed that when I would go to the Jacksonville Navy Exchange (an on-base store like an Army PX), the staff struck me as being kind of rude to me. I asked other sailors with whom I worked, what they thought was the reason for these snubs or "... was I just imagining it?"

The sailors said, "No, what you are experiencing is quite common because most of the sales jobs at the Exchange are filled by Navy spouses, (who were mostly women at that time) and they do not like Navy women working with their husbands. They feel really threatened by this because it was something they did not have to worry about before."

Shocked by this new information, I made an effort from then on, to be extra nice to sales people at the Exchange, which helped improve their treatment of me. As I think of this now, I realize that the Navy spouses had a point to their worry. Many years later, when women were allowed to work on ships, there was a case in point. I had a civilian friend, called Claudia, who was a trainer for a Naval education program delivered to ship personnel out at sea. When she was chosen to deliver training on one of our ships, she was happily married. She went on a six-week tour on a carrier to deliver drug and alcohol education to the sailors on board.

Unfortunately, Claudia got involved with one of the sailors there, who was also married and it broke her husband's heart. I believe my friend and her husband were divorced soon after she came home. I hate to say this as someone who firmly believes women should deploy on ships like men, if they do a job requiring a deployment at sea, but there are problems with fraternization between members in those close quarters on a ship. Now that many of our ships are co-ed, pregnancies occur, which is a nightmare for the Commanding Officer (C.O.), who has to arrange for the pregnant woman to be taken off the ship (usually by helicopter and/or a passing boat going back to the U.S.), due to the greater safety risks on ship for an expectant female. After that, somehow, the C.O. needs to get a replacement, which is difficult, once the ship is out at sea.

Mixed gender crews are even harder to manage for the C.O., if we are talking about a co-ed submarine crew. The quarters are so tight, personnel have to do what we call in the Navy: "hot rack" it. Sailors are often on three eight-hour shifts around the clock to keep the ship in great operational shape. Consequently, when the ship has the "hot rack" system, the racks (single bunks) need to be shared by three sailors, one sleeps while the other two are on duty and so on, all throughout the deployment.

Even though I think an all-female-crew ship would be the answer, to avoid these problems, that solution is not practical. These decisions by top brass are not as uncomplicated as strong feminists would have you believe, but they are finding more ways of working out solutions to these types of issues in today's Navy.

In Jacksonville, FL, I was asked to create a slide presentation for the base Admiral called, "The History of the Navy in JAX" by doing historical research in our Navy photo lab archives. I found and included great pictures taken during WWII of comedian Bob Hope entertaining the troops with his cavalry of movie stars and real

German prisoners of war working on base at JAX (We were nicer to prisoners of war than other countries like Japan and Germany were to us.) I had a lot of fun making this slide presentation because I was able to pick great old pictures from the lab collection and research what important events had happened at that base over the years.

Interviewing the base Admiral and his wife helped to give me insight that was valuable for enhancing the slide presentation. An added benefit was being invited by Mrs. Admiral to lunch at their quarters on base and getting to enjoy her company. When I decided to apply for Officer Candidate School during my tour there, she really supported me in that goal. When she met her husband, they both were Lieutenants early on in their military careers, so she knew what it was like to be a woman in the Navy. Incidentally, Mrs. Admiral had to get out of the Navy herself when she married her military husband because those were the rules in her time. I never forgot her kindness and encouragement to a "lowly" enlisted girl, who was stationed far away from home. Later, when I graduated from OCS, I was able to send her a card thanking her for believing in me and telling her how much her support meant to me.

Loving history as I do, and obviously being creative, as demonstrated by my degree in Art Education, the slide presentation was a perfect project for me; therefore, I really went to town and seemed to please the Admiral and his wife with my work. Often, there were important people visiting the base, so we broke it out to show them and it awakened their understanding of how important NAS JAX was to Naval history and to the present-day mission.

Being in a barracks at NAS JAX with other Navy women, at least in my experience, was not at all like being in a college dorm. First of all, many of the inhabitants had been around the world and had experienced things that never happened to the average college student.

Second, being that I was kind of sheltered growing up, I was shocked at the behavior of the enlisted women I lived with. Items in my part of the barracks were stolen and we were warned to secure our personal lockers in our shared rooms because no one knew who the culprit was yet. Contemplating the fact that one of my roommates could steal from me was something I had never experienced in my small midwestern college dorm rooms.

Third, another one of my roommates was an open lesbian, when that was not allowed in the Navy. If one was a lesbian or gay, one had to keep it quiet or be kicked out of the service. Obviously today, that scenario would not be an issue, however, in 1977, it was kind of shocking to have a lesbian living in my small dorm room. Many of us did not know a lot about the lesbian lifestyle then because it was not well-publicized or talked about in my naïve circles.

Fourth, another one of my other bunk mates, (We had bunk beds, with one person sleeping above the other, and four women to a room.) was what was called a member of the "Mile High Club." Since NAS JAX was an air base, this club concept was significant. Basically, to be a member of the Mile High Club meant that you had gone up in a plane with an aviator and when it was above the clouds, about a mile up in the sky, you had sex with that partner on the aircraft. Being somewhat naïve, this concept was also news to me.

Fifth, the fourth bunkmate in my room, had an obvious drug problem. Around this time, almost everyone who had enlisted had at least tried drugs, but even though it was spelled out as prohibited in the regulations in writing, many sailors didn't pay attention to the rules because drug use was so rampant in the society at large and there were few penalties if caught.

A few years later, in 1980, there was a survey of drug use in the military, which was anonymous, so people would answer truthfully. And they certainly did! This was a time that Officers and Chief Petty Officers had been telling their troops it was OK to do marijuana (MJ) only off base, but to be careful because the drug stays in your system thirty days and it was possible that a random pee test would be given. These types of things would never be allowed today.

Before the 1980 survey, those random pee tests (called urinalysis tests) were not given frequently because the Navy higher-ups were a little naïve about how much drug use was in fact going on among the troops; however, after the survey, when it turned out that close to twenty-eight percent of those surveyed used drugs, mostly marijuana in the last thirty days, the upper echelon knew they had to take action right away.

Urgent action was especially needed, since the upper echelons of the Navy also found that some of the accidents that had happened aboard ships and planes involved sailors, who had MJ in their systems, when the mishap occurred. Case in point: on May 26, 1981, there was an aircraft accident on the carrier USS Nimitz. Six of the fourteen sailors killed were found to have marijuana metabolite in their systems. The investigation report declared that drug use was a contributing factor to the cause of the accident.

Eventually, after President Ronald Reagan took office in January 1981, steps were taken to stop the increased use of drugs among military troops through education, regular urinalysis, and use of dogs to sniff out drugs on ship and on base. Additionally, the First Lady, Nancy Reagan joined the effort by starting a campaign against drugs called, "Just Say No!" We had had a Navy-wide evaluation, counseling and treatment system in place. In actuality, with presidential attention and a beefed-up random urinalysis system in position, drug use started to decrease.

All those steps concerning chemical use are important to my story because by 1980, I had obtained a Master's Degree in Human Resources Management (HRM) under which the categories of drug prevention and counseling came, as part of my Naval career path. Accordingly, when I was ready to transfer in 1982 from Naval Training Center, Orlando, Florida (my first duty station after OCS) I asked for an assignment in the field of drug and alcohol evaluation and counseling, which I received; however, I am a little ahead of myself. While still at Jacksonville an interesting set of incidents materialized that warrant telling before moving on.

My first duty station after Boot Camp in 1977, was as a Navy Photographer's Mate at Naval Air Station. Jacksonville. I went there, after finishing several months of initial and advanced training at Naval Schools of Photography in Pensacola, Florida. Three duty stations and I had not left Florida yet! Throughout my time in the Navy, I have re-encountered people I knew from many bases in the U.S. During my three-year tour (assignment) at NAS JAX, a few things took place, which influenced the course of my career and my attitude toward it.

Soon after I arrived in Jacksonville for my first Photographer's Mate assignment, I ran into the Senior Recruit Company Commander (Senior C.C.) who was one of my two Orlando Boot Camp instructors. She had transferred there after her Recruit Instructor/C.C. tour, where I had first met her. Her partner (Junior C.C.) was strict, but not unnecessarily pernicious like Senior C.C. was to the eighty recruits they both supervised in our recruit company. Both were Petty Officers Second Class (equivalent to an E-5 enlisted pay grade of the nine enlisted grades in all the services (see INDEX A, pp. 307-308) but Senior C.C. was the one in charge because she had more time in her pay grade. "E" stands for Enlisted, meaning not being a Commissioned Officer.

Usually, most Commissioned Officers have college degrees or equivalent experience, depending upon the program they enrolled under when they were commissioned. Commissioned ranks consist of ten pay grades, where "O" stands for Officer, starting out as an Ensign (O-1 all the way up through O-10) equivalent to an Admiral in the Navy and Coast Guard and equivalent to a General in the Army, Air Force and Marines. Rarely do we have the rank of O-11, Fleet Admiral, even though it exists during special times, like WWII. Warrant Officer pay grades (W-1 through W-5) are officers that fall between the Enlisted ranks and the Commissioned Officer ranks. Warrant Officers are produced from programs that do not apply here. Our basic pay, also seen in INDEX A, pp. 307-308, is determined by our rank/pay grade plus time in service. Added to basic pay, those who live off base can get monthly housing and food allowances and some, like pilots and Navy SEALs can receive hazardous duty pay. Moreover, when sailors are at sea, they receive sea pay.

Being a college graduate and entering the Navy as an Enlisted sailor, was an opportunity for those of higher seniority, like Senior C.C., to take advantage of me or to treat me poorly because they had more power. This situation didn't happen to me too often, but it brings up a question several have asked me over the years, "If you had a college degree upon enlisting, why did you go to Boot Camp instead of Officer Candidate School?" Good question, but the answer is simple: if I wanted to be a Navy Photographer, I had to start out as a blue collar-like Enlisted sailor, requiring Boot Camp because Photographer's Mate is not a job in the Commissioned Officer ranks, similar to white collar managers and requires completion of OCS.

Anyway, back at Boot Camp, Senior C.C. found out I had a college degree, which was rare among Enlisted ranks at that time and she proceeded to give me the most thankless job in the company, called "Yeoman." Senior C.C. knew that with a college education, I could probably write well and most likely prepare Company 3049 paperwork with high precision, which was needed in the Yeoman job.

She was correct in assuming I could write and spell well, but I did not want the job for several reasons:

First, I had to carry the company paperwork in a heavy briefcase everywhere we went (all eighty recruits in formation) while marching in step together, on our large base in Orlando. Because of having to carry the Company 3049 Briefcase, I was placed at the end of the formation, where my short legs had trouble keeping up with the pace of the marching in formation.

Second, I had to be available to all eighty recruits in our company, "twenty-four-seven" and I hated it because I never had a minute to myself, even when one time, I was confined to bed because I got sick. There are no sick days allowed, if you have the Company Yeoman job. I was still required to stamp chits (permission paperwork) while lying in my bunk. Furthermore, the job obligated me to be available every time one of the eighty recruits in our company had to go somewhere, like on an errand for the C.C.s, to Medical, or on any other assignment away from the company.

Third, I was required to clean the C.C.s' office to pass the white glove test, answer their phone and be available to them for further administrative duties as needed. These duties were all on top of doing the regular work of every recruit in Boot Camp, including cleaning the barracks, going to class, studying for exams, practicing marching drills, shining our belts, polishing our shoes, doing difficult physical exercises as a group and taking care of and stowing our uniforms properly.

Unfortunately, after about four weeks (half-way through the Boot Camp regimen in Orlando), when Senior C.C. reassigned the big jobs in the company to other recruits, I was not one of those reassigned, so I had to keep the Yeoman job for the whole eight weeks of Recruit Training. It was a difficult, unrewarding job that no one wanted to take on, especially because they would have to work under at least one malicious C.C. (bossy Senior). It was obvious to the other recruits that Senior C.C. treated me badly, so why would they want to subject themselves to that in the Yeoman job?

I knew nothing about, nor did I want to engage in the number one job of a Commissioned Officer, which is leadership – being in charge. Growing up, I never saw myself as a leader and had no idea I would be good at it. Even though being a teacher requires leadership of the class, I still did not understand what specific duties leadership entailed until my training in the Navy. Anyway, when I enlisted in 1976, I wanted to literally "do" art for the time being, as a photographer, rather than teach it in the school system, and that is why I initially opted to join the Enlisted ranks.

Inevitably, there was a part of me that did not fit in during my enlisted time as an E-3 and E-4. My workmates, who were of the Enlisted ranks too, teased me a lot about being a college graduate. Some sarcastically asked me why I did not know about this or that because "Don't all college graduates know about everything?" It got tiresome, but by the time I reached the rank of E-5, I found the job suited me well, especially, due to the creative aspects of it. Gradually, I fit in with several of the people at the photo lab, which melted the ice with my colleagues and my bosses, who were mostly E-5s through E-8s. They even gave me an award as Sailor of the Quarter for my performance as a Navy Photographer's Mate.

What helped is that I didn't act like I knew everything and seemed to really listen and respond to the teaching and to the wisdom of my bosses and colleagues. After all, they were more experienced with photography and leadership than I was. My co-workers felt my respect for them and that is what caused the turnaround from hostility to acceptance of me becoming one of them. That was one of the most important lessons I took with me when I moved on to my other Navy jobs: Even if you seem to have had more schooling and intelligence than the average sailor, still be teachable because anyone can instruct you about something valuable, if you let them. That lesson has turned out to be true in every job I have had since.

Not long after I had made Petty Officer Second Class, my boss at the lab at NAS JAX put me in for OCS, since he had just received a message saying that the Rhode Island-based school was looking for new women candidates. I had also just was promoted to the E-5 pay grade myself and the traditional arm "tacking" had been done by my colleagues. This is where you sew the new pay grade E-5 patch on your upper left sleeve and everyone takes turns punching your arm over the patch. Of course, the new E-5 rank (called Petty Officer Second Class) is happy, but has a sore and often bruised arm to show for making the new rank.

Leaving the photo lab in Jacksonville to attend sixteen weeks of Boot-Camp-like training in Rhode Island at OCS was bitter sweet. I had no guarantees that I would ever return to see my colleagues and now friends in Jacksonville again, but I felt the satisfaction of winning them over and they in fact wished me well. The first thing I did when I got to Rhode Island, as did all other "priors" (those with Enlisted service before OCS) was staple my old E-5 rank patch onto a board kept in the lobby of my new OCS company for that purpose.

In 1979, I graduated from OCS and was given thirty days leave to include travel to my first duty station as a Commissioned Officer. I was assigned to Personnel Support Activity (PSA) at Naval Training Center (NTC) in Orlando, Florida, which was part of the base that also contained the only Recruit Training, where Navy Enlisted women received initial instruction at the time. So, I was to be stationed in Orlando for a second time, but on the main part of the base (NTC), separate from the more restricted part of the base, where I had attended Boot Camp (RTC) before. Orlando was about two and a half hours from Jacksonville, Florida (where NAS JAX was located). I knew Senior C.C. and my old photo lab colleagues were still stationed there.

Knowing that I wanted to see my old colleagues and let them see my new rank on my uniform, I decided to drive up to Jacksonville for a day. In my mind, also was the thought of revenge concerning the malevolent Senior C.C and to get revenge, I would hardly have to say a word. My new Ensign uniform would do it for me. I drove up there and first I visited the photo lab. All my friends at the lab were sincerely proud of me and "oo-ing and ah-ing" over my gold chinstrap and the Ensign stripe on my dress blue uniform, displaying my Commissioned Officer rank.

Unlike the Army, Navy personnel never salute the higher ranks without their covers (hats) on. Outside, where it is required that all Navy personnel in uniform wear their hats, the junior person passing the senior person (Commissioned/Warrant Officers only) initiates the salute and says a greeting like, "Good morning, Ma'am (or Sir)." Then the senior person (Commissioned Officers/Warrant only) returns to the junior person, a snappy salute and appropriate greeting. We are very polite and civilized in the military. One is taught that even if the person you are greeting is someone you don't like, you still give them the respect by saluting if they are a Commissioned/Warrant Officer or by returning a verbal greeting, if they aren't. You are told that the point is that you are saluting the uniform and rank, not the person. I think that if everyone observed politeness protocols in society like this, we would not have as many of the bitter, uncalled-for disputes anytime, anywhere that we see all over our country. There would be more room for civil and logical discourse in place of petty disagreements and rage.

Anyway, while I was still visiting the lab that day, my friend Debbie thought it would be great fun to play a trick on my old immediate boss Gary, an E-6 (First Class Petty Officer). He had not known I was there to visit and was on his way back to the lab from lunch, when Deb spied him walking up the sidewalk in front. Suddenly, she grabbed my cover (hat) off her desk and plopped it quickly on my head, opened the front door and shoved me out onto the sidewalk. The front of our covers sit a little low on our foreheads and sometimes it can be difficult to recognize the person walking toward you at a distance.

That is exactly what happened to Gary as he walked up the front sidewalk. Seeing the gold stripe on my sleeve of my dress blue uniform and the gold chin strap on my hat, he immediately initiated a salute, saying, "Good afternoon, Ma'am." I returned the salute and greeting and stopped in my tracks so he would have to stop too. He then looked up and saw whom he had just saluted and started to laugh. We went inside and caught up on all that had happened since I had left four months ago and talked about old times. Then I walked over to the Air Control Tower to seek out my Boot Camp nemesis, Senior C.C., who worked there as an Air Traffic Controller.

Since our ranks are obvious by the colors, patches and other insignia on our uniforms, I knew I would not have to rub it in that I now outranked Senior C.C. by seven ranks (to include Warrant Officers), whereas I had been two pay grades below her last time we met. In the meantime, she had also been promoted to E-6, which is why I said I was only seven instead of eight ranks higher than she was. Since her office was inside, I knew she would not be required to salute me, since when we are working inside, we do not usually have our covers on our heads (our hats/covers must be on our heads in the Navy to render a salute). It looked as if my dream to see her now act respectful toward me was within reach, with or without a salute.

As I walked into her space in the Air Control Tower where she worked, I knew she was really surprised when she saw my uniform and it seemed to take everything that she had to paste a smile on her face as she watched me casually walk toward her, smiling so sweetly. Luckily for her, being inside we were not wearing our covers, so there was no need for a salute; however, my point was made and I wondered as I left if she had remembered what she had said when I graduated from Recruit Training about NEVER, EVER having to salute me and if somehow required, it would be "...over her dead body."

Revenge is sweet, but this kind of action is usually not in my modus operandi; however, I needed to show her the error of her ways regarding her treatment of junior personnel for those coming through after me. Even the other Company Commander (Junior C.C.) who had worked with Senior C.C. in my company was strict, but fair and didn't have tendencies of taking advantage of her position being in charge of recruits by treating college graduates worse than the others under her charge, just because she could.

A couple of years later, I had lunch with Junior C.C. when I was stationed in Orlando, where she was still working. During a lunch we had together, Junior C.C. admitted that the two C.C.s almost got relieved (taken out of their jobs) for cause as Company Commanders because their recruits (meaning our company) were not performing up to par. I believe we didn't do as well as the other recruit companies because the two Company Commanders were not on the same page as to how to approach and train us, which was cryptically indicated to me by Junior C.C. at our luncheon. Because Junior C.C. was promoted to Second Class Petty Officer later than Senior C.C., she really had to go along with Senior C.C.'s ideas, but she often did not agree with how the recruit training was conducted.

From the incident in the Air Control Tower and having lunch with Junior C.C., I learned two leadership lessons that I would use later: Lesson One: Treat your people right for the situation and you will create a more productive and loyal team. The Second Lesson involves listening to not only your underlings, but also to your colleagues, even though they are junior to you. Listening gives them respect, even if you cannot always do what they suggest at the moment; however, perhaps you can use that person's ideas later in another situation. The fact that you are willing to listen is the key. I talk about treating someone right for the situation because one would be stricter with a recruit, since they are new to the Navy way of life and that attention to detail and strictness is helpful in training people new to the military situation. But that does not mean cruelness, (just because you can) is ever a correct approach, even with recruits. On the other hand, I learned later that one would not treat senior, experienced people the same way. Even if someone has positional power, it is not enough to be successful. They must have other essential skills and know when to apply them effectively.

According to "Situational Leadership Theory" that's described in the book *Management of Organizational Behavior* (1982) by Paul Hersey and Ken Blanchard.[54] To be most effective, the leader needs to choose from several approaches according to the requirements of the organization and the readiness of the employee. It requires flexibility on the part of the leader to be able to adapt his or her style to the work maturity of the employee. For instance, a Commissioned Officer would not interact with a recruit in the same way he/she would interact with a senior enlisted person like a Master Chief (E-9) when trying to lead them. While in the Navy, I was trained on this approach and I found it to be practical and useful in any organization, military or civilian, of which I have been a part.

(Left) Kathleen front row, second from left, holding the first flag with the round seal (Some faces are shaded for privacy.)

(Right) NTC staff, in Orlando, FL, Kathleen is in the middle, standing in the second row, to the right of the civilian with the black coat and tie, 1980.

(Below) Officer-in-Charge of NAS JAX Photo
Lab, promotes Kathleen and her good friend
Debbie to Petty Officer Second Class.

(Above) Barbie is dressed in her formal
occasion "Mess Dress Uniform"
as a Lieutenant Commander, like
Kathleen in the framed picture.

(Left) Kathleen learning audio visual
techniques at Photo Mate "C" School, and
(Below) at Photo Mate "A" School, 1977-1978

(Left) Kathleen with her Art student,
Linda F., who wanted to join the
Navy, but she never did, 1976

Chapter 17: *A Little Family History Explains A Lot*

We change our behavior when the pain of staying
the same becomes greater than the pain of changing.
Consequences give us the pain that motivates us to change.

— **Dr. Henry Cloud**[55]

During the early seventies, my little brother Terry was not even a teenager yet. Sadly, even though he was busy with friends, sports and school, Terry was left holding the bag with my parents' growing alcoholism. I was away at college in Wisconsin and my brother Mike (almost two years younger than me) was soon to be living on his own taking drugs, drinking and getting into trouble. But first he came home after one year of high school as a freshman at St. Thomas Academy, a military school in Minnesota. My parents meant well sending him there because they thought it would straighten out his behavior and improve his grades. Like my parents sending me to an all-girls Catholic school, it was a decision that had many repercussions for years to come.

Cracks in our demeanor as a family were beginning to show my senior year of high school. Mom started drinking daily at home, to cope with the growing financial pressures during a big recession and Dad would drink to excess, usually on weekends or at social events to deal with all of this. Due to a recession in the seventies, which impacted negatively on my father's business, I suspect my parents were deathly afraid that their nice lifestyle was in danger of collapsing. Dad's small business had been very profitable in the fifties and sixties, but in the early seventies it was in jeopardy.

The seventies ushered in two recessions caused by several factors including the quadrupling of spending by the U.S. government on the Vietnam War, the OPEC oil crisis and a stock market crash. For two people raised during the Great Depression of the nineteen-thirties and the threat of not having enough, their fear of being poor would be understandable and palpable, especially if they thought they were on the cusp of going back there again. The two recessions caused my dad's business to lose a lot of money, which fed into their fears. This caused an upheaval in our house regarding lack of funds.

Of course, in hindsight I have been able to piece together what was happening in our home from my own observations and experience at the time. Later through discussions with other family members like my aunts, cousins and uncles, I came to understand much more about my own family dynamics.

While in my thirties, through study, personal therapy and being a drug and alcohol counselor with the Navy, I began to understand, in a visceral way, what caused all the chaos in my growing-up years. What also helped in writing this story, was my having been an amateur genealogist for the last twenty-plus years. I have spent hours reviewing census documents, vital records, Catholic school records, ship's passenger lists, pertinent on-line records and communicating with distant cousins that I met through doing family research, so I have a lot of information about both sides of my family to include into this memoir.

After reading historical novels by Dr. Andrew Greeley, a Catholic priest in Chicago, I learned about the idiosyncrasies of the Irish who came to Chicago for a better life after the 1850s Famine in Ireland, when Irish citizens started immigrating in huge numbers to the United States. According to the Library of Congress website, the Irish were still emigrating in large numbers (approximately four and a half million) between 1820 and 1930.[56]

My Grandmother Johanna Spillane's family made Chicago their home between 1889, when her father, Roger Thomas Spillane arrived alone and when the rest of the family came after 1891. He was probably trying to pave the way by earning money and staying with kin, so he could pay for the rest of his family's passage to the U.S. That was a common strategy for new immigrants then.

Roger T. must have had a trip back to Ireland at least once because my grandmother, Johanna (sometimes called Josephine) was born near Kenmare, County Kerry in June of 1889. Johanna, her older siblings, sister, Catherine and brother, Thomas arrived with their mother Mary Anne O'Shea Spillane in 1891 to permanently settle in the U.S. with Roger. My dad remembered that his mother, Johanna said that she learned to walk as a toddler coming over on the ship.

Like I did, you can find a lot of information on ships' manifests and the census microfilm in your local library's genealogy section, the U.S. National Archives,[57] local Mormon Churches, genealogy resources on-line and anywhere there are genealogy

140

records. There is so much on the Web now, which was not available when I was doing my research in the late nineties. FamilySearch.org is a free website, which adds new records all the time. The relatively recent free website called irishgenalogy.ie has been one of the best I found for Irish research. You can also use the expensive Ancestry.com in your local library, so you do not have to pay for it.

My parents came from low-income families that did not have much in material things. Both families never even owned a house. Instead, Tom O'Brien and Elaine Robinson individually grew up in small apartments in Chicago. Maternal Grandpa, Dewey Robinson was a cab driver and Grandma, Sylvia Kocka Robinson worked at Marshall Field's in the candy department to make ends meet. Paternal Grandpa, John J. O'Brien was a motorman (like a street car conductor) and Grandma, Johanna Spillane O'Brien worked at the Graymere Hotel as a switchboard operator.

My dad graduated in 1937 from Chicago's St. Mel's High School, an all-male school run by the famously strict Christian Brothers. Earlier, he attended the nearby St. Mel's Grade School for the first through eighth grades. Sadly, his father, John J. O'Brien died of a sudden heart attack at sixty-four years old on Christmas Day in 1945, when my dad was twenty-six. Dad continued to live with Johanna for at least three years of college, when he attended DePaul University, until he married my mom, Elaine Ruth Robinson on November 24, 1951 at St. Jerome's Catholic Church in Rogers Park, IL.

As an amateur genealogist, I can't help putting in all the vitals and details in this story because if anyone ever takes over documenting our family where I left off, they will have enough information to prove that these people are really a part of our family history, when and if they are able to uncover new facts in the future, considering there's at least seven-hundred thirty-seven names of O'Brien families listed in the *Nineteen-Hundred Donnelly Chicago City Directory*.[58] Of the O'Briens listed, at least one-hundred-forty-three were named John (my paternal grandfather's name). It took me several years to find out who my O'Briens were. Through addresses on death certificates and the census, I traced back and authenticated my ancestors to Ireland.

For the Scotch-Irish Robinsons, I was able to trace back all the way to England. I hope to write a proper history including a

141

pedigree chart of both families someday for documentation and for posterity, as a result of my twenty years of research. Scotch-Irish people are mostly from Northern Ireland, controlled by the British, which are predominantly Protestant areas of Ireland, now a separate country from the Republic of Ireland to the south.

The Irish-Catholics are mostly located in the Republic of Ireland and that's where my dad's family roots begin. In the Republic, many of the records were kept in the local Catholic parishes by the priests with no extra copies. During my genealogy research, I found it to be difficult to go very far back in Catholic Church records to trace family history before 1800. So far, I have been able to uncover records relating to only five generations of my dad's (O'Brien-Spillane) family. Not only are Catholic Church records lacking, it has been especially difficult to find which ancestors are mine because many of the first and last names are the same, like John O'Brien.

Additionally, I knew nothing about the Catholic side of the family because my dad rarely kept any of his own records or pictures. His parents were already dead by the time I was two years old and nothing much appeared to be passed down to my cousins, except my cousin Mike found and gave me a picture of my grandmother, Johanna. The resemblance to me is phenomenal, especially in the smile. A smile with a slight overbite, I noticed it in my dad and my brothers and my daughter too (before braces).

Many of the anecdotes my dad told me before he died in 1987 were flawed remembrances, with only a few clues as to any family going farther back than my Grandparents, Johanna Spillane and John O'Brien. Cousin Mike O'Brien went to Ireland in the late 1990s and brought me back Johanna's baptismal certificate, so I had her original to verify against the other records I had found. One interesting fact that my dad told me, which I later verified was that "two brothers had married two sisters." As a result, he and his first cousins Roger and Marguerite (Peg) were called his "double cousins."

The two sisters were his mother, Johanna C. Spillane and her older sister, Catherine Hortense Spillane (called Kitty). After they arrived in the U.S. and became teens, they met the two O'Brien brothers (John Joseph and Daniel Francis) and then married them in Chicago around the turn of the Twentieth Century. I do not think my dad ever knew about the two sisters having an older brother, Thomas

142

Spillane, who died in 1913 in his twenties in Chicago, six years before Dad was born. If they did, no one ever mentioned it to me.

I found my Great Uncle Thomas Spillane's death record, which explained at an inquest that Thomas Spillane was a night watchman at some firm near the corner of Clinton and Harrison Streets in Chicago and to quote the record, "...was shot by one Archie Carroll, with whom he had some trouble."[59] That's all it says and his obituary/death notice gave me some more names to research, which I did, but found nothing else about his manner of death. I could not find an article about the shooting/killing in any Chicago newspapers around the December, 1913 dates of his death. I wonder if it was covered up. At the time of his death, Great Uncle Thomas Spillane had been married to Catherine Fiedler for about a year and had a son whose name was Roger Daniel Spillane, born in 1910.[60]

Roger D. Spillane grew up in Chicago, not too far from my dad and Uncle Ray. Again, my cousins do not seem to know anything about Ray and Tom's double cousin, who lived a long life into the 1980s. Besides the shame that is common to Irish families, when unpleasant events come to light, there does not seem to be a good reason for double cousins to never meet in their lifetimes, when they lived so close by. The only other explanation could be that Catherine Spillane remarried and her son Rodger Daniel Spillane grew up with a step-father and half-siblings surnamed "Bochek" and the family wanted to forget their Irish ties to their past.

I did find the Joliet Prison record of Archie Carroll, which shows that for the crime of killing Thomas, Mr. Carroll only spent one year locked up in prison. The reason I don't think my dad knew about his Uncle Tom is because the shooting or even the existence of his uncle was never mentioned to me by him or my cousins. My father was born in 1919, six years after the Spillane's death. Consequently, I have concluded that my dad must have been named after his recently killed uncle because there were no other men named Thomas in our family at that time. Dad's brother, Uncle Ray (short for John Raymond) was only four years old in 1913, so he probably didn't know about it either. Was Thomas Spillane doing something wrong or shameful to have gotten shot that night? Moreover, the killer, Archie Carroll, who knew his victim personally, only spent a year in Joliet Prison for the incident. I hesitate to call it "murder" because none of the records I researched did and in the absence of good documentation outlining the circumstances, I have hit a genealogy wall ... for now. New family information is not out of reach for me because I can always do more research - there are so many libraries and so little time.

Kathleen's paternal grandparents, (Left) Johanna Spillane and (Right) John J. O'Brien

(Left) Kathleen's maternal grandparents, Dewey Robinson and Sylvia Kocka Robinson

(Right) Thomas J O'Brien about 1920

(Left) Kathleen's grandmother, Sylvia Kocka Robinson with younger brother, John about 1905

(Right) Thomas' older brother, Ray O'Brien with wife, Anne Reynolds O'Brien

144

Chapter 18: *The High School Counselors Were Wrong*

Leave your pride, ego, and narcissism
somewhere else. Reactions from those
parts of you will reinforce your
children's most primitive fears.

— *Dr. Henry Cloud*[61]

It is important for me to talk about what was going on in my life around 1974-1975, before I was a teacher, as well as, my first two years of teaching because the atmosphere and setting are important to my reasons for joining the Navy two years later. The first job I landed after graduating from St. Norbert College was as a waitress. Working at a large popular specialty burger restaurant called Hackney's on Lake was not only fun, but the lone job choice I had in 1974. It was not my dream job of being a teacher, the one the high school counselors recommended we get into because there had been a teacher shortage.

Guess what? We listened to those counselors, so, many of the Baby Boomers (BBs) applied for teaching jobs upon graduation. But they were wrong because many of the good jobs were already taken by the first third of my generation born after World War Two. Being at the end of the first third of the BBs like me, was making it much harder to land the most desirable teaching jobs. In order to not be what we used to call a "deadbeat," "slouch" or a "freeloader" living back at home with our parents, many of us chose to take any job to at least make money until we could land a good position in our field.

For me, it took about a year and a half after graduation to get my first real teaching job and even then, it was more low-paying than other teaching jobs because it was in a parochial school. Parochial schools were known then for offering employees lower salaries because well, they could. The salary I was offered was even lower than other schools in the same parochial category: I only received a salary of five thousand dollars for the whole school year. Indeed, at about five hundred dollars per month before taxes on a ten-month teaching contract, I could barely make ends meet. So, I obtained a roommate to be able to afford to live in an apartment away from my parents and closer to my new job.

When I left waitressing to start the school year in the fall of 1975, I told myself, "I will NEVER be a waitress again!" There were a few times I wanted to pick up some extra money and almost caved in on my pledge, but since 1975, I indeed never had to go back to waitressing. Waiting tables was fun for a while, but for me it was not the kind of career I desired for the long run. I needed more intellectual stimulation in a job, something I realized in college, where I obtained a love of learning after getting some study skills and starting to do well in school.

My parents were still paying on loans they took out for my college education, and I wanted to use my B.A. degree in my next job for which I had worked so hard. We all just assumed my dad made too much money to get financial aid and it was not something we pursued because it wasn't talked a lot about at my private college in those days. Most of the parents we knew were paying the tuition out of pocket.

If I am honest, I think my dad's pride was a factor in not pursuing financial aid. He had made so much money with his own business in the sixties, I think he thought that this was just a bump in the road and the loans would be able to tide him over until his business revived to what it had been only a few years before. Dad was wrong. Unfortunately, his business struggles did not go away. Mom told me later that during this time Dad had lost confidence in his own abilities. It was unfortunate that his younger business partner was giving Dad trouble.

We will call this younger guy Bob (not his real name), whom Dad took on when sales revenues were high. Funny how people forget who first taught them all they know about a business, like young Bob did. He started pressuring my father to make more sales, when Dad was at his lowest point, driving my dad to go into a depression, which did not increase Dad's sales ability. My parents never used the word "depression" to describe my father's low self-esteem during this period, but since I have had similar issues, I recognize the symptoms.

Thomas O'Brien had never been this low, being that he was a generally happy man, always telling us that if we had our health and our family, nothing else really mattered. He never lost that attitude, but this so-called partner would not stop putting pressure on him to bring in more new business. Mom said that when Dad took on Bob as a partner, he taught the young man everything and carried him (the man drew a salary, even though he was not bringing in any revenue for quite a while, as he was in sales training); however, the man was obviously not grateful. He should have been, since Bob had learned the business from a pro like Thomas O'Brien, who was so highly thought of in his field. Dad had been on the board of his business association for many years and knew all the movers and shakers.

My father eventually became the President of the National Business Forms Association (NBFA) which had hundreds of members from all over the country. His platform was "Education" during his year as President because it was his hope and desire that the small business owners who were the members of the association would continue to learn and grow in their field. His picture was on the cover of their trade publication, with his plan for the year.

Unfortunately, partner Bob was "too smart" and felt he did not need Dad anymore, thus the trouble between them started. Mom said she talked Dad into breaking up the partnership because it was literally hurting my father and causing him to lose confidence in himself. In addition, Dad was already on his way to having his first heart attack in his fifties. Tom, needing to regain his confidence by eliminating the stress of working with arrogant young Bob, agreed with my mom on what needed to be done. Thomas then went to work with his nephew, Mike O'Brien, who had taken over for his father.

Ray, his wife Anne and some of their sons, (including Mike) had formed their own company doing the same type of business as Dad's company did. This all came about because when Mike was a teenager, he had started working in the office, helping my dad and eventually learned the business. Mike's own father, John Raymond, (my dad's ten years older and only brother, who went by Ray), had been working in the stationery supply business. Ray saw how well his younger brother, Tom was doing, and desired to be a part of it.

Tom and Ray became partners and later served on the National Business Forms Association (NBFA) board together. This took place years before even young Bob was in the picture. Everything was going fine until my Uncle Ray expressed a desire to bring more of his sons in addition to Mike into the business. It may have worked, but Ray had ten sons, so it had all the evidence of being impractical! In general, Dad felt that one should not really put a lot of family into a business because he saw the potential for fights and rivalries. Moreover, the business could not handle many more employees at this point; therefore, Ray formed his own company with his sons and my dad stayed in the original company.

Even though they formed their own separate companies, Ray and Tom were still family and close brothers. If there were any hard feelings about breaking up their partnership, they learned to deal with them. After all, Chicago was a big town and there was enough business to be had by all.

Adding a partner would spread the risk among more stakeholders than just Thomas J. O'Brien on his own. At this point, I surmise that running his company alone and suddenly taking on all the business risk is why Tom was willing to bring in a new partner, such as young Bob, who applied for the job. It makes good business sense to spread the risk, so in case of a loss in revenue, one person would not have to shoulder the whole burden alone.

In the early seventies, when my Uncle Ray was diagnosed with cancer, he knew he was terminal. Dad advised Ray's sons to pick a company President, so my uncle's business would have a successor to keep the firm solvent, when he eventually passed away, which happened soon afterward in the fall of 1974. However, before Ray's death, the infighting started, when the sons were trying to vote on a new President for Ray's company.

Rivalries became clear and several of the brothers formed their own companies, taking their accounts with them. This appalled my father, who had hoped these types of actions would never come between family members. Dad was saddened by this situation. Shortly before Ray's death, the infighting prompted Uncle Ray to remark, when they were alone, "Tom, you were right." Ray now conceded that it had been a mistake bringing too many family members into a small business.

When I was older and my father told me about this rift among family members, I never forgot the leadership lesson I learned and tucked into the back of my mind: If possible, do not work with family, especially if you are worried about causing a rift. The more family members involved, the more potential problems that can result. As my dad wisely surmised himself, he hoped he never would ever see brother against brother as had just taken place. This situation went against Tom's favorite old adage that if we have our health and our family, nothing else matters. My dad was a big part of helping the brothers come back together as a family after their father died. After that, for the rest of his life, Dad was like the statesman uncle and father figure to all those boys. It just goes to show, if there is a rift in a family, it can usually be healed, if people are honest with each other and really try to make it work. By the way, Thomas J. O'Brien started gaining back some of his confidence in his sales abilities later, when he worked with Mike at Uncle Ray's company. Interestingly, I believe the brothers were a big part of my dad regaining his business confidence after his fiasco with young Bob.

Dad fittingly became their advisor and sales trainer, as well as handling and even adding to his own accounts. He was still working there when he died of heart failure at age sixty-eight in 1987. when I was thirty-five years old. We have never really recovered from the loss of this lovely man, who was taken from us far too soon.

I have already talked about some of Tom's flaws, and none of us is free of mistakes, so it has been easier to accept that he was not perfect. Thomas Joseph Peter Aloysius Kevin Barry O'Brien's (Dad had me believing this was his full Irish name till I was twenty) love, grace and influence in our lives far outweigh any flaws he had. Remembering the good times with Dad serves me well because writing this book caused me to delve into much of the sad episodes already. As a result of many years of therapy, I obtained hard-won, good mental health. This thankful daughter truly believes that if she had not had Tom O'Brien as a father, a normal life with marriage and children might have been out of reach for her.

(Left) J. Raymond O'Brien, brother of (Right) Thomas J. O'Brien, who were business partners in Budd Business Forms in the 1950s and 60s.

Thomas O'Brien (Left) working with NBFA
Board Members, including
brother, Ray (Far Right) 1960s

Thomas J. O'Brien, about 1950

Kathleen and Debbie P. at Trinity H.S.
in the Art Classroom, 1975-76

Elaine and Thomas O'Brien being
announced at the NBFA Ball, 1960s

(Left) Tom, Elaine, Ray and Anne O'Brien at an NBFA Costume Party, 1960s
(Right) NBFA President Tom O'Brien passes the gavel to the new NBFA President, 1970

Chapter 19: *Pattern of Bad Relationship Choices*

*People will hurt you. But don't use that as
An excuse for your poor choices, use it
as motivation to make the right ones.*

— LeCrae[62]

It took me thirty-plus years to heed the message in the quote above. This will be a hard chapter to write, but I need to, so I can be honest with myself and so the reader can see the amazing changes I have made in my life. One must deal with pain and sorrow to understand how beautiful life can get, once you come out on the other side. And it "isn't no picnic" to deal with either.

In the title, "Pattern of Bad Relationship Choices" I mostly mean that a great deal of decisions I made in relationships were not the best; however, to be clear, I did not mean that the men I have talked about already and will talk about in following chapters are bad people. I just mean that they were either the wrong person for me or more commonly, I made bad choices within those relationships, which contributed greatly to break-ups or hard feelings.

I also do not mean that all my bad relationships are dealt with in this chapter. I just want to point out that a pattern exists, and hopefully, you will see an improvement in my attitude toward the handling of relationships, as my life unfolds in this book. In the end, I have fond feelings for most of the men with whom I have been in personal affiliations because they were good people. I take responsibility for my own issues like ADHD and low self-esteem, which got in the way of forming good relationships with a boyfriend or a potential mate.

I mentioned a high school era boyfriend I had named Keith Donahue earlier. I am starting there because it was my first serious relationship and because I was so gob-smacked by the interest this boy showed in me that I let him sometimes get away with some not-so-good behavior. One big one was that I let him pick me up for dates really late, sometimes, even as late as two hours. Today, I see how NOT OK this was.

I had such low self-esteem, but seeing Keith's interest in me put me on such a high because I never thought a popular guy like Keith would be interested in me. This caused me not to say or do anything to rock the boat. Also, I was inexperienced with being honest with boyfriends, like you can when you have had experience with candid friendships of the opposite sex. Yes, I hung around with the boys from my neighborhood in west Glenview, but our relationships were more social, not really mature.

Being with Keith changed everything for me regarding the girls at my school because he had gone to grade school with them and was well-liked. We all were maturing in high school and because of dating Keith, ironically, it was the first year I had felt I was more accepted with the girls at my school, Regina. Before, I had not felt as if I belonged with most of the girls with whom I went to high school because they were from well-off families and had known each other since grade school in Wilmette, IL bordering Lake Michigan, one of the most expensive neighborhoods in the Chicago suburbs. Those girls were in the same crowd that Keith had known well from his Wilmette neighborhood, his church and his grade school. Wilmette was an area very different from where I had grown up in the northern suburbs, a region not as well-to-do as the upscale area where Keith and most of his childhood friends lived.

A great number of the girls at my high school had gone to Catholic grade schools in those northeastern suburbs along the lake and had formed their little groups and cliques there. Naturally, when they started at Regina, they kept a lot of the same friends from their close-to-the-lake (Lake Michigan) neighborhoods and parochial schools.

The Donahue family consisted of Keith and his twin brother Jack, an older brother, Randy, a younger sister Mary Jane and three younger brothers Tom, Pat and Kenny. Along with their parents, Mr. and Mrs. Donahue, there were seven kids in all, living in an old, but rambling, well-kept, large white house. Living five blocks from Lake Michigan, the Donahue family was well-known and popular in their Wilmette neighborhood.

When I met Keith during our junior year of high school, Kenny was only a baby and Randy was about ready to graduate and go on to Harvard University. Keith's dad, Mr. James Donahue was a lawyer and later a judge in Chicago. His wife, Ellen, was a stay-at-home mom, which was essential for managing such a large family. Mrs. Donahue's father was a well-known doctor in Chicago. Evidently, the Donahue family came from good stock and it sure seemed that way to me because the older boys (like Keith) were all taught a good work ethic, which included sharing the load with their younger sister Mary Jane, the only girl.

Consequently, they all had chores around the house, took turns babysitting the younger kids and each Donahue child was expected to attain high grades and then go to Ivy League Universities. At the time, with my mediocre high school grades, except in Art, English and History, I would be lucky to get into a decent college, much less an Ivy League school. Keith was a good influence on me as we spent a lot of time on the phone discussing what we wanted out of life, while we were both babysitting our younger siblings at our respective homes. One of our record-setting calls lasted seven hours!

Keith knew I hated to do schoolwork and he would spend a great deal of that time on the phone with me, trying to get me to commit to studying, even just half an hour each night. It helped somewhat, and I think Keith's influence was good for me; however, I graduated from Regina, only smack dab in the middle of my class. I did win an Art Award my senior year, and was often complimented about my writing abilities by the nuns, getting "As" most of the four years I took English and Art. I usually got a B in History; ironically, I did not know that I would love the subject of History so much until later in college and I still do. It is common for my friends and family to shake their heads when they see me still reading history and historical novels for fun. My love of history blossomed even more, when I got into genealogy in the late nineties.

From the spring of my sophomore year, through the end of my junior year in 1969, when I met Keith and until I started college in August of 1970, many events already discussed like U.S. leader assassinations, the Vietnam War, and the moon walk were in play. This was the background of my first serious relationship.

Notwithstanding the exhilaration of the moon walk, the Baby Boomer generation was the first to experience so much death and destruction being shown on television and it numbed us to seeing horrific events in the future. In many ways, these events felt distant because it was happening so far away and we could forget about it, at least if we did not watch the nightly news.

I met Keith at a basketball game at his all-boys' Catholic school, Loyola Academy, Wilmette, IL on March 22, 1969. Handsome and tall at six-foot-two, Keith had short brown hair, smiling Irish brown eyes, a square-shaped face, and an arresting smile. He was usually preppy in attire: typically, seersucker light blue pants, a button-down shirt with brown loafers and a light jacket. Soon after we met, Keith asked me on a double date with his friend Steve and Steve's girlfriend Debbie to go see his high school (Loyola Academy) musical play. From then on, we dated for a year and a half until we both left for different colleges in August 1970.

It was a magical time in my life because Keith had a great personality and was very attractive, smart and we had fun. I know he thought about becoming a priest and I have always wondered why he did not because he never married, at least until today, when we are both going into our late sixties. He was a very devout Catholic and would have made a fine priest. My father and mother really liked him too because he was Irish like my dad, very respectful, smart and was destined to go to a good university.

We kept contact for many years and later in our forties, Keith and I had been talking about how some of us did not live up to our own potential, like being doctors or lawyers, as pictured by our parents. He said, "Your dad thought I was going to be the U.S. President someday, didn't he?" It was true, my dad thought Keith was an ideal man. In addition, I really liked my cute, fun-loving boyfriend for deeper reasons. I admired him because he always tried to live by his faith's good values and principles. We had long discussions about what was important in life, like: family, friendship and love.

In challenging my study habits, Keith really did me a big favor, influencing my academic awakening and which showed when I started taking classes that I was really interested in during college. Because of his encouragement and our discussions. when we were in high school, as well as his good academic example, my interest in academic subjects increased ten-fold. I believe the encouragement from Keith and my later discussions with my college roommate, Patti M., who was an excellent student and role-model, developed my new-found desire to learn about as many subjects as I could. All this new love of learning, as a by-product, also multiplied my love of reading.

Going out with Keith and being treated better by my Regina school mates because of it, was a dream come true. I fell totally in love with him and finally felt like I was worthy of someone as good as my father. We went to activities in Lake Geneva, Wisconsin;

dances at our respective schools, parties at friends' houses and then, both our proms that were held at fancy hotels in the city of Chicago.

Two of the most popular movies in 1969 were "Butch Cassidy and the Sundance Kid" with heartthrobs, Robert Redford and Paul Newman and "Cactus Flower" with Goldie Hawn. Because we didn't have a lot of money then, I am not sure if Keith and I saw them together or separately, but they were the talk of the town that year.

That fall of 1969, Keith was on the field wearing number eighty as a tight end when his all-boys' high school, Loyola Academy, won the Chicago City Football Championship. The game was held at Soldier's Field in downtown Chicago. It was thrilling and I was so inspired, I sculpted a statue out of clay, a figurine of Keith running with the football as number eighty in Loyola garb, with hands reaching up from the ground to grab him. I think his parents were impressed and Keith really loved it. In turn, he gave me a gold pendant of a football on a chain I wore around my neck. I think it was a way for him to claim me as his girlfriend and like many besotted young girls, I never wanted it to end.

My most fervent daydreams included always hoping that someday we would get married and have a big Irish family like his. As college drew closer in August of 1970, I started to worry that we would break up at some point because our respective colleges were thousands of miles apart; his college was on the East Coast and mine was near Green Bay, Wisconsin. This thought saddened me and put a damper on my excitement for starting college. Trying to sustain a serious relationship that far apart was almost impossible, especially at our young age and without the added technology we have now like: cell phones, FaceTime, Zoom and cheaper airline flights.

Keith and I did not have lots of cash to spend on dates, but we had good times in ways that I doubt kids would enjoy today. Simple activities like going to O'Hare Airport and watching the planes taking off and landing on the runway were fun things to do. One time, Keith said he would take me to eat at McDonald's. It is mind-boggling to think that he bought me a hamburger, fries and a coke and the total bill including tax was only thirty-seven cents! Also, we walked down Isabella Street, the dividing line between the suburbs of Evanston and Wilmette, jumping "to-and-fro" to each side of the pavement, saying, "Evanston, Wilmette, Evanston, Wilmette," laughing as we landed on the appropriate side. It looked like a hopscotch game.

Moreover, we would go to Gillson Park, a beach on Lake Michigan near Keith's house and take a walk. That year, work was being done at Gillson Park for several months with huge concrete pipes about five feet in diameter. Several were just sitting there for a few weeks, while the work was going on, right on the sand near the shore. In summer, Keith and I used to crawl into these large pipes and make out, no one being able to see us from most angles, especially in the dark. We kept our clothes on, kissed a lot and there was a little petting taking place, but I would call it very tame by most standards.

Even before I met Keith, I learned of Gillson Park and the great beach there, when I started high school. My tight-knit neighborhood group, to include Val and Lorraine, used to ride the bus all the way down Lake Avenue to go to the beach on the west coast of Lake Michigan in Wilmette, when it was still free. We would pass by the house that famous actress Ann-Margaret grew up in. Many good times were had by us there in the summer, playing guitar and singing on the beach as well as eating our picnic food and swimming.

I took guitar lessons when I was thirteen and played all through high school and college, including for guitar masses at church. I enjoyed singing and writing songs too. After singing in several choirs as a soprano, I gave up singing and playing at the end of the seventies, when I was the Navy for a couple of years. I think I would have stuck with it, had it not been for stage fright and my insecurity singing with a harmonizing partner. Due to being distracted by someone harmonizing with me, I could not stay on key.

Jamming with my cousin Dennis O'Brien (see his picture on p. 302), who still performs around the Chicago area, I usually did the melody because I could not hear or even sing the harmony. Extremely frustrated, I thought it was hopeless for me, so I quit. However, things changed many years later, when I was in a church pew singing along with the congregation. I had just taken my ADHD medication and realized it was the first time in my life that I could hear, in reality, all the different parts, including the harmony.

ADHD medication, such as Adderall or Ritalin, helps the ADHD person to focus and sort between different competing sounds, feelings, visual images, etc. Now they aren't a jumbled-up mess in my head like before taking medication. Since I now understand this, I am planning to take guitar again. I missed out on a lot of good years playing and singing because of my ADHD. Who knew? Perhaps

156

someone should study this phenomenon for future musicians who are having trouble learning how to sing and hear all the parts like I did.

My friends and I were not kids looking for trouble, did not do drugs, have sex or do things many of our older Baby Boomer cohorts were doing in the sixties; at least not yet. It was an apple pie life, before the 1969 Woodstock Festival and violent demonstrations against the Vietnam War were even in our consciousness. How innocent and grand those lazy summer days were. Little did we know, a more rebellious time was coming. I am glad I didn't know what was to come because for a time I still could be an innocent kid.

In September, 1970, about two weeks into my first semester at St. Norbert College, I received a "Dear John/Jane Letter," from Keith, which devastated me. Around this time, my small acne problem started to get worse, so I was really on a downhill spiral with my self-confidence again. Having my boyfriend break up with me during my first weeks of college, put me into a depression, especially when I felt such low self-esteem already due to my growing acne problem and my uncertainty about my academic ability at the university level. I secretly pined for Keith on and off for years, even into our late thirties and early forties, when we dated again sporadically. Profound sadness came over me for several months after the initial break-up and beyond because I did not think I would ever deserve or find another man like Keith, with so much good character and high integrity, which now seemed out of reach for me.

Kathleen (second from right) hanging out
with her Glenview gang, 1967-68

Kathleen's sketch of Keith
Donahue about 1969-70

(Left) Kathleen, age 15, playing guitar

(Right) Mark, Kathleen and Brother, Michael before leaving to go to Kathleen's graduation, June 1970

(Above) Kathleen's High School Logo[64]

(Below) Drawing by Kathleen Iverson,[63] of a Vintage McDonald's meal like the one Keith bought for Kathleen in 1969. Prices back then for a burger, fries and a coke cost 35 cents plus 2 cents tax = 37 cents total.

(Below) Sign of Gillson Park on Lake Michigan, where Kathleen and Keith enjoyed hanging out (Wikimedia. Commons) [66]

(Above) Picture of Keith, far right, Tight End, #80 for Loyola, ramming a player from Gordon Tech. High School, Fall of 1969 [65]
Photo by Brian Hodge (paper source unknown)

Chapter 20: *Acid Rock, Acne and Agnew*

The pain I feel now is the happiness
I had before. That's the deal.

— *C.S. Lewis*[67]

Starting collage with a break-up, initiated by Keith, did not help my self-esteem, or help me want to study. If it was not for starting a new chapter in my life, such as college was for me, I may have sunk much deeper into melancholy than I did. But the new experiences and people I met at St. Norbert College lifted me out of the abyss long enough for me to keep striving for new growth as a person.

Unfortunately, at eighteen years old, rampant new hormones appeared to be taking over my body, resulting in severe acne on my back and on my face to push me back down. I didn't have a big acne problem in high school, so being the late bloomer that I am and probably due to nerves over my new circumstances, my acne appeared to be uncontrollable with my usual methods. My whole college freshman year, I had trouble controlling the acne and felt like my face looked like a pepperoni pizza. Knowing I needed to do something to feel better, I finally went to a doctor, who gave me tetracycline, which cleared up the acne cysts with minimum scarring on my face and back. I was so excited with the progress that I wanted to shoot for improving my appearance in bigger ways and in my mind, I needed a goal to keep me on track.

After losing fifteen pounds to go with my cleared-up skin, I entered the Miss Glenview Contest in June of 1971. I didn't win, but I felt triumphant that I could enhance my appearance so much and be numbered among those beautiful and talented other contestants. For my talent, I sang a song in French, accompanied by my guitar. Due to the Miss Glenview Contest, I felt more confident in general, but not totally because I still pined for my first love, Keith Donahue. After this, I dated mostly anyone who asked me out, regardless if I really liked him or saw potential there. I did not realize this until many years later, but my self-confidence seemed to depend on other people or situations, not on my own intrinsic self-worth, so it never seemed solid. It was among all these positive changes and renewed (although flawed) self-confidence that I started my sophomore year of college.

As I write this, my daughter, Christina has just turned thirty-three-years old. In September, 2001, when she started high school, her generation (the Millennials) witnessed something horrific in one big surprise swoop: the destruction of the Twin Towers in New York by Osama bin Laden and Al-Qaeda. It was even more shocking than nightly Vietnam combat because it happened on our continental soil, where we always felt so safe due to two big oceans separating us from other countries. Even though we were attacked by the Japanese in Hawaii in December of 1941, heading us into WWII, Hawaii was not part of the main continent, so it still seemed too far away to hurt the average American until the draft started.

After we were attacked on the North American continent in New York in 2001, many Americans started to feel unsafe and it caused a lot of anxiety that has never gone away. The Vietnam War was different, in that we got used to it gradually. It struck me as being ingrained in us, little by little, making us less innocent as the war went on. The first part of my generation, the Baby Boomers (B.B.), started protesting the war and some even went to Canada to wait out the draft.

As I was part of the end of the first third of the B.B. generation, I was not caught up in protesting the war, etc., as I was still in high school. My section of the Baby Boomers was still a little young to get involved yet, but it would definitely affect me more, when I got to college in 1970. Since St. Norbert was a Catholic College in De Pere, a little agricultural town near Green Bay, Wisconsin, at the time it was more conservative. At first, we did not see large demonstrations against the war, like those already taking place in big cities. However, subtle signs of young people's discontent were showing.

At St. Norbert's annual Ice Sculpture Contest during our big Winter Carnival, my sorority decided to sculpt our Vice President, Spiro Agnew, with his foot in his mouth. It was popular to make fun of our government leaders because they were blamed for getting us into this mess. Our parents, who served in the military during a more patriotic time, were shocked at all these demonstrations against the war by their own children.

In addition, the drug culture was heating up during the war too and we were seeing a lot of the upperclassmen using marijuana at parties. Drugs and Vietnam looked like they were inextricably linked during this time. That was because there was a huge disconnect between what the young people wanted, who in many states were eligible to drink liquor and to vote at eighteen years old, and what government officials wanted.

Most of the B.B.s thought that if they were old enough to be drafted, they were old enough to drink and vote, which helped change many state laws, allowing those behaviors for people under twenty-one years old, which for a long time had been the age of majority. After all, it was my generation who were going off to war as soon as they left high school or college and they were the most affected.

Unfortunately, those who dropped out of college, or graduated from high school in those years were the first to be sent over to Vietnam and later, Cambodia. There was a deferral for those men who attended college. Remember, it was only men who were eligible for the draft because women were not allowed by law to be put into combat. Those laws for women not allowed in combat were only changed by Congress in 1994, so I was never eligible to serve aboard combatant ships at the time I served in the Navy.

Just like I had in high school, again I felt out of step with my college peers, finding myself a little more traditional than many of my age. For instance, I wanted the old-fashioned idea of college: big dress-up dances and events, more conservative dress; no marijuana-laden concerts or football games. Most of my usual tame-by-most-standards-today attempts to fit in just did not work for me. I tried to go braless once (all the range in the nineteen-seventies) while wearing a halter top. My dad looked at me and said, "If you keep going without a bra, you (your bosom) will be down to your knees by the time you are forty years old." I was horrified that he noticed that I am well-endowed. What Dad said turned me off to going braless and I have not done it since.

Police did not seem to do anything about unlawful activities, like smoking marijuana, unless they in fact saw who was causing the cloud of sweet-smelling dope above the crowds. Most people did not dance anymore at performances by the bands of the day because many of those performers were playing un-danceable songs influenced by "Acid Rock". So, those who attended sat down on the floor and smoked marijuana. Out of the mid-sixties "Psychedelic" culture, Acid Rock is aptly described by Wikipedia: "...The style is generally defined by heavy, distorted guitars, lyrics with drug

161

references, and long improvised jams," https://en.wikipedia.org › wiki › Acid Rock.[68]

Extremely bored by this behavior, it almost ruined the college experience for me. If I had not joined a sorority, where the old-type events—like dances, activities, such as: "Winter Carnival" and concerts with singers, like John Denver, were common like they were in the sixties, I think I would have been bored out of my mind during college social events. I had hardly ever used any alcohol before college and even that was not a source of excitement for me when I started St. Norbert College.

Besides marijuana becoming more prevalent as the early seventies wore on, the old standby, twenty-ounce draft beer was everywhere to be had for only twenty-five cents, even in the St. Norbert Union. I got really drunk one time only during my freshman year, and I was so hung-over when I had to play the guitar at Catholic Mass the next morning, in addition to having a terrible headache. The picking of the strings sounded like loud ringing in my ears and I was nauseous as I tried to sing one of the "Guitar Mass" songs like, "Shout from the Highest Mountain" in church. I never did develop a taste for beer and haven't had one since college, nor have I ever become that plastered again.

During college, one unexpected positive thing happened. I started to become more intellectual and it showed in increasingly good grades. My love of learning acquired in undergraduate days has never stopped. I have read over five hundred books on my Kindle reader, not to mention library books I have checked out, as well as, magazines and newspapers I have devoured. I am now a voracious reader (Who knew?) and my mother had gone as far as to call me: "The Professional Student" and she was not far from wrong. I love to take classes, especially to learn new skills.

As I already mentioned, I went abroad to France for one semester in the fall of my junior year at St. Norbert. Since my parents really wanted me to experience this once-in-a-lifetime chance, they didn't tell me how dire the family finances were, due to the recession in the early seventies that I already talked about. Literally unaware that my study abroad dream would be putting such a heavy burden on my parents' financial situation, I applied to study in Paris, France, starting in September of 1972 and lasting through January of 1973. There was an arrangement in place for a reciprocal transfer of credit between St. Norbert College and Schiller College in Paris, France. This arrangement made it possible for me to study for a semester abroad without losing any credits in order to graduate at St. Norbert on time in 1974.

I was given the choice by Schiller to fly directly from Chicago to Paris or to take a ship from New York harbor to France, then get on a boat train that went to Paris. I chose the latter. In September of 1972, having just turned twenty years old, I flew to New York and boarded the largest luxury liner ship in the world at that time, called the U.S.S. France.

During the five-day journey crossing the Atlantic, I met a twenty-eight-year-old man named Larry Parnell, who would become one of the most important loves of my life. He was an American from St. Louis, Missouri. Larry was blond and handsome, with blue eyes, and I was smitten. He seemed so sophisticated in contrast to the younger men I knew and he had a good sense of humor. Larry was on the shorter side, five-feet-seven inches to my five-feet-three and a half, but his personality was wonderful, and he treated me well, so his shortness wasn't a factor in my wanting to know him even better.

Larry was on his way to visit his brother Rich in Europe. Rich was first going to study in Scotland and then travel to southern France to stay for a few months, totaling a year abroad. Larry had planned to stay with Rich and his wife, Bonnie in both countries for several months altogether.

Back in St. Louis, Larry had worked part-time in a wine shop while he was trying to finish his bachelor's degree, so he taught me a lot about wines as we took in the sights of Paris. This included dining together on fabulous cuisine in the small French cafés that we both favored. Our connection became serious for a good part of our three-year-long relationship. When returning to the U.S., we traveled back and forth among the cities of Chicago, St. Louis and De Pere, when I was still in college and beyond.

Larry and I were inseparable during the whole cruise on board the S.S. France, eating gourmet dinners together, dancing every night in the club and taking long walks on the deck. We stayed up the whole final night so we could be outside on the bow at sunrise when the tugboats escorted our ship into le Havre, France. This way, I got my first glimpse of the European continent. Larry was romantic, giving me cards and flowers, "just because" during our time together.

Before completing his plan of going to Scotland to see Rich and Bonnie, Larry stayed in Paris for a few weeks to be with me.

While I was still in school, Larry came back to Paris several times to visit me. We learned about French culture together. Candlelight dinners, red table wine, strolls along the Seine (the river that divides Paris in two) and scrumptious food at local cafés were our regular activities in the glorious and romantic City of Light. At twenty-years-old, I had never been treated so much like a grown-up woman, as I was by Larry Parnell. Thus, it was inevitable that we fell in love.

Upon Larry's upcoming return to St. Louis after the winter semester, he planned to start classes again and work part-time in the wine shop in order to finish up his education. But before that, while I was still in France and he was in Scotland, we made rough plans to go for Christmas Break to Nice, France, where it was considerably warmer on the French Riviera. From there, we planned to go to Italy and Sicily for the rest of the Christmas Holidays.

In those days, the fall semester didn't end until late January, so I was due back in Paris after Christmas Break to finish up my classes at Schiller and take my final exams. As a consequence of the frequent mail strikes in France, Larry and I didn't get each other's letters suggesting plans as to exactly where and when we were supposed to meet for our vacation. To make it worse, he never got my letter telling him that I had given up my apartment in Paris, so I could save money by staying with my French friend Alixe Regnier and her family, until I went back to the U.S.

As a result of those crossed mail issues, Larry was having trouble getting a hold of me and I did not know how to get a hold of him because his brother was traveling in Europe with his wife and was not at the location I knew about in Scotland. Most of the places we lived in Europe did not have individual phone service; therefore, since I left the school for vacation and our letters crossed in the mail, we didn't know how to find one another.

Alixe and her family came up with a plan so Larry and I could find each other. They suggested I go to the Gare du Nord (North side Train Station) every day and wait all day until all those Paris-bound trains arrived, to see if Larry was on one of those. Not knowing in which station that he would arrive, Alixe's family joked that if Larry never arrived at Gare du Nord, we could always go to the several other Parisian train stations and wait there for him. We did not know any other way to do it, so every morning, I went to Gare du Nord to wait for Larry as soon as my Christmas Vacation started.

Madame Regnier was kind enough to make my new favorite sandwich every day for me to eat while I was waiting at the train station. It was commonly found in cafés around Paris and they called it "un sandwich au jambon et au beurre," which consisted of thin slices of ham and lots of butter slathered on a soft fresh eight-inch baguette with a hard crust. I brought a book to read while I waited at the train station many hours until all the trains from the north had arrived for the day.

It took three days waiting at Gare du Nord for me to spot Larry getting off one of the trains. We were so happy to find each other that we hugged, kissed and held hands non-stop until we boarded our own train later at Gare du Lyon, leaving for Nice in the south of France. There, we planned to spend most of our vacation.

At this point, I was still a virgin at twenty years old and planned to remain so until marriage, like I had been taught during my Catholic upbringing. But being away from home for four months at this point (as well as having been so worried I would never find Larry again) weakened my determination to wait for marriage. Also, the cultural climate was geared towards being looser on those morals we had all grown up with, telling us to "Love the One You're With" as the popular contemporary song by Stephen Stills was titled.

After the Woodstock Festival in August of 1969, which was shown on T.V. for all to see, with young people walking around naked, (albeit with black rectangles over private parts because of the restrictions of network television) and couples wrapped horizontally in blankets on the ground during the concerts of the three-day festival, it seemed normal not to wait to have sex until marriage. We heard peers often remarking, "These are the days of free love and sex and let's not be square about it; we are really in love, so why not partake?" After all, we had the "pill" now to avoid pregnancy.

When Larry Parnell and I arrived in Nice by train the next morning after I found him, we were so emotionally caught up in the joy of finding each other again that we let ourselves get carried away when we checked into our hotel. Looking back, I really didn't understand then what a monumental decision I had made that day, but I was living for the moment, instead of thinking of the future, just like

165

the rest of my generation was doing. I never knew what a large toll that decision would take on me in future decisions and relationships until many years later. I had not agreed with a lot of the lessons I had learned during my Catholic education, like the ban on birth control, the infallibility of the Pope's major decisions, or the marriage ban for priests, so why buy into the prohibition against having sex before marriage?

Around this time, I started to rethink belonging to the Roman Catholic Church, in which I had been raised. My spiritual mores took a dive and eventually, I did not take God as seriously as before. It was an insidious slide south as I bought into the "Sexual Revolution." But it all started with my decision to have my first sexual intercourse with Larry Parnell. I am glad it was Larry who experienced sex with me for my first time because we were in love, but I wasn't ready to be that close to someone or for marriage. Moreover, even though I went steady with Larry for three more years, it was in the back of my mind that I didn't live up to my own ideals or that of my mother's, a virgin until she married. Once that line is crossed, you cannot go back, so it colors all the relationship decisions going forward.

In the end, our relationship was not meant to be. I was too immature, not ready for marriage and started seeing someone else as an unconscious and unhealthy way of forcing the breaking up of the relationship. I now regret how much I must have hurt him by ending it that way. Even though I did not want to let him go by breaking up, my actions did it for me and of course Larry couldn't trust me.

For the next ten years, I made poor decisions regarding men because I did not even know what my own boundaries were and no one appeared to be able to tell me how long you should wait to have sex after you got to know someone. I thought I was a modern woman and I could handle having sex with different people, just like many men could. But it was a NO-GO. There was a piece of my heart torn away every time I got too close to someone sexually, whom I didn't end up marrying. Besides tearing pieces off my heart, these sexual encounters without permanence chipped away at my self-worth, little by little. As a result, my personal integrity took a dive and I wondered if my dreams of having a good permanent relationship were again out of reach for me.

(Above) Kathleen's cousin, Casey O'Brien with Larry P. (Right) at a family wedding, 1974

(Above) Kathleen standing in front of the Arc de Triomphe in Paris, France, 1972, Photo by Lawrence Russell.

(Above Right) Marché Mouffetard—Market across the street across the street from Kathleen's apartment in Paris.

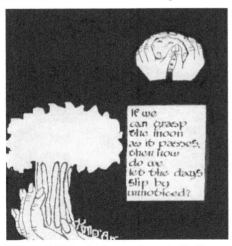

(Above) 1972 Yearbook cover drawn by Kathleen, along with the poem she wrote at St. Norbert[69]

(Above) St. Norbert College Yearbook, 1973[70]

THETA PHI

Kathleen, second from left, third row, in striped sweater with sorority sisters, 1973[71]

PARIS, FRANCE –
(Left) Gare du Nord,
with national
and international
destinations, it is
the busiest railway
station in Europe —
Photo by pxhidalgo,
https://en.wikipedia.org/
wiki/Gare du Nord[72]

Nice, France - retrieved on
3-4-2021 by Kathleen Iverson
https://en.wikipedia.org/wiki/Nice[73]

(Left) Kathleen learning
photography during
college, 1973–74

Chapter 21: *Love the One You're With*

"If you cannot hold me in your arms, then hold my memory in high regard. And if I cannot be in your life, then at least let me live in your heart."

— *Ranata Suzuki* [74]

The above words seem to be the story of my love life from the time I broke up with Larry Parnell in early 1975. Without the strict rules from the Catholic Church to live by, I was floating in a rudderless boat. I let a lot of my searching for the "right one," be left to chance and proximity. By this point, I was twenty-three years old with no boyfriend prospects in sight. Working in my first teaching job instructing high school classes in Art and French at an all-girls Catholic High School, like the one I graduated from, did not help me meet any eligible bachelors. Furthermore, I could have won a prize for attendance at the most weddings without meeting anyone marriageable.

Going back home to the Chicago suburbs to live after I finished St. Norbert College in 1974, there were no professional teaching jobs to be had the first year, so I worked as a Glenview Park District Arts and Crafts teacher during the day in the summer, while living at home to save money. After rushing home from my day job, I would arrive just in time to go to my second job as a waitress at night to help put away money to eventually move out into my own apartment. These circumstances were also not conducive to meeting eligible men my age with a similar education and background, as I had already obtained; therefore, I did not move out of my mom and dad's place until 1975, when I started teaching at Trinity High School.

Going to bars and clubs with my girlfriends did not do it for me either, because I was mostly meeting alcohol-imbibing men. At the time, my other sibling, Michael was in drug and alcohol rehab for the first or second time trying to get clean and sober. To encourage his sobriety, I used to visit him there at what we will call "Synergy House" in Chicago on the northwest side. The program was not an easy one, requiring daily group and individual counseling, nightly Alcoholics Anonymous (A.A.) meetings and a stomach for humiliation, when discussing with others how you ended up there. Synergy was a long program that required a nine-month stay at the facility and of course continuous sobriety. Surprisingly, I liked all Michael's friends at the Synergy House treatment center. Like Mike, they were working hard to beat their addictions, so they could go back to being a productive member of society. One of Mike's friends there was named David Gray. He had been a daily heroin user at a cost of one hundred fifty dollars a pop. By the time I met him, he had been doing well and was almost ready to graduate.

I started spending a lot of weekends at Synergy, attending meetings for family and friends of addicts/alcoholics called AL-Anon so I could understand my brother's issues better and learn what I should and should not do to help him. Synergy House would also have a lot of interesting activities for the clients to replace the fun and crazy times they often had while they were high. These included dances, dress-up parties, games, outings and generally good times that most had left behind when their substance abuse became a priority.

If you walked into an A.A. dance even today and didn't know that the attendees were recovering alcoholics, you would think that they were all drunk and having a great time. These sober people were learning how to have fun without alcohol and for many, these kinds of activities were helping them realize that their lives were not over, just because they were living sober. They were discovering other ways to have fun. For the first time, in a long time, I was having fun and enjoying the deep discussions these clients were willing to have about life, since they had also given up a lot of healthy intimacy with others when they collected the baggage of addiction.

It was at Synergy House that I first saw how the cycle of addiction worked and what part family members and friends played in enabling the addiction to continue unabated. It was a revelation, getting to know these people, who were working so hard to improve their lives by kicking their addictions and learning new ways to find joy in life without a chemical substance. My eyes were really opened to what the secrets of good relationships were and what behaviors were essential to building healthy intimate connections.

These desired behaviors were essential and the same, whether you kicked an unhealthy addiction or whether you ever touched a drop of alcohol in your life. By getting to know these people and my brother better, I was also learning how to improve my own abilities to have successful close relationships in the future. During the months I was involved at Synergy House, I got to know David better and enjoyed our soul-searching and intimate conversations together and started to wish I could find these attributes in a life partner.

Dating David for about a year, I learned a lot about the ups and downs of addiction. He stayed clean and sober for most of that period, until unfortunately, I found some hard-core drug paraphernalia among his things. In addition, David and some of his friends stopped by my father's office and after they left, an employee's purse was missing. The stress of this caused us to break up. Unquestionably, I had chosen to date him, even though I knew he was wrong for me on so many levels, but I was lonely and having low self-esteem, I thought I needed a man in my life to make me whole. But really, I was just a broken woman, with parents who were drinking more every time I went to see them in Glenview, about forty-five minutes away from my new apartment.

Many years later, when I was in the Navy working as a drug and alcohol counseling center director and counselor, I returned to Chicago for a convention on this subject to learn more about addiction. I had just taken on a new job as a Navy program inspector for the same kind of counseling centers I had worked at only a few years before. This field was quickly becoming one at which I was obtaining a lot of expertise. At this convention, I ran into a person that I knew who had been in the Overeaters' Anonymous program with me in Orlando, Florida. Her name was Janie and she was now a psychotherapist. She was standing next to a display of her great book that I had already read about addiction and overeating.

When I had read the book a few years earlier, I suspected my old friend may have written it because it sounded like her and the author had the same first name as the girl I had known in Orlando. I was not sure if it was indeed the Janie that I had known because it had been about ten years since I had last seen her. Also, she had gotten remarried and changed her last name. It was so great to talk to Janie again; she was just as down to earth as she had been, when I knew her before.

I congratulated Janie on her book and on how far she had progressed in her career. She was standing in an area of counseling service providers with displays about their programs. After our impromptu pleasant reunion, I saw a display for Synergy House, the place both my brother, Mike and my old boyfriend, David Gray had gone to for drug and alcohol rehabilitation.

When Janie turned to greet another attendee at the conference, I struck up a conversation with the person running the booth for Synergy House next to Janie's booth. I asked if he had known David Gray there and he looked surprised as he indicated that he had. This man saddened and shocked me when he quietly told me that David had died several years before because of a drug overdose. Today, because of the common opioid drug problem wreaking havoc with our young people, it does not seem as shocking. But back then, only a hardcore few were using drugs like heroin, which in fact belongs to the same opioid class of drugs as fentanyl and morphine. I suspected David overdosed using heroin because that was his drug of choice, before he got clean for close to a year at Synergy House. David's death disturbed me, as I thought of this fun, adventurous, full-of-life man, who wasted his life on drugs.

As a teacher, I kept my little brother Terry's picture on my desk because he was so darn cute and to remind me to always check in with him, while he was the only one left at home with my parents. By then, Terry was thirteen years old and I still adored him and did not want him to be tainted by what my family later called the "Irish Virus" (alcoholism/substance addiction). Terry had been so darling and smart as a little kid, I became very attached to him, since I was with him most of the time while babysitting. Undoubtedly, I had practically raised him from the time he was born, when I was ten years old until I moved away after college.

When I left home for good at twenty-three, as I got my first teaching job and started living in an apartment, I felt helpless to do anything to help my baby brother, except to tell him the unvarnished truth, however painful. It was then that I started to explain in more detail how my parents' drinking was not his fault and how it had affected the whole family. Terry said that those talks and immersing himself in sports saved him from unhealthy use of substances then and later in life, which he only told me about when we were older.

I was so fond of Terry that I would have done anything then and even now to protect him from hurts and sorrow if I could. I never forgot about his quick-thinking responses and funny actions, when he was a toddler. One time, my father was babysitting at night for us, while Mom was out playing Bridge with the girls. Dad became frustrated because Terry, who was about two years old and already dressed in a yellow fleece one-piece pajama with feet, did not want to stay in bed. Somehow, the little stinker had figured out how to get out of his crib, even if the sides were as high as they could go.

After about the third time putting Terry back in his crib and trying to find a way to get him to stay in bed, Dad thought that he finally had it under control, so he sat down in his easy chair to watch television and relax after having a very tiring workday. My father had built up a barrier so high on each side of Terry's crib with pillows and other items that he thought this toddler would never be able climb out. Thomas J. O'Brien was tired, but all he and the rest of us could do was laugh, when Terry came downstairs again, looking triumphant and said to our father, "I'm out again, Dad!"

Another time, the family was on vacation at a resort called Wagon Wheel, when Terry was only four years old. My mom was putting her make-up on in the only bathroom, while Terry was trying to take a pee. He was splashing urine all around the toilet and seat. Mom yelled, "Terry, why are you being so messy? You are getting pee everywhere!"

He responded in an exasperated voice, as if she should already know the answer, "I am TRYING TO WRITE MY NAME, MOM!" It was these kinds of family incidents, before my parents' drinking got out of control that endeared Terry to all of us in the family, especially to me.

One other time, when Terry was about ten years old, I was home from college in the summer and the whole family was watching T.V. together. One of the characters on a show we were watching mentioned the word, "virgin." Terry looked at me and asked, "Kath, what is a 'virgin?'"

I casually looked back at him and said, "Well, 'virgin' means someone who has not had sex yet."

He replied, "Oh." and we both nonchalantly went back to watching the show. By the looks on their faces, it was obvious that my parents were amazed because those kinds of things were not usually discussed out loud in our home and I think they were surprised that Terry and I had such a close relationship.

There were many more instances, but after over fifty years later, I cannot remember them all; however, those experiences stand out and were typical of Terry's openness, intelligence and creative know-how. Is it any wonder that my baby brother is very successful in sales as an adult? Terry could sell most people anything and as my other brother, Michael used to say about the members of our family and I am specifically applying it here to his adorable eight-years-younger sibling, Terry, "He has the gift of gab!" It seems to be a family trait. So, there were happy times in my childhood, interspersed with chaos and loud arguments, due to the negative effects of alcohol in my family, especially during puberty and when I was a teenager.

During my senior year of high school, Mom turned forty and had a meltdown of sorts, causing her to increase her alcohol intake. My poor little brother Terry had to deal with the brunt of their worst behaviors after Michael and I were out of the house and on our own in the early-to-mid-nineteen-seventies. I am surprised Terry turned out as well as he did, given that he grew up in alcohol-infused chaos, with Mom's daily vodka intake and Dad's periodic weekend binges. Again, thank God Terry had his love of playing sports to keep him busy, so he did not get caught up in our family's downward spiral. I'm sure he was still negatively affected by all this turmoil in the house, but he weathered it better than I imagined because he kept busy with sports, contributing to his high, healthy self-esteem.

When not drinking, my parents had good senses of humor, were properly protective of us, seemed like they were in love with each other and enjoyed being parents to three kids. As a couple, our parents seemed happy together most of the time. Dad brought mom a flower every week and took her out on dates a lot. She was still beautiful and was keeping a nice home for Dad to come home to. Both of my parents were functioning fairly well in life, so these ups and downs made it difficult for us to determine if alcohol was the real problem in our home.

A few years after Michael and I were out of the house and in careers of our own, my mom had some kind of accident with the car and Mom told Dad that it was not her fault, which he believed. Dad later told me that when he first talked to the policeman about it, who had been on the scene, he yelled at him. Later, after Dad heard the true progression of events during Mom's accident, he told me how bad and how guilty he felt for yelling at the young, on-scene policeman, who was just trying to do his job. Of course, Mom was probably drinking, but during those days, the authorities were not so strict about DUIs, unless it was clear the person was intoxicated, and by this time, she held her liquor well.

After college, Terry started a business career in sales, albeit selling different products until he settled into selling air time on radio and now, he has branched into T.V. Terry's newfound business career at twenty-four was going well and he met with Dad regularly to help guide him on a good sales career path. He had been getting wise advice from my dad's own sales experience and business acumen, unfortunately, my youngest brother suddenly lost my father to a fatal heart virus. Sadly, Terry suffered the loss of Dad's stabilizing and wise influence too young, just when he needed his father the most.

Learning about A.A. and addiction through the troubles of Michael and David and then grasping the wisdom of the teachings at Synergy House, started me on a journey of self-discovery and improvement that has lasted for over forty years. I had hoped that it would help me be a better partner to a life-long mate, if I ever found one but that was out of reach for me until my mid-forties, even though I had several false positives along the way.

(Left) Picture of Terry at 13 years. old, which Kathleen had on her desk at work

(Right) Christina and Kathleen, 1989

(Below) Mike & Karen O'Brien, late1970s

(Right) Terry at 2 years old

(Below) Terry visiting Kathleen
in San Diego, 1987

(Above) Michael & Karen O'Brien, 1980s

(Below) David Gray & Linda F.,
Kathleen's student, 1976

(Above) Carole H., Kathleen and another
contestant dressed in costumes for the opening
act: "Countries of the World" at the
Miss Northshore Contest, 1975.

(Above) Tom, Terry and Elaine O'Brien, 1980s

(Left) Elaine and Tom, 1960s – 1970s

Chapter 22: *The Marriage-Go-Round*

*The dark thought, the shame, the malice, meet
them at the door laughing and invite them in.*

— Rumi[75]

In May 1977, my parents hosted a big going away party for me, as I
had signed up for the Navy to be starting Recruit Training (Boot
Camp) Center, Orlando, Florida shortly on May 20, 1977. Keith
Donahue was there from my old high school days, as we had started
dating again around that time. As I had outlined in earlier chapters, it
took me a long time to get over him and we saw each other
periodically off and on after we broke up my first year of college in
September of 1970.

Something I didn't know in 1977 when I signed up for the
Navy, was that Keith was sad and upset when he realized that I was
really leaving this time. Keith never told me until many years later
that he had decided then that he really did not want me to go. It is not
clear to me that if I knew how he felt about us as I was about to leave
that I would have broken my contract to go into the service in order to
stay and continue seeing Keith. To this day, in our sixties, Keith
never married.

Since I didn't know what Keith was feeling when I left for
Navy Boot Camp, I never had the chance to feel torn and uncertain
about my decision to become a member of the military. Even though
it was a long while before I later fulfilled my dream of finding the
right man with, whom to spend the rest of my life, my experience in
the Navy really influenced the healthier self I am today and it suited
me perfectly as a career. Furthermore, I needed the structure and the
adventure to keep me engaged in productive activity as I moved
forward in life.

After Boot Camp in Orlando, which at the time was the only
recruit training facility for women, I was stationed in Pensacola,
Florida, in order to attend Navy Photographer's Mate "A" school.
Located in the Florida "Panhandle," I had a lot of fun on that aviator
base, called Naval Air Station, Pensacola. It was located in a small
town, very southern and dedicated to proudly supporting the mission

of Naval Aviation, Cryptology and the other commands stationed on the base. Pretty, white sandy beaches, which were rarely crowded, ensured that sailors and aviators had quiet areas to study, as well as, having places to catch a ray. Good southern comfort food could be found nearby at small restaurants that served family-style fried chicken, corn on the cob and mashed potatoes smothered in butter.

Photo Mate "A" School in Pensacola was the first training I went to after Boot Camp. Fortunately, all the great training I have received in the Navy on a multitude of subjects, not only prepared me for my career, but for life in general. In addition, this training enlarged my intellectual capital and it furthered my aspirations, giving me a desire to try harder in new endeavors. I had no idea that I had it in me. As much as I had loved Art, English and History in high school, I never thought of looking into other subjects. Nothing then seemed to appeal to me, but that was before I was bit by the curiosity bug. The courses I took in the Navy opened my eyes to new possibilities and stoked my desire to learn more. This is one of the greatest gifts the Navy has given me, as well as, helping me to abundantly boost my self-confidence.

Some of the best courses I have taken that were part of my Navy training, include: Drug and Alcohol Training, Drug and Alcohol Counselor, Advanced Drug and Alcohol Counselor, Organizational Effectiveness (Development), Equal Employment Opportunity, Prevention of Sexual Harassment, Planned Maintenance System, Military Leadership, Instructor Training, Curriculum Development, Situational Leadership, Civilian Personnel Management, Division Officer, Urinalysis Officer, Physical Fitness Coordinator, Legal Officer, Officer Candidate School, Recruit Training, Total Quality Leadership (six courses), Quality Control Inspector, Photographer's Mate, Advanced Photographer's Mate, and Photojournalism.

I put that valuable training to good use most of my Navy career and after I retired from the Navy, when I worked in the business world for five years. During that time, my first civilian jobs included working as a freelance Organizational Management Consultant and as Manager of Organizational Performance at a worldwide fine art object collector company, which I really enjoyed. All that training and relevant experience came in handy and made me more confident in my own abilities managing business performance.

The last career I had, which was teaching French to high school students for twelve years, prepared me even more for dealing with difficult situations and challenging circumstances.

All the courses I had had in the Navy, as well as, experience teaching courses like Officer Rank Recognition and Total Quality Leadership (TQL) to sailors, really solidified my own performance in the education field. Moreover, after hours on my own time, I taught Equal Employment Opportunity at Chapman University and Organizational Behavior, a graduate course at Roosevelt University. Through all encounters with teaching adult sailors and civilians, I came to appreciate the priceless education and experience I obtained from the military.

An important discovery for me during that time was that it was possible to increase professional confidence by working hard and doing one's best, while at the same time having low self-esteem when it came to personal relationships and a love life. Ironically, I was often complimented by my parents, professors, bosses and friends about the success I had had in my career, but it seemed a satisfying long-term permanent boy-girl relationship was not ever going to be within my reach.

This personal versus work contradiction in my life seemed to take years for me to comprehend. Part of the problem was the ongoing battle with ADHD symptoms that I didn't understand until I got help in my forties, like: impulsively talking in social groups or not being able to read personal cues from others well. My attempts to establish healthy personal relationships, outside of the well-established military social norms I was comfortable with, were rendered difficult by my ADHD symptoms.

Fortunately, I had a decent Naval career despite my issues because of my good work ethic and the strong military structure that guided my decisions and behavior. More so, the symbols worn on military uniforms were easily readable and the Naval protocols I learned in training became second nature because they were used repeatedly. These helped me to perform successfully, as expected of a Naval officer. My unhelpful ADHD symptoms that could have had a more negative impact on my military career were often mitigated by my good overall performance. Some of my performance was impacted negatively by my ADHD, but that mostly happened later in my career.

As I explained earlier, I really liked the modern way photography was taught at the Navy Photographer's Mate School, using modules that we completed with personalized instruction at our own pace. Each module lasted about one week, so you got to know your instructor well. One of my favorite classes was learning about Ansel Adams and his "Zone System." I admired the instructor, Petty Officer Troy Camwell because he was so intelligent and explained the nuances of photography very well. The examples he showed us blew me away and later, we found out the examples were from his own photography work. He also showed us some new technology to make crackerjack slide presentations using the latest rear projection screens and multi-part slides. In his work, I saw an artistic sensitivity, technological expertise and a hunger to keep learning new things about his own field, which attracted me.

Troy was about five feet nine inches tall, had brilliant blue eyes and thinning red hair, cut military style. He wore gold aviator-style wire-rimmed glasses and a well-pressed blue uniform shirt and dungarees. At almost twenty-six, he was one year older than me and we seemed to have a lot of interests in common. I was really surprised and flattered when Troy asked me out on a date. Today, going out with your instructor would be frowned upon, not to mention I was two ranks below him in seniority; however, most sailors hadn't dealt with many women under their purview yet. Because females were just being allowed into the military services in larger numbers, our bosses did not have a lot of experience dealing with fraternization. Unless you openly flaunted it, they mostly ignored it.

At that time, the fraternization rules had either hardly been used or were not well defined yet, due to limited experience with female peers in the Navy workplace. It was an unwritten tradition that sailors were not charged with fraternization unless they had already had other similar charges pending like adultery. However, during my era, as the big influx of female enlistments occurred, these rules would eventually become tighter and applied more often.

This push to sign up more women was because the Vietnam War had ended a couple of years earlier and many sailors, soldiers and marines had left the service already, so the force was smaller. It was thought that women would fill in the gaps. Within a few years, I saw my first female Admiral. Around the same time, I first saw the new maternity uniform being worn by a female sailor. Before that, there were comparatively so few women, they had to wear civilian clothes during their pregnancies because the services did not have any maternity uniforms.

For over two hundred years, not many women served, compared to the rest of the total military service population. Part of the reason was the Combat Exclusion Law and part of it was because culturally, it was thought that the military jobs required work for men, not women, which wasn't totally true. Except for work requiring height and brawn, the rest of the jobs can be done by women. who have the desire and the skill to do them.

Anyway, Troy Camwell and I started a relationship, so I began spending all my free time with him, both on and off base. We started staying together all the time at his house and I hardly came back to the barracks to sleep. Troy began talking to me about marriage after we were seeing each other for only two months. Again, the conditions were ripe to make a bad decision here because I was away from home and lonely in a new career. Moreover, although I admired Troy and his accomplishments greatly, it wasn't a good reason to start a serious relationship because I would be leaving after the ten-week Photo Mate "A" School ended. My impulsive nature won out, becoming deeply involved with him anyway.

Troy was taking classes to get his degree at the local college and we were always having deep discussions. We got serious fairly quickly. He talked me into not waiting a long time to get married by reminding me that if we got married, the Navy would try to station us together. In addition, we would get a big housing allowance added to our pay. We loved each other, right? So, why not? Troy also thought that we knew each other well (after only two months) because we had lived together. Again, I was starting to put the cart before the horse.

Troy and I started shopping for rings and I called my parents telling them that we would be getting married two months down the road on November 5, 1977 and asked them to come to Pensacola for the wedding. I thought that when I told my parents that I was getting married so soon after joining the Navy that they would be surprised and question me more to make sure I was being wise. But all they said was, "If you love him, then we love him too." Thomas and Elaine O'Brien told me later that they thought I would get married anyway, so why question me about my decision? They didn't really know how much their opinion counted with me, but I know that if they had asked me to wait, I am convinced that I would have.

Since then, I have seen how many young people make mistakes and get into trouble or make immature decisions, when they first come into the military like I did. Unwise commitments are made in a rush due to loneliness, or lack of life experience with big decisions. Family and friends were not close by to talk these decisions over with, so many of us took leaps of faith with our lives that did not turn out so well in the long run. These are all factors that contributed to the demise of my own marriage to Troy three years later.

Moreover, conditions are not exactly right for other life commitments, when enlisted members first come into the service because they have to go to Boot Camp right away, which is designed to break the sailor down, so they can be built back up again the "Military Way." That is true one way or another for all the military branches. Many new sailors still have trouble with self-esteem until they have been in the service for a while. Finishing Boot Camp doesn't always build them back up.

It takes time to adjust to the unusual stresses and rigors of military life. Additionally, it is such a different way of life from the average person's that it is necessary to start recruits off with a lot more discipline than is required later, when sailors have some time in the service under their belts, after a proper period of adjustment. Recruit Training is the start of that adjustment time, immediately followed by technical schools to learn their specific new jobs before they are sent out to the fleet. If the sailor is trying to make fast, big life-changing personal commitments, while trying to adjust to the Navy culture, there are bound to be bad decisions taken.

Later, when I became the Officer-in-Charge of different Naval technical schools, twice a week, I was required to conduct a kind of court called Officer-In-Charge-Mast to hear cases presented about infractions incurred by our "A" School students ("A" School is usually the first school sailors are sent to, with the purpose of learning their specialty before they go to their first duty station or another school). The students I encountered at Mast were usually suffering from the same kind of low self-esteem that I had suffered from earlier in my life and career, but that still plagued me from time to time.

Seeing the Mast students making bad decisions (as I did) I tried to talk with them about the choices they were facing. I had gotten myself in trouble with relationships because of low self-esteem, but it hadn't often affected my career because I had good mentors and role-models. Instead, I seemed to thrive under the discipline. Able to come up with creative solutions and to use those abilities in order to handle difficult situations or to deal with people, boosted my self-confidence tremendously.

Fortunately, for a sheltered girl from the Midwest, I was able to develop much higher self-confidence in my career than I would in other areas of my life because the Navy expected us to learn many things and learn it quickly. One thing that ensured our wealth of new abilities in the service as young Naval Officers, was that we rotated jobs at least every three years to get maximum variable experience. The powers that be wanted Naval Officers to learn as much about operations in different departments, so that one day, they would have enough variable experience to use, the higher they climbed the promotion ladder.

Conversely, high self-esteem in my personal relationships took me much longer to master and seems to be an on-going process the longer I live. I wondered if having high self-esteem and good personal relationships were out of reach for me. That attribute was hard-won by good and bad relationships over forty or fifty years, but "... having the ability to pick yourself up, dust yourself off and begin again..." as my mother described me one time, can be directly credited to both my Naval service and my many years of psychotherapy. But for now, there is the rest of the story concerning relationships and me in the coming chapters.

(Left)
Kathleen
With Troy,
1978
in Orlando,
FL

Kathleen as Division Four Officer and her
staff at Recruit Graduation, 1988

(Above) Kathleen on her first liberty at Sea World during Boot Camp, 1977

(Above) Kathleen (front far left) graduating from Quality Control Inspector School, Orlando, FL 1979

(Below) Kathleen's Navy Going Away Party, May, 1977

(Below) Kathleen (third from right) and other recruits wearing dungarees, chambray shirts, and holding ditty bags at Boot Camp in Orlando, FL, 1977

(Right) Keith and Kathleen, the night before she left for the Navy, May 1977

(Above) Kathleen as Sailor of the Quarter at NAS Jacksonville, FL, 1979

(Right) Friends and Family at Kathleen's Navy going away party, May 1977

Chapter 23: *The Marriage-Go-Round Again*

"Second marriages show triumph of hope over experience."

— Samuel Johnson[76]

Ever the optimist, at the end of my second tour in Orlando, Florida in 1982, I asked to be stationed in San Diego, California. After I finished the twelve-week Naval Drug and Alcohol Counseling School, (NDACS), I became the Director of the Counseling and Assistance Center (CAAC), Naval Air Station (NAS), Miramar, CA. CAACs are local base drug and alcohol evaluation and counseling centers. Markedly, I was totally in my element in this job and it was one of my favorite assignments of all my Navy career.

This assignment also clued me into the fact that I actually had some leadership ability. Perhaps I picked up something from my dad, who always talked about his time as a Captain in the Army. A lot of my dad's lessons to us about life were about how important it was to treat people well and with respect. Thus, I think learning that lesson is half the education required to be a good leader.

One of the counselors I worked with was named Burt. He was a First-Class Petty Officer (E-6) who wanted to be promoted. However, he had problems with writing English, which was needed to become a Chief Petty Officer (E-7). In order to help him, I started giving him writing lessons after work. The following year, he became a Chief Petty Officer and told me it was all because of me helping him with his English. The lesson I learned as a leader was to look deeper into a problem than what was on the surface. I knew Burt didn't have much confidence, and I had to probe deeper to find out why. Once I learned that English as a Second Language (ESL) was his problem, we worked together to solve it.

Besides running the CAAC, I was responsible for giving presentations around the base about our services, as well as, about what addiction really is and how it affects the family and the workplace. I would evaluate and counsel clients myself as a trained paraprofessional counselor, as well as manage a staff of four other counselors. I dreaded the day I would have to leave this job because I

185

loved it so much. I really enjoyed working with the staff because they cared so much about our clients and gave one hundred ten percent, assisting the sailor clients to get the right help for their substance abuse issues. Little did I know that one of my friends at Miramar would eventually be the one to take over the CAAC when my tour was up.

Krystal DeMarcus was another Lieutenant like I was and we got along very well. She was married to an aviator named Jerry DeMarcus, who was an instructor for the U.S. Navy Fighter Weapons School (nicknamed Top Gun), located at the time on my base, NAS Miramar, CA. Not dating anyone seriously, I told Krystal that I would like to meet someone special. It had been two years since Troy and I had divorced and I was now close to thirty years old. I was worried about being able to have children and time was running out, not to mention that I was lonely and felt ready for the plunge.

Krystal said she knew a single guy who worked for the Navy as a civil servant, managing the F-5 Tiger Fighter Jet program, the program her husband Jerry oversaw. Top Gun used the F-5 Tiger for its adversary fighter training plane. Manned by the instructors against the students, who were flying their F-14 Tomcats during dogfight simulations, the F-5s were similar in fast maneuverability to Russian MIGs, as seen in the Tom Cruise movie, "Top Gun". Responsible for the operation and maintenance program for the F-5s within Top Gun, Jerry worked closely with the civilian Navy Program Manager for the F-5 Tiger, Salvatore Frank Causarano. Sal was located ten miles south at NAS North Island on Coronado Island in San Diego Bay. He was the guy Krystal was thinking of, when she offered to fix me up.

Because of his Aeronautical Engineering degree from Western Michigan University, Salvatore was a knowledgeable program manager of the F-5 Tiger fighter jets. His general schedule twelve (GS-12) job title was Aviation Logistics Management Specialist. This meant he oversaw the money to buy, repair, write and administer the contract with Northrop Grumman, a company which produced the fighters for the Navy. Basically, Salvatore was responsible for logistically keeping those fighters in tip-top shape to be able to fly when needed.

Jerry and Krystal DeMarcus thought Sal and I might have a lot in common, since he worked for the Navy. He seemed like a steady, very intelligent guy, who understood well, some of the tough requirements of being a Naval Officer. Moreover, Salvatore had had his own experience in the Navy in the early seventies as a student at Naval Aviation Officer Candidate School in Pensacola, Florida. His dream was to be an aviator himself, but it was dashed when after five months of the training, he was found to have a cyst on his spine, which became an issue, hindering his ability to sit in a cockpit.

Because of the cyst on his spine, Sal was considered "not qualified" for the aviation field as a pilot. Deeply disappointed, he was offered other Navy non-aviation jobs so he could stay in, but he declined, due to his burning desire to work in aviation in some capacity. Instead, he applied to the Navy Civil Service and was accepted to work in Aviation Logistics. He had been working in that capacity for more than a decade, when I was introduced to him.

Instead of the pressure of a blind date, Krystal and Jerry decided to have a party at their house and invite both Sal and me for us to meet in a more casual atmosphere. The DeMarcus's party was a success and Sal and I started dating soon afterwards. Around this time, my parents decided to visit me in San Diego. While they were staying with me for a few weeks, before I went out on a date with Sal, I had been casually seeing two different guys, both Naval aviators of my same Lieutenant rank, whom I individually introduced to my parents. Each night I went out, my mom casually joked, "Who's the contestant tonight?"

Toward the end of their two-week visit, Tom and Elaine also met Sal, one of the "contestants" that Mom had joked about. For a few days during the visit of my parents, I had to go to the Naval Medical Center, San Diego for some minor gynecological surgery. Sal was the only one of my suitors who visited me in the hospital and brought me flowers. This impressed my parents and when asked towards the end of their stay which guy of the three "contestants" that they liked best, they resoundingly agreed that hands down it was Salvatore F. Causarano.

Because of their approval, I started looking at Sal a little differently, with more interest than I had at first. He had been very quiet during our dates and I was having trouble figuring out how much I liked him because I really had to draw him out. I was attracted to Sal, a good-looking Italian-American male with almost-black thick, shiny hair; he had dark brown eyes and was about five feet nine inches, with an average body weight.

His Roman nose was somewhat large like many Italians, but it looked fine on him. I met both of his parents around this time too. His mother, Antoinette (also called Nettie) was born in Sicily and came to America when she was four years old. Sal's dad, Frank, was actually born in St. Louis, but his parents came from Sicily too.

After Antoinette and Frank Causarano were married on July 9, 1944, they had lived in New York, where "only child" Sal was born and raised, but then they moved to San Diego, CA when Frank was diagnosed with Parkinson's disease in his fifties. Frank was told by his doctor that Southern California, with its dry warm climate, was perfect for him to fend off the symptoms of the disease. In the early seventies, Sal and his first wife, Linda followed the elder Causaranos out to San Diego, specifically, to the suburb of Mira Mesa. That is where they raised their two children, Joey (now likes to be called Josef), born in 1971 and Lisa, born in 1975.

When Salvatore and his first wife, Linda moved to San Diego in the early seventies with their new baby, Joey, Sal started working for the Navy as a civil servant. Sal traveled a lot for his job (which put a strain on his marriage) as the years passed by. Linda and Salvatore had very different interests and a decline in their relationship set in. Sal eventually told me that the divorce was his fault because he had had a girlfriend that he met on a business trip to Washington, D.C. He broke up with the girlfriend, but not before the marriage was destroyed.

At the end of 1982, I met Sal right before his divorce from Linda was final. He and I had been dating steadily for about five months, when one night, we were talking in his car. Nervously, he turned to me and said, "Kathleen, I love you." I told him that I loved him too.

Not long after that, we were on board a plane flying to Cabo San Lucas in Mexico for a vacation that we had planned to take together. When the flight attendant told us we could put our tray tables down, Sal pulled out a pen and a little card he had in his pocket and started to write on it. A few minutes later, he handed me the card, which said, "¿Te quiero muchísimo? ¿Te casarías conmigo?"

Confused, I looked at him and indicated that I did not really know what those Spanish words meant. I asked, "What does it say?"

He answered, looking straight into my eyes and said, "It says that I love you very much and will you marry me?"

By that time, we were really in love and so I said, "Yes, I will." and we kissed to seal the deal.

Shortly afterward, I told Sal that I wanted us to have been seeing each other a whole year when we would tie the knot because that is what I promised myself I would do if I ever got married again. I thought that was the solution for a lasting marriage: to know each other a whole year first. I knew that I rushed into it the first time and did not want the problems created by that scenario, so I thought that a year knowing each other before we walked down the aisle would prevent us from making a mistake. Since I also had had twelve weeks of group therapy as part of my counselor training to work at the CAAC at Miramar, I thought I had dealt with my issues well enough to make a good decision about marriage.

Moreover, during our engagement, in order to get married in the Catholic Church a second time, both Sal and I were required by the Church to write pages about ourselves and what went wrong in our first marriages. In addition, we had to go to counseling with a priest. We each had to admit our parts in the dissolution of our marriages. Indeed, there were tons of paperwork and questions to fill out before the priest could be assured that he could religiously annul our first marriages.

The Roman Catholic Annulment process takes about six months, which is the only way we could get married in the Church again. It does help the divorced person to get insight into their own issues and how to prevent problems in the second marriage. Anyway, I thought this annulment system and an upcoming "Marriage Encounter Weekend," run by the Catholic Church, would be added insurance against the possibility of Salvatore and I breaking up in the future. We set the date for December 30, 1983, about a year and two months after we first started dating." This time, I wanted a large wedding with my close friends and family present in my original hometown, Glenview, Illinois.

Accordingly, I arranged for the ceremony to take place at the little chapel on NAS Glenview and the reception to be held at the base Officers' Club. It turned out beautifully and this time I had Val as my maid of honor, my sister-in-law Karen (Michael's wife) and my last college roommate, Jean B. in the wedding, as well as my two brothers Mike and Terry and Sal's best man, his cousin, Ralph.

In my heart, this was the way a proper wedding was supposed to be: old friends who had known me for years, my parents, and my cousins, all being present at my wedding. All these special people in attendance and having the ceremony taking place in my own hometown would make it "legit" in the eyes of God and the world according to my flawed thinking. I had received the blessing from the Church, so I felt cleansed of all my sins and free to marry again. What could go wrong if I was doing this so right?

I met Sal's kids when Joey was eleven and Lisa was seven years old and fell in love with them. I thought it would be great to have this built-in family in case I could not have my own children, due to my many gynecological problems that started coming about after I turned thirty years old. Joey was a very good artist, so we had that in common. I loved to look at his artwork because he was certainly talented, even having his drawings chosen to be in the Del Mar Fair, near San Diego. Lisa loved to dress up and play with dolls, which appealed to my girly-girl nature, so we got along well too.

Before I had any children of my own, Lisa overheard me say that I loved the new Cabbage Patch dolls that had just come out in the stores and were flying off the shelves. When the stores ran out of these popular baby dolls in the eighties, Lisa paid a lady, who made "look-a-like Cabbage Patch dolls," twenty-five dollars of her own savings to get me one for my birthday. Lisa was only nine years old at the time and I just could not get over her sacrifice and thoughtfulness. How could you not love a kid like that? Before Sal and I were married, the four of us spent a lot of time as a pseudo-family and it seemed to me that we were all compatible. I did notice that Joey was very quiet and to himself a lot when he came over. Later Joe told me it was because he didn't enjoy being with his dad. I believe there were unresolved issues that Sal had to work on with his son.

For me, I really enjoyed Joey's company when we were all together, but Joe has since told me that he and his dad never truly worked out their problems. He also said that even though, father and son never really became close before Sal died in 2006, they had learned to tolerate each other, as the years went on. To me, that is a shame. I know Sal was not really equipped to have a good father-son relationship because he did not really know how to have one with his own quiet father, who had health problems. In addition, throughout the years, Frank had more trouble speaking because his voice was negatively affected by his Parkinson's disease, which made it more difficult to have those father-son discussions.

Sal's family was attractive to me because of their Italian culture. I liked how they all gathered regularly for great family dinners, which included their scrumptious Italian cuisine. I found it cute how they called their red sauce "gravy" instead of spaghetti sauce. Also, his Aunt Sarah's homemade bread was to die for. They always toasted with wine and had lively conversations, interspersed with Italian phrases at the table, just as depicted in the 1972 movie, "The Godfather." These endearing ways made me want to be part of their Italian family.

Often, the extended family would come over and my mother-in-law would go to the part of San Diego where there used to be a cannery, an area where most of the early Italian immigrants had migrated to find work. During that time in the early eighties, there were still plenty of Italian features in that part of downtown San Diego, like Italian bakeries, fish shops, pizzerias and restaurants. In fact, since it is a custom in the Italian culture to serve fish on Christmas Eve, my mother-in-law, Antoinette (Nettie for short) would go to that area to buy her fish, bread and other supplies to make her Italian holiday dinner.

Being away from my O'Brien family for the holidays was difficult, so having Sal's family there was a blessing. In addition, Antoinette was kind enough to let me invite single Navy girl friends of mine (a couple of them were Italian too) who were away from their families on a holiday. Antoinette taught me how to make Italian red sauce, lasagna, and cannoli, which really made me feel part of the family. And they never drank excessively like some of my Irish relatives.

After Sal and I were married, for several Easter holidays, we had the whole extended family over at our house and I made lasagna for dinner. Thanks to my mother-in-law, I knew how to make the same lasagna and sauce that she made, which took five hours to simmer. One time though, I substituted "Ragu" sauce from the store because I did not have time to cook the "real" sauce. Unbeknownst to everyone (except Sal), I served the Ragu version. Sal winked at me when the aunts and others were raving about my sauce. Aunt Sarah said, "Kathleen, you are really getting good at making the gravy for the lasagna, keep up the good work!" From then on, I never made the five-hour genuine sauce again. I always used the store-bought Ragu and none of Sal's Italian aunts nor Nettie, ever knew the "secret" to my sauce.

During my seven-year marriage to Sal, we were both able to do well in our respective careers, travel to Europe, make close couple friends like our daughter's godparents, Rod and Linda W. and buy a nice house in Poway, CA. I became pregnant with our daughter, who we named Christina Marie Causarano. She was born on January 21, 1987 by caesarean section at Naval Medical Center, San Diego (nick named, "Balboa") in the old building before the new Balboa Park hospital was built next-door in 1988. The first building was a dispensary built in 1917 for WWI sailors and veterans. By the time of the Vietnam War, it had become the largest Military hospital complex in the world. Celebrating its Centennial Year in 2017, the Naval Medical Center, San Diego is now made up of many buildings, employs 6,600 people and cares for 125K military patients.

By this time, I was working as the Recruit Training Command (RTC) Administrative Officer on board Naval Training Center (NTC), San Diego. RTC was one of three in the Navy - the others were located in Orlando, FL and Great Lakes, IL and I have worked at all three, as a result of my Navy Training Subspecialty.

When I was only three months pregnant, I had to start wearing maternity clothes because I didn't fit into my uniform anymore. The Navy had just come out with maternity uniforms, so I bought a set to wear for the rest of my pregnancy. Because I worked at the main Administrative Building, I was often tasked to show people around, especially those, who had gone to Boot Camp there. This base had been around since the nineteen-twenties and some of the older men (Remember, many women were not yet in the Navy then.) would come around for a tour of the premises. Not only was the Administrative Department housed in one of the ancient buildings that the old guys remembered, but we had set up a display in the lobby showing the old Boot Camp. Available for public viewing, the exhibit consisted of artifacts donated, mostly by U.S. Vietnam POWs.

One time, one of the Chief Petty Officers that worked for me, we will call him Chief Halperin, was in the lobby showing a group of older men around, who had graduated in the nineteen-twenties or thirties. I was a Lieutenant (LT) at the time, dressed in my new summer white maternity uniform with navy blue shoulder boards (sporting two LT gold stripes) and wearing my everyday ribbons above the top left pocket. Instead of the uniform blouse being tucked into my skirt and form-fitting, like the regular uniforms, it was an A-line white maternity blouse that was wide and worn over the skirt without a belt.

After I left the lobby, one of the older men Chief Halperin was escorting said to him, "Was that the Lieutenant you work for?"

Chief Halperin responded, "Yes, why do you ask?"

The older gentleman said in almost a whisper, "Gee, Chief, your Lieutenant didn't look very much squared away."

Chief Halperin asked the man, "Sir, why do you think that?"

The old man replied, "Because she let her shirt-tail hang out!"

The Chief smiled and said, "But sir, she was wearing the new pregnancy uniform, so it is made to be worn outside her skirt." The man was blown away. I guess he had already accepted that there were more women now in the Navy, but just could not believe there could be a pregnant one working at his old Boot Camp, wearing a regulation maternity uniform.

Another interesting tidbit that took place in the Administration (Admin.) Building that I was responsible for as the Administrative Officer of RTC, was that our bathroom, just off the lobby in that old building, was famous. Why? Because just the year before, the movie *Top Gun* with Tom Cruise was partly filmed there. You know the scene where Cruise follows Kelly McGillis into the Ladies Restroom? That scene was filmed in *my* washroom (under my purview as Admin. Officer).

Of course, normally it was the standard plain gray Women's Head, but for the movie it was spruced up with white, fluffy hand towels and vases of flowers. My boss, the Executive Officer of RTC, who happened to be an aviator, made sure I had a brass plaque constructed and put on the outside of the door that said, "Top Gun Was Filmed Here." These incidents all happened while I was married to Sal and we had a good laugh over them before the marriage soured.

During the painful divorce proceedings that I went through with Sal, I couldn't believe I was getting a second divorce. It just did not compute. In my mind, I, that girl-next-door-type, should never have had to go through a divorce in the first place, much less two. It did not fit the image I had of myself growing up in a Catholic home where "Divorce" was a dirty word. The events leading up to that divorce are a separate story, which I will tell about later in this chapter. To this day, on the O'Brien side of the family, four total have gotten divorced in my B.B. generation and in our parents' generation.

As of 2022, out of the ten sons of Dad's (Tom) only sibling, Ray and his wife Anne, three of the ten have been divorced. Those three that are divorced are interestingly the closest of the ten brothers to my age and incidentally, they are also Baby Boomers. One was born, like me, in 1952 (the seventh son of ten) and the next was born three years later in 1955 (the eighth son of ten) and finally, the last one (the tenth son of ten) was born in 1959. Besides my cousins, I am the only one that has been divorced of Tom and Elaine's three children (which adds up to thirteen first cousins total on the O'Brien side).

Raised as a devout Catholic, Sal had few divorces in his family. I only know about two of his cousins, who were divorced. On my mom's side, the Robinsons, there were eighteen first cousins, (including my two brothers and me) several of whom I don't know well; two never married (one of which separated from his common-law wife), six have been divorced, and I don't think any are divorced in my Uncle Dewey Jr.'s and his wife, Shirley's family, who together had six boys. Of the twenty-five first cousins on both sides, only four have died, two on the O'Brien side, and two on the Robinson side. Counting my two brothers and me into the mix, the O'Brien side has a thirty-one percent divorce rate and the Robinson side has a thirty-eight percent divorce rate. Since I calculated my divorce rates differently than Wikipedia, they aren't really comparable; they were calculating it for one year and my rates were calculated for the long-run. However, looking at Wikipedia can give you an idea.

The Divorce Rate for 2020 (the latest figure) in America was paraphrased by me like this: of the U.S. married population, a skosh over forty-five percent were divorced, according to Wikipedia.[77] I surmise that the lower divorce rates on both sides of my family have to do with the importance of religion, especially, the O'Brien side, who were Catholic, a religion that really frowns on divorce. My Grandpa Robinson's side, even though, not really religious in his generation, had been a religious family before that, as his grandfather, Shuah S. Mann was a minister in the Protestant tradition. Going back at least three or four generations, I could not find many divorces on the O'Brien side, where the Catholic "no-divorce" religion ruled the day.

Whether you are a proponent of religion or not, I think most agree that if there are some moral principles to follow, like religion purports, there is a much better chance that people in the family will try to stay together. If you look in the Protestant Robinson-Mann background, there are a greater number of divorces going back from my great-grandfather, Shuah Mann and even further back.

Markedly, the divorce trend had stopped with my grandparents and my parents, but the Baby Boomers picked the trend up again, probably due to their tendencies to rebel. However, I am not a sociologist, so all I am saying is that the divorce trend in my family matches my limited research of the Baby Boomers, who are getting divorces at greater rates than their parents or grandparents did.

According to Wikipedia, "...in the US, since the mid-1990s, the divorce rate has increased among Baby Boomers to fifty percent." As contrasted to the general "...divorce rate of 45.1% in 2020." [77]

On paper, Sal's and my demographics certainly looked like winners, but there were underlying forces at work that took several years to show their full repercussions. When I married Sal in December of 1983, I knew he was quiet and that I would have to draw him out more than usual, but I felt I could handle it. He came from a good Catholic family, and I knew he had a conscience because, when he knew he was in the wrong, I had observed him feeling guilty about it and admitting to his misdeeds. In addition, he had really good children, Joey and Lisa, who were well-behaved, polite, kind and seemed like normal, healthy kids. They were close to their parents, their grand- parents, and integrated well into the extended family.

Even though, there seemed to periodically be tension between Joey and his dad, I thought it would work itself out, as time went on. After all, Joe was approaching the teen years and it was hard to tell if that tension would last. I knew Antoinette was a little overbearing, but she was a wonderful grandmother to the kids, and that continued later, when Sal and I had our own daughter, Christina. My father-in-law, Frank, was very kind, but he really could not talk that much because his Parkinson's wreaked havoc with his voice. I was very touched that Frank was the first to give me a hug, when Sal and I announced our engagement. Moreover, I especially liked the extended family, aunts, uncles and cousins and certainly felt a part of the close-knit Italian family I had married into. I was impressed that Sal's ex-wife, Linda, stayed close to the family after Sal and she were divorced, which made things easier on the kids.

Sal and I had our problems, but overcoming them seemed very doable. We had some good times too. Every so often, it was comical, when we had to attend school events for the kids. When both Sal and I had to attend one of those school activities and his ex-wife, Linda was there too, occasionally, it could get awkward. One time, all of us were standing in the same row to view a school event and Sal ended up standing in-between his ex and me. I don't remember why, but everyone was holding hands and of course it made him truly uncomfortable to hold both of his wives' hands at the same time.

A year after Frank had passed away, when Antoinette died, Linda and I, who got along well, took it upon ourselves to put on the funeral reception at Nettie's house because there didn't seem to be anyone else there to do it. We went shopping together and bought the food for the guests. As we were both sitting next to each other during the reception, Sal and his last wife came in. Since some of his friends were already there, he started to introduce people. Trying to keep his three wives straight, he said to his friends, pointing to Linda, "Now this is my first wife, Linda." Then he looked at me and pointed saying, "And this is my second wife Kathleen." He looked at his present wife and said, "This is my third wife…" and he never finished because she gave him daggers for his thorny presentation and for putting her at the rear of his line of wives. Linda and I looked at each other and tried not to laugh at the situation, but it was difficult to stifle our giggles because it really was funny.

Regarding my in-laws, Antoinette and Frank, there were a few humorous things that happened during our years together, but the following one takes the cake. If you have ever watched those old WWII movies made at the old Naval Hospital in San Diego, like the one called, "In Harm's Way" with John Wayne and Maureen O'Hara, you would recognize the area at the hospital I want to talk about.

When I was pregnant with my daughter, Christina, I was put on bed rest for the last seven months of my pregnancy. Even though I was confined to bed at home, I was required to come to the Naval Hospital once per week, to see my doctor for a check-up because I had what was called a "complicated pregnancy," which required more monitoring. For most of the pregnancy, I was at home on bed rest and I was not allowed to drive. Consequently, the only people that were home during the day and could drive me were my in-laws.

Antoinette was about four feet ten inches and Frank was about five feet four. Due to my complicated pregnancy, I was not allowed to walk far. Once we parked the car, they had to push me in a wheelchair on hilly walkways outside. Nettie was so short that she didn't want to park the car in tight spots because she could barely see over the wheel or out the back window. Antoinette would drive and when we got there, I would switch seats with her and park the car. No matter how big "with child" I was horizontally, at five-feet-three-and-a-half inches tall, I was certainly taller than my mother-in-law and could see over the wheel. To make moving around difficult, I had a condition called pre-eclampsia (excess water weight), so I was huge, especially near the end, at about one-hundred-eighty-nine pounds that all came pouring out after I had the baby. The doctors said I dropped thirty-seven pounds of water weight, as soon as the baby arrived.

After I parked the car, my short and lightweight in-laws would do their best to push my wheelchair into the hospital to see the doctor. The problem was, the old Naval Hospital was all made up of steep sidewalks leading to the many buildings that were in the large complex. This one time, Frank and Nettie lost control of the wheelchair on a hill and it started rolling quite fast down the steep sidewalk, due to my extra pregnancy weight and the sharp incline. We were heading straight for a full Navy Commander (0-5), who was crossing my path. Altogether, we yelled, "Look out!"

The Commander was able to see us just in time and instead of me slamming into him, he was able to reach out and help stop the runaway wheelchair at the last minute. I tell you, we laughed and laughed about that incident then and for many years to come. Those good memories are priceless, especially since Nettie and Frank both have since passed. They have been gone for over twenty-five years, but I still share good stories with Christina about her grandparents.

Unfortunately, there were other things that I learned about Sal that I would never have imagined. Close to a year into our marriage, Sal and I took a vacation to New York to see some of his family. Again, my lack of discernment was alive and well when it came to trusting what Sal told me about his past and what he was thinking in the present. As I was sitting there talking to his mom's sister, Aunt

Mary, she asked me if Sal was feeling OK after the scare that he had experienced the past April, while on a business trip to New York and had stopped by to see them. I had no idea what she was talking about.

I said, "You mean April, while I have been married to him?"

She answered, "Yes. Didn't Sal tell you?"

Sal and I had been married about four-and-a-half-months at the time, when this incident that I knew nothing about had occurred. The one while he was visiting his relatives in New York during a business trip. I was shocked to learn that he started having chest pains and couldn't breathe, so he was taken by ambulance to the hospital. Sal thought he was having a heart attack, but it turned out instead to be a full-on panic attack, so he was sent home without further treatment. I found out that he had other panic attacks before I met him. It was then that I started to suspect that he kept a lot of important things from me. There were other dark stories told to me by Sal's son, Josef (aka Joe or Joey) but I choose not to share them here because I don't have his permission to write about them. They remain Joey's stories to tell.

Another issue was that Sal was harboring a lot of anger about all sorts of things that would come out in unhealthy ways. For example, if he was angry at me, he would not tell me. As I mentioned before, I do not easily notice non-verbal cues unless I am specifically looking for them, like when I have been a counselor, so I thought everything was going along fine with our marriage. But I would soon find out he was unhappy with me, not by him telling me, but by him being passive-aggressive toward me or being more quiet than usual.

For instance, if we were at a wedding or doing something he knew I really enjoyed, he would purposely not participate, like dancing with me at special events. Dancing is one thing I really relish and since we had taken dance lessons to prepare for our wedding reception, we had had a lot of fun doing it and I had thought we would dance a lot more during our marriage. But if he was angry at me, I found out about it when we were at some event and I said, "Sal, let's dance," and he refused to do it the whole evening, thus he knew I would have a terrible time, which I did. Neither did he talk to me or tell me why he was treating me that way.

Another time, we planned a picnic for just the two of us on Point Loma, in San Diego, and I spent the morning baking chicken to take with us to eat while we would be enjoying the sunset. Just as we were about to leave, he suddenly refused to go, without telling me why, and I ended up going by myself. Because of incidents like these, I started to become very lonely. The worst thing was, even though we usually enjoyed a healthy sex life, he would withhold it on purpose, without telling me why, and when asked, he further manipulated me by refusing to explain his actions. It seemed like this was the way he was trying to control me and I started to resent it. In addition, my self-esteem took a dive. I was only in my thirties and I thought, "If this is going to be my life, lonely in my marriage, with no conversation or sex, I am going to have a very sorry life for the next forty or fifty years."

The sad part was that when we were alone and he wasn't angry, we would talk a lot more. His natural demeanor was quiet more when he was in a group or he didn't know the people we were with well. Other times when we were alone or with close friends, he could be a delight to be with. So, I know that had he not had those anger issues, I could have been happy with a quieter husband because he was very intelligent and we would talk about a lot of things. Unfortunately, I realized too late that his brand of quietness (which was not only his demeanor, but a way of purposely withholding information) was hard to deal with because of the manipulation.

In addition, Sal's deceitfulness did not help our trust issues either, as evidenced by his not telling me he was sent to the hospital, when he was on that business trip to New York. And since I do not always pick up on cues, due to my having ADHD, I felt blind-sided, when I was finally told about his anger. My step-son, Joey, did tell me things (after Sal and I had been divorced for a while) that happened in Sal's marriage to Joey's mom. Had I known those things beforehand, I would not have married him; however, that saga is not my story to tell, so I will not talk about it here. It just goes to show that either I did not question Sal enough about his past, or was not picking up the "whole picture cues" that I needed to understand before I married him. And I still wasn't picking up on them after we were married.

Sal started ordering me around and telling me what to do and he knew that that did not sit well with me because I was very independent; however, he did it anyway as another way to control me, instead of telling me how he felt. Case in point: we had a newly built house in Poway, CA near San Diego that was landscaped, but it needed some tending. He usually did the yard work while I did the housework. One time, Sal went on a business trip and he indicated to me that he would do the yard, when he got home. At that time, I suggested that we could hire someone so he didn't have to worry about it while on his trip. He replied that he wanted to do it himself, even though I knew he did not have time.

After Sal left on the business trip, I was talking to the girl who helped clean our house about what needed to be done in the yard. She said her brother did that kind of work and needed a job, so I got his number and called him up to hire him. He came over within a few days and proceeded to pull the weeds and tidy up the landscaping. Her brother did a good job, but what I did not realize was that he pulled out one or two small shrubs that looked like weeds to both of us.

When Sal came home late at night after his business trip, he went outside and inspected the yard, even though it was dark. Sal obviously saw the two missing shrubs that looked to me like weeds. He came inside, woke me up yelling, and started pushing me around, shouting at me because of the changes in the yard. He was in fact throwing me around the room and hurting me, causing me to bruise. That was the first time I was really scared of him and I did not know what to do, so I ran into our nanny's bedroom to get away from him and asked if I could sleep there with her. She asked me what the banging was that she had just heard and I told her that it was me hitting the wall due to being repeatedly thrown into it by Sal.

Needless to say, Sal and I couldn't go on like that. I was so afraid of him, that I made him take the gun he had for protection in the house, outside and bring it to a mutual friend of ours, so I could feel safer, knowing it was gone. I asked for a divorce, but instead, he agreed to go to counseling, something I had been asking for several years. That led me in good conscience to feel obligated to try one more time; however, I think I was kidding myself that we could ever go back together because I did not trust him anymore and lost respect for who he was.

Even so, we had been getting along better after a few months of counseling, when a crucial event happened that changed my life forever. Not knowing what was soon to be in store for me, I changed duty stations, even though I was allowed to stay in the San Diego area for my next three-year tour. There were at least five Navy activities in the San Diego area, plus other places close by, at which a sailor could work that were not on a typical Navy base. I had already been in my job at Recruit Training Command for three years, so it was time to call the detailers (officers in Washington, D. C., who transfer sailors to a good position for one's job progression, when a tour is up). Detailers are kind of like personnel/human resources officers who help guide your career.

They found a good position for me at Naval Station San Diego (nick-named Naval Station Thirty-Second Street), where most of the surface ships on the west coast are located. On Thirty-Second Street, there was a small inspection team called DAPMA (Drug and Alcohol Program Management Activity) to which I was assigned. They performed inspections of drug and alcohol counseling centers like the one I used to direct at Miramar. The inspection teams reported to the main drug and alcohol program head for the whole Navy in Washington, D.C. The team's purpose was to ensure records, procedures and policies at all the Navy base counseling centers were done correctly and within regulations.

In the fall of 1988, I arrived at the DAPMA inspection team. It was a great place to work and our boss, Commander (CDR) Pete Sanders was a very capable leader, with a wonderful sense of humor. The small tight team was very sociable and consisted of about five Naval Officers and about the same amount of Civil Service personnel, who worked well together. Commander Sanders insisted we all get these Date Timers, with faux leather covers. It sounds old-fashioned in today's world, doesn't it? Since we traveled a lot domestically and overseas, we needed to be organized and keep track of the inspections and the traveling that we were required to do.

Obviously, these day planner beauties were the latest in organizational technology, since we did not have iPhones, electronic pads or any of that type of technology then. Being the ADHD person that I was, even though I didn't know it yet, I resisted at first, but came to love having the planner and used it until I eventually got my first i-Phone in the twenty-tens. For a person with ADHD, it was a life-saver. All these little strategies to organize myself, along with the Navy's own intrinsic organizational structure were very essential to my success as a Naval Officer and leader.

While at DAPMA, I became very close friends with a GS-7 (General Schedule Seven) Civil Service employee named Karen

Perry (now Foster). Karen and I just clicked and since we met thirty-three years ago, she has been my champion, confidante and wise counselor through all the ups and downs in my life and I have been the same for her. Commander Pete Sanders also ensured all of us got to know each other well on the team. He did this by planning team-building activities we could do during lunch, while in San Diego or on travel in another city, or after hours that really made the team cohesive. At the time, I was traveling more than I ever had in my Navy career (about twice a month all over the U.S. and Europe), so I had to get a nanny for two-year-old Christina.

In the fall of 1989, I was due to travel with my boss, CDR Pete Sanders to Europe for a big conference in Bavaria, Germany; however, he was going to soon be retiring in January of 1990. The new DAPMA boss, Commander John Wilson had just arrived four months early to take CDR Pete's place, so CDR Pete thought it would make more sense for the new guy to accompany me to Europe, instead of Pete, in order to introduce him to all the inspection sites there. He told John something like this, "Take Kathleen, she knows everything about this operation and you will get great experience for your assignment as the new leader of DAPMA. I don't need to go, since I am retiring when you take over." As the European site inspector, it made sense for me to go too.

According to the plan proposed by Pete Sanders, John Wilson and I proceeded to go to Bavaria, Germany together. I had been getting to know CDR John better for the last two months, since he had arrived early to take CDR Pete's job. When John arrived at DAPMA, he asked me to carpool with him, since we lived close to each other. Funds were tight for both our families and we needed to save money and share the pain of driving in San Diego traffic, which was getting more congested every day. Before we left for Europe, I had gotten to know him better because we had been already carpooling together for two months. When we left for Germany, I had no idea how my life was about to shift. Little did I know the world was about to change too on my November 1989 trip to Germany, as the Berlin Wall came down while we were there (I never seem to do anything in a small way).

Arriving in Europe by plane, we then had to drive to the Armed Forces Hotel in Bavaria, Germany which took many hours, so we got to know each other even better through our long conversations in the rental car. Leadership Lesson Number One: If you are married, don't spend hours talking about personal things, when you don't want to have an inappropriate relationship with a co-worker of the opposite sex, especially if it is your boss.

On the way to the hotel, after driving long hours through picture-postcard countryside, dotted with Swiss chalets, we stopped in Innsbruck, Austria to go up to see the highest peak of the Austrian Alps. Snow-covered mountains, the sun shining against a blue sky, the view near where Julie Andrews was filmed singing "The Sound of Music" were all unforgettable and unfortunately, it was quite romantic. As we boarded the cable car to come down off the mountain, it was really crowded, so we were crammed in together, with John standing behind me. You know when you hit a moment where you could have made the right choice, but you ignore your instincts to get away? Well, it happened to me then.

Pressed behind me on the tram car, John said, "Don't worry, I won't do anything improper up here."

At that crucial moment, I could have responded with an, "OK," and would have been done with it. But no, I suggestively responded with, "It's not YOU I am worried about."

Well of course, that changed everything, and the next day we started an affair. There is no excuse for having an affair on your spouse, but looking back, I could have avoided the whole sordid deal if I had just been aware of how vulnerable I was to a man's interest, attraction and kindness to me at a time in my marriage when Sal and I were teetering on the edge.

John made me feel valuable professionally and personally, something that had been lacking for a long time in my marriage. Even though our few months of counseling sessions before I left for Germany had improved communication between Sal and me, our marriage was still in bad shape due to Sal's physical and emotional abuse towards me for the many months leading up to this trip to Europe. I can't say I never provoked Sal, but nobody deserves abuse, *ever.* When John and I went to Europe, I think I had already emotionally left the marriage, even though I hadn't yet admitted it to myself.

Later, it was clear to me that if I, the "girl next door" could have an affair, anyone could if they put themselves in the right circumstances of vulnerability. Long afterwards, I had a close friend argue with me about this point. She was married, yet getting dangerously close to a man she was taking night classes with. I told her she needed to cool it with this guy, like stop meeting alone for lunches and telling him intimate things about herself. She told me an affair could never happen to her because she knew better and that "she wasn't like that." Well, a few months later, it happened to her and she had to eat crow by admitting to me that she had had an affair with her night school classmate, even though she was still married to someone else. Since then, I have heeded my own advice and have never allowed myself to be in such a vulnerable and unwise situation again.

Going back to my story, a few months after John and I returned from our European trip, our office had a government holiday. Since we were unwisely continuing our affair after we had come home, we decided to make up an excuse for our spouses and meet for coffee nearby on our day off. What we did not know was that our spouses were starting to suspect the affair. When I left to meet John that day, Sal got a call from John's wife. She had been going through John's briefcase and had found a couple of romantic love cards from me.

When I arrived at the coffee shop, John rushed up to me and told me that I had better get home right away. Apparently, after already leaving his house to meet me, John had immediately gone back to get something and his wife told him then what she had found. That day, I was humiliated beyond description because Sal proceeded to take my personal phone book and call up all my family members and friends who lived all over the country to tell them I was having an affair on him.

As soon as I returned home from my short meeting with John, the calls started coming in from everywhere. For example, my mother called and asked what was going on, telling me Sal had reached out to tell her about my affair. My brother, Terry also phoned. I will never forget that they both still loved me and stood by me, even though I was the one who had had the affair. Then people, like my friend stationed in Hawaii and others all over the country called and I was on the phone for a couple of days afterwards answering for my marital "crime."

I started having nightmares because Sal kept coming to my room (I had moved out of the master bedroom), telling me that he was going to call up the head of the Navy's substance abuse program in Washington, D.C. (John's boss) to tell them about our affair. Sal knew he would put the fear of God into me by doing that because I could be sent up before a court martial for adultery and fraternization, an ancient law still on the military books.

Eventually, Sal stopped threatening me with going to the authorities to get me into trouble because he knew if I was given a court martial, I could lose my job and have no money or retirement check to help support our daughter. By this time, I had asked Sal again for a divorce. Moreover, John's wife took matters into her own hands to humiliate both her husband, John and me, so the whole local DAPMA office heard about the incident. Even more humiliating was that John's wife came to work with him every day and sat in his office the whole eight hours, so she could make sure John and I were not communicating any longer.

With good reason, John's wife wanted me transferred out of there, so John called the detailers to find me another job. I did not complain or argue because I knew it was required to diffuse the situation and kept me from being sent over for a court martial. Also, one of my good girlfriends in the Navy happened to know the detailers well in Washington D.C. who were in charge of getting me a new job. They told her that the female Admiral in charge of our section of the Navy knew all about the affair and since I was the junior person in the illegal liaison, I would be allowed to transfer and not overtly punished. The military is traditionally harder on the senior person of the affair because the senior person has undue influence over the junior person's career. Unfortunately, this time it didn't work that way; I was the one who would have to move and it was my career that was permanently damaged by this.

John was allowed to stay in my beloved San Diego, where all the friends and colleagues I had cultivated there for nine years, like Karen P., still lived. A few years later, when my name came up for advancement, the same female Admiral from my old outfit was now in charge of the promotion board in Washington D.C. All she had to do was put my record aside without explanation and it would never be considered for promotion and apparently that is actually what happened. From then on, I knew that I would never be promoted again.

Knowing about my lack of promotion possibilities caused me humiliation again later, when at other jobs I was given, the Commanding Officers told me what a good officer I was and they just could not understand why I wasn't promoted to the next level, Commander (O-5). It was out of reach for me and this was a hard pill to swallow. So, I did not tell them the reasons, but I knew *why* and it hurt. Sadly, I knew I had done it to myself and John was close to retirement, so he probably wasn't going to be promoted again anyway. What seemed unfair, was that John was allowed to stay in his job, in the place I loved and I would have to leave my position one year before my tour was supposed to end. It was a job I adored and in which I had done very well.

After having spent nine years working in the San Diego area, I had made some really good friends, so it was painful to leave. When I told my best friend there, Karen Perry that I was transferring up to the San Francisco area in 1990 because of the affair, she was devastated and started to cry. The good news is that she stuck by me, not critiquing me harshly because of my lapse in judgment by having an affair. I am blessed to still have her as a very close friend to this day.

From the incidents I outlined above, I have learned an important lesson. Take care of business close to when it is happening, like: make the necessary changes, apologize, go to counseling or whatever you have to do to handle things in a more mature manner than I did at the end of my marriage to Sal. I had agreed to go to counseling, even though I was not honest with myself that my heart really wasn't in it anymore. Because of that, I was vulnerable when John came along, offering me a way of not facing my misery. I should have either given it my all during therapy for Sal and I to stay together or made a clean break by asking for a divorce right then. By going to Europe with my new boss, someone I could see being attracted to, I put myself in a very bad position, given the way things were going in my marriage.

When I finally left the marriage, Sal gave me a letter, which I refused to read right away because I was afraid it would torture my mind about divorcing him and I was truly through. Reading it later, I still believe it wouldn't have changed my mind because instead, it made me angrier. In the letter, he admitted that he had really done all those things I talked about on purpose to hurt me, like: withholding sex, not dancing with me at events, not being kind to me or not telling me what was really on his mind when I asked. In the letter, he told me that what I told him about his despicable actions in our marriage was true. He apologized for his other actions too and wanted me to take him back.

Unfortunately for him, I had already figured out that he had purposely tried to hurt me with his behavior, so even when he gave me the letter, I would not have wanted to get back together. The hurt and the anger was just too far gone. Not only that, before I started the affair with John, I had felt worthless for being rejected in bed by my husband all the time and not being told the truth about why Sal was always so angry, even though I begged him to. Of course, I blamed myself for not being good enough to be cherished both in the bedroom and everywhere else. My sin of having an affair while still married was despicable too, so I had trouble forgiving myself for it.

Sadly, I know there was a piece of me who got just a little satisfaction when Sal was hurt by my affair. I think affairs are often about power, and during my affair with John, I think there was some of that going on there for me. I wanted to hurt Sal, like he hurt me. Not initially, but as it went along, I found myself glad that he finally felt some hurt and rejection too. It helped that I went back to counseling to figure out why the affair happened and how I could avoid this kind of mistake in the future. A year or more after we were divorced, I sent him a letter making amends for my part in things because I was not proud of how I acted during the whole ending of our marriage.

He called me up and said, "I don't understand, Kathleen, what do you want me to say to this?"

I answered, "Sal, I just wanted to say that I recognize my part in our breakup and am very sorry for all of it."

My apology letter seemed to give us both peace. I am glad for it because I was able to forgive him and I think he forgave me too. I do not know for sure how he felt, all I know is after that, we got along better while coordinating Christina's visits, vacations, school work and whatever good parents are supposed to do.

One thing I had done that I had promised to myself, was to never say anything derogatory about Sal in front of the kids. I never said a bad word about him in front of Christina, during and after our divorce until his third wife started bad-mouthing me to Christina, and she didn't even know me. I had stuck to my vow from when we divorced, (Christina was three years old and Joey and Lisa were teens) until Christina was about ten years old, when I finally felt that I had to defend myself. Christina had just visited her dad and his third wife in another state. As soon as Christina came home from this trip, she said, "Mom, Daddy and Sue (not her real name) told me you and Daddy broke up because you had an affair with your Commander. Is that true?"

I am not sure she even knew what an affair was, but how inappropriate of Sal and his wife to tell that to our little girl at her young age. I had refrained from telling his kids about his abuse toward me or his affair during his first marriage and now I had to explain to Christina, something she was too young to know yet, *if ever*.

I did not tell her that Sal physically abused me, but rather how unhappy I was and that having a relationship with my Commander was wrong and I shouldn't have done it. I told her that I had already apologized in a letter to Sal for doing that. Mutual friends of Sal and his ex-wife, Linda told me later that his new wife had been going around asking them how they could allow their kids to be around me, a deleterious person; after all, I had an affair on Sal. Maybe, she thought I had "cooties" too.

Even now, to everyone who does not know the whole tragic tale, according to Sal, I am the *only* one responsible for our divorce because of my affair, <u>period</u>, end of story. When Sal phoned all the people in my personal phone book and they started calling me, I felt like I had a big red "A" printed on my shirt for "Adulteress" like the heroine, Hester did in the classic public domain book by Nathaniel Hawthorne, *The Scarlet Letter,* as summarized in SparkNotes: "She will not reveal her lover's identity, however, and the scarlet letter, along with her public shaming, is her punishment for her sin and her secrecy. On this day Hester is led to the town scaffold and harangued by the town fathers."[78]

The Scarlet Letter quote says it all. I felt publicly shamed. John Bradshaw, a psychologist and author of the book, *Healing the Shame That Binds You*[79] explains how shame works: "When we are exposed without any way to protect ourselves, we feel the pain of shame: If we are continually overexposed, shame becomes toxic." It becomes toxic, whether it is intended or not.

Earlier, I told "The Cookie Story" about me at five years old, being turned away from a group of kids playing a game in a friend's house. The mom felt sorry for me because she had to turn me away, so she gave me a fresh-baked cookie to make me feel better. What I was feeling bad about was caused by shame that I was not good enough to be let into the house to play with the other kids. That is how young children interpret events like that because they only understand that they can't play with the others, not getting that the mom didn't want too many kids in the house at one time, even though there wasn't anything wrong with the kid (me) that the mom turned away. But as a little kid, I saw the incident as a confirmation that there WAS something wrong with me. This is the first instance of shame that I can remember in my life and because of the cookie given to soothe my feelings, I developed a life-long tendency to soothe hurt feelings with food.

Developing a toxic shame within myself was caused by many exposures to being shamed. When my mom was screaming at me all the time in childhood and I was told later by my next-door neighbor Lorraine, that she and her family heard it, it became an exposure. When people called me, "Motor Mouth" in college in front of all the students who were changing classes, it was another exposure. When John Wilson's wife came to sit in our office all day until I was transferred and everyone there knew why, it caused another exposure. When Sal found my phone book and called all my friends to tell them about my affair, I had more exposures and these are only some of the examples. But all the toxic shame exposures added up and after a while, I learned to operate out of that damaging place.

That detrimental part of me is where all my trouble with self-esteem began. My shame is telling me, not only that I might have made a mistake, but that I AM the mistake, so I lose confidence, even though I may be very competent. And since my ADHD made me impulsive, then I could not predict if I would say or do the wrong thing or when, so my exposure to shame reached toxic levels over the years, for which I lost self-esteem, etc., etc....

Not knowing I had ADHD yet; I didn't understand this injurious cycle that often got me into trouble. Moreover, for over twenty years, I tried to soothe myself with my own medication—the cookie or other food. And then when I inevitably gained weight, I felt another unearthing of my "shame place" to add to the toxicity. Thank God for author John Bradshaw and other experts, ADHD therapy and medication, to which I was finally introduced around the age of forty.

Therapy helps someone like me untangle all these overlapping and interacting factors that caused my unhealthy ways. Through all the pain, I learned unhealthy coping mechanisms like denial, defensiveness, overeating, overworking or being compulsive about word and deed, which seemed to help me manage when I was in pain. But that type of coping is deleterious and definitely wouldn't work for me now as a healthier individual. Through years of therapy, attending recovery conferences and voracious reading of books by people like John Bradshaw, Harville Hendrix and Father Joseph Martin, I developed good coping skills to add to my toolkit. Some of them are: talking to a friend, crying when I need to, admitting to my errors and even laughing sometimes when I make a mistake, like rolling my eyes and saying, "ADHD at its finest!"

After the shock of dealing with the guilt created by my affair and subsequent shaming through Sal getting a hold of my phone book, things calmed down, even though we went to court one more time for child support issues. However, I also took responsibility for my part in that whole end-of-marriage-scenario, without being as hard on Sal as I could have been when forced to explain the unexplainable to our daughter.

All in all, my daughter didn't seem to love me any less and has turned out to be a mature, lovely lady at the age of thirty-three, as I write this chapter. I have told Christina that I am sorry for my part in things about that situation and since then, whenever we have had conflict, I would try to make sure I say I am sorry and then try to improve. Therapy and medication have helped me to be a better mother too; however, there was some more unhealthiness to come before I can tell you what besides, medication and therapy, helped me turn my toxic ways around. Bear with me, there is a happy ending, with me finally finding my wants and needs within reach, but I must go through this next part first.

(Left) Admiral Mack Gaston, Commander, Naval Training Center, Great Lakes, IL (Wikimedia Commons) [80]

(Right) Admiral Jeremy M. Boorda, Chief of Naval Operations (Wikimedia Commons)[81]

(Below) US Navy DT-38A at U.S. Navy Fighter Weapons School (Top Gun), Photo from Wikimedia commons [82]

Kathleen working at her desk.

(Below) DAPMA staff— Kathleen, front row, far left, Karen P. is second row middle right, 1990

Kathleen and Christina, 1989

Karen P. and Kathleen in Sand Diego, late 1980s

(Right) Kathleen, Karen P. and CDR Sanders, OIC, DAPMA

Kathleen O'Brien Iverson

Grandpa Dewey Robinson,
Father of Elaine.

Lisa, 7 yrs. old and
Joey, 11 yrs. old

Kathleen with Linda,
mother of Joey & Lisa

Kathleen with bird on her
shoulder & Christina, 1989

Kathleen with Lisa's Cabbage
Patch birthday gift.

(Left)
Frank and Nettie
Causarano, Sal's
parents

Antoinette & Frank Causarano.
July 9, 1944

Elaine Robinson & Tom O'Brien's wedding, 11/24/1951

Joey, Lisa, Kathleen with Sal and
Christina in his lap, 1989

212

Chapter 24: *The Marriage-Go-Round Help Me!*

Third time's a charm until it's not!

— Kathleen O'Brien Iverson

This memoir is getting harder to write by the chapter. I had forgotten a lot of the difficult events that happened in my story. Some of my friends and relatives will be surprised when they read about what happened at this time of my life because for me, this upcoming story is a hard one to tell, especially after all I had been going through up to this point, so I haven't shared it with a lot of the people in my life. People reading this may be thinking, "When is this girl ever going to learn? Is she a glutton for punishment?" Again, my ADHD and my related lack of discernment and ADHD impulsivity were the culprits.

Sometimes I think of this upcoming episode in my life and even though I have had more than thirty-five years of therapy and medication, I still sometimes have shame come up as my go-to feeling. Honestly, I am sharing everything in this book, especially this chapter because I hope someone will read it and feel that they are just like me or going through many of the same things that I have talked about or going to talk about below. If someone else feels they are not alone and can get comfort and help after identifying with my story, writing it, however painful, is worth it. Here goes.

In the prologue of this book, I outlined an episode in my life about how I longed for a blue sweater I saw hanging in a window in a store, but told my boyfriend I didn't think I deserved it, especially because it was so expensive. Well, that story could be placed at the beginning of this chapter instead of the prologue because the time period is when this chapter starts. The boyfriend in question in the prologue is named Ian Brady and he has a starring role in this drama.

It all began when I moved to the San Francisco Bay area in late 1990. If you remember from the last chapter, I was required to leave the job and the people I loved in San Diego, due to one of my bad decisions (the affair). Bad decision-making seems to be a gift in my life that just keeps giving. At least by moving to the San Francisco Bay area where I knew no one, I could start fresh.

My new job entailed being the Director of Surface Missile Systems (SMS) school at Mare Island, California. I arrived there as a Lieutenant Commander (LCDR 0-4) (equivalent to a Major in the Army, Air Force or Marines), a rank I attained just before meeting John. Unfortunately, because of that affair, I still realized that no matter what I did, I would never be promoted again. Even so, I still did my best as Director of a large department (about 300 Sailors), responsible for training those who operate and maintain missile systems on ships. It was a job I really enjoyed.

Arriving in August, 1990 at the Naval Shipyard, Mare Island, I was struck by all the buildings (about five) that my school encompassed. Impressed by all the missile system paraphernalia that I saw mounted on top of those buildings; I was eager to get started in my new position. It sounds crazy that someone like me, who never at this point was allowed to be stationed on a ship because women were still barred from combat assignments, was given such an important assignment related to ships' systems.

For this new job, at Mare Island, I would be in charge of training for these systems and the staff and students to go with them; When looked at more closely, one can see it makes sense. I have a Navy sub-specialty in the Management, Education and Training field, so I know how to run a technical school, what the main components should be, what kind of manuals should be present for reference, and how a training department should be set up. With that background, the Navy felt I would be qualified to start this assignment and would learn the ins and outs as I went along.

Those enlisted instructors who would work for me on Mare Island, were the cream of the crop in their field—Radar and Missile Systems on surface ships and would be doing the actual training. Basically, someone in my position is like a school principal, responsible for ensuring an excellent curriculum is being written and good instruction is being delivered. That must be done within the timeframe set for the students completing the courses under my purview. With all my educational experience inside the Navy and out, I was excited, confident, and felt that I could make a difference there.

The Chiefs (like blue-collar top supervisors) would in reality, run the school under the Master (E-9) and Senior (E-8) Chiefs (see Index A, pp. 307-308) who would be overseeing and administrating the department. Those Master and Senior Chiefs in turn, worked directly for me and were part of my planning and advisory team. They not only had the technical knowledge because they had done the job of operating and maintaining these systems on ships, but also, they worked their way up to Chief Petty Officer (E-7 through E-9), highly respected enlisted ranks in the Navy (sort of like foremen in the civilian world).

Most people know that the Chiefs are the ones who really run the Navy. Here are their ranks in ascending order: Chief (E-7), Senior Chief (E-8), and Master Chief (E-9). If there are more than one E-9, the senior E-9 is the Master Chief of the department, school or command and everyone else takes orders from him except the top Officer in Charge, in this case: me. I say, "him," not "her" because at that time there were no women in the Surface Missile System (SMS) field. Women were still not allowed to go to sea and those working or going to school in this field were only in sea-going pay grades. I was the only woman who worked in my department.

When I arrived at Mare Island, I first got what I call "the speech" from the senior people already there who would work for me (I have had this speech given to me more than once at different duty stations). It goes something like this: "Welcome, Commander. My name is Master Chief Granger. I have never worked for a woman before, so I am not sure how things are going to go, but I am at your service. What do you want me to know about how you run things?"

At first, I suspected this was just lip service to impress the new boss; I would respond, "Well, Master Chief, it is simple. I expect you to do your job by keeping me informed of the important issues, like budget, need for supplies, equipment that is broken down, need for parts, required training and problems with instruction, students, administration, curriculum and security. You may run the department and part of that means supervising and training the junior Chiefs and Petty Officers (E-4 through E-6), so that when they leave here, they are ready to pass exams as needed and to take over a higher-level job on a ship when the time comes. You wouldn't be here if you hadn't already proved yourself, so I will only say once that if you don't do your job or keep me informed about the important things, I will be on you like white on rice. Otherwise have at it. I will trust you to run things as you see fit within the Command and Department Directives, the Training Plan and the Security Manual. And I will back you up if you don't blind-side me. Is that understood?"

Don't I sound like I have a lot of confidence in the "speech" situation above, after I have been complaining about my lack of confidence in this memoir *ad nauseam* (loosely translated in Latin as: until I throw up)? Seems contradictory, but it isn't. By this time in my career because of the Navy's superb organization and instruction throughout my tenure, I knew what was expected of me and the sailors who worked for me. I also had had special training in Human Resources Management, (a Master's degree) which includes the subjects of Education and Training, along with a graduate course in Workforce Education. In addition, before I entered the Navy, I have had experience as a teacher and in writing curriculum development, not to mention the great leadership training inside and outside of the Navy that I have been privileged to attend.

The Navy did wonders for my confidence, even with my set-backs, like being transferred early from my last job because of my affair. The structure of the Navy is perfect for ADHD because you hardly know you have the affliction, when you can operate so easily in the military. Even though I knew I would never be promoted again because of what happened with John Wilson in San Diego, I knew what I was doing in my specialty (as a leader of technical schools) and it was noticed by my bosses. In fact, the most self-confidence I have ever experienced, was as Director or Officer-in-Charge of technical schools in the Navy. Anyway, it was while I was having these contradictory feelings that I took over as Director, Combat Systems School at Mare Island, CA.

In order to keep my personal life healthy, I found a therapist named Mark right away to support me in my working through what happened in my last workplace with John and my new endeavor at Mare Island. My new therapist also supported me in being a single parent with no family around like I had in San Diego to share the load. To help me continue to grow as a person, I also started going to Al-Anon meetings in Benicia, CA, a small town near the base.

Not knowing that I had ADHD yet (Support for that would come a few years later, when I was officially diagnosed), I embarked on the road to self-improvement with the only tools I had at the time such as: the great structure in the Navy, my new therapist, Mark, and AL-Anon meetings (for friends and family of alcoholics and addicts to help them cope with the addict in their lives). These tools were getting me through life.

Speaking of AL-Anon meetings, I met one of my very best friends there named Bonnie F. She is still a close friend to this day and last year, I spent some time with her in California and earlier this year, she spent time with me in Florida while I worked on this book.

During my tour at Mare Island, which happened to be the oldest U.S. West Coast base in the Navy, I was fascinated with its history. The main command headquarters building (H-1) used to be a hospital during the Civil War and there were rumors that there were ghosts up on the third floor. I never encountered those types of phenomena, but I did learn that Abraham Lincoln had signed the Construction Bill for that building. In addition, going through the Mare Island base cemetery, I noticed that there were mostly Civil War graves interred in the place, so it gave me a sense of the reality of death and war during that period.

Anyway, on Mare Island, I really started healing from the fiasco with John because I felt Christina and I were in a safe cocoon there. The base was an island and the only ways on or off were boats or the two bridges, so it felt protective to me as a single parent. Christina, three years old, and I had a lot of fun when I strapped her onto the back of my bike in her special seat and we would explore the historical base together, riding up and down the hilly isle.

Because Mare Island is surrounded by water, it pretty much was self-contained, with our own living quarters, a quaint chapel down the street with original Tiffany-made windows, servant's quarters for officer housing (a relic of the past because *we* didn't have servants), a McDonald's restaurant and other eateries, a base movie theatre, a gym, library, recreational facilities, horseback riding (sailors boarded and fed their own horses there) and many other activities. These facilities are not unlike other full-service bases, but at Mare Island we were somewhat isolated, so they were used a lot more by the military residents than in bigger bases closer to metropolitan areas.

Moreover, all events like trick-or-treating, dances, Christmas tree-lighting at the base Commander's house and other activities were much better attended than on bases where people mostly went home off base at night. I lived in what was called Lieutenant Commander Row; my residence was a large half of a duplex built in the nineteen-forties, with hardwood floors, three bedrooms and two and a half baths, a detached two-car garage and a fenced-in large yard with swings for Christina. Unfortunately, after my tour ended, in 1993, the base was slated for redevelopment because the Navy moved away, as part of the Base Realignment Committee directed by Congress.

Not long ago, when I visited Bonnie F., we went over to Mare Island to see how the building of new civilian homes there was going. It had not been going very well, even though the base had officially closed more than twenty-three years ago. Whoever owns it now is letting most of the historic structures deteriorate and it is a shame because some of the old ten-thousand-square-feet grand senior officer houses are just looking shabby. I hate to see waste like that. Many were beautiful, stately and as old as the base itself that was built in 1853 and closed in 1995. During my time there, the base was still operating as a military complex; therefore, the senior officers who stayed in those large historical mansions had to sign for beautiful antiques that came with the house. My old duplex on the main drag, Cedar Avenue is still standing, but they changed the street name and it looks like they are using my old house for offices. They don't build them like they used to. How sad.

In the fall of 1990, I met Ian Brady through a personal ad in the newspaper. At that time, we did not have computer ads or dating services that I knew of. In fact, I got my first personal computer at Mare Island, delivered by my new boss, the Executive Officer (XO), second in command, when he found out I did not have one of my own. He had asked me if I had received his email and I told him I didn't have a computer, so he had one sent over the next day.

The new XO was ahead of us with technology because most of us were not using our own personal computers at work yet. In the eighties and early nineties, computers were mostly used by the secretaries to type letters that we wrote in long-hand or to type up the Command Directives and Manuals. I had recently taken computer classes and had one at home, but I was not used to using it for everything like we do today. In fact, the average person used the computer for word processing and email only. The Web was hardly developed at that time, being that it was only invented the year before in 1989 by British Scientist, Tim Berners-Lee.[83] When I arrived in 1990, we used a Local Area Network (LAN) on base for communication until the internet (called the Web or Net) was set up.

I liked Mr. Brady's personal ad in the newspaper because we seemed to have the same interests; he was Irish-American like me, mature (being seven years my senior), and enjoyed conversation, coffee shops, theatre, music and traveling. Ian had his own business as an insurance agent and lived in the town of Berkeley Hills, which was a thirty-three-minute drive from the base. We exchanged pictures through mail, and although I didn't find him gorgeous, Ian was attractive enough to make me want to meet him.

When I eventually saw Ian Brady in person on our first date, he looked about ten years older than he was, so I was a little concerned, since I really looked about ten years younger than I was. In fact, when we were out on dates or met each other's friends, they first thought I was his daughter. In reality, I was thirty-eight years old and he was close to forty-six. Long-time divorced, Ian had two grown girls that lived on the East Coast with their own families, including Ian's grandchildren. Even so, he had a great personality and we were able to talk about almost everything, so I wanted to know him better.

Moreover, Ian was wonderful with my three-year-old daughter and enjoyed taking her with us on outings. I was happy that he was truly spiritual, belonging to a well-known church in downtown San Francisco where many seemed to know him. Known for its charismatic leader, whom Ian knew well, and for feeding the poor and tending to the drunks and addicts downtown, the church was often acknowledged for helping others. Ian told me he was a recovering alcoholic, with about fifteen years of sobriety and he took me to a few of his Alcoholics Anonymous (A.A.) meetings. Also, we were both interested in helping others stay sober. Most of his friends were from church and the A.A. meetings and I fit in well with them because of my Al-Anon meeting attendance.

Because of these similar interests, I thought that I had finally found "the One" and so I fell hard for Ian and thought I had died and gone to heaven. Not only that, but he made a good living and owned a gorgeous upscale house overlooking the hills of Berkeley and Oakland. Generous with his resources, Ian took Christina and me everywhere we hadn't been to yet in the area. With him, I went to the Black and White Ball, (a formal event where everyone wears either black or white), the San Francisco Opera, Chinatown, wonderful area restaurants and anywhere you could think of. We took Christina with us to the zoo, on miniature train rides, playgrounds and anywhere kids were happy. Christina loved him and even called him a pet name, "EE-nee," for Ian.

After about nine months of dating, Ian asked me to marry him by giving me a very expensive almost two-carat diamond engagement ring. I had already met his older girls and we seemed to all like each other. Ian was also always working on himself by going to his meetings, seeing a personal psychotherapist and sponsoring other recovering alcoholics. All those actions added up to someone I could respect and trust to always be working a program of improvement with good insight because of his fifteen years of continuous sobriety and his commitment to working the Twelve Steps of continuous self-study, (an important part of A.A. that helps the Alcoholic stay sober).

Accordingly, I brought Ian home to Chicago for Christmas and my mom and my brother Terry really liked him, although my brother Mike was living in Indianapolis at the time, so they hadn't met yet. But since like Ian, Mike was a recovering alcoholic, I think they would have really liked each other. Also, my dad, who had died three years earlier, would have liked Ian too. After all, they were both one-hundred percent Irish, with a wee bit of the blarney in them.

Anyway, our wedding date was set for September 1, 1991. We decided to have the wedding and ceremony at Ian's house in the Berkeley Hills, with stunning mountain views. Bonnie and Karen and my friends from Al-Anon, my brother Terry and his then-girlfriend, Stacy (now his wife) as well as my coworkers from Mare Island were in attendance. My mom walked me down the aisle and I thought I had truly made the best marriage choice this time. The decision to marry Ian was based on his good character, which I truly admired and sound reflection on what I wanted and needed in a man and step-father for Christina. I was not only excited about this marriage, but I felt at peace with the decision to be with this man for the rest of my life, believing that this time, the third time, I had done it right.

What else could I have done to ensure he was the right guy for Christina and me? We dated one year, we spent a lot of time together as a couple as well as with Christina. Also, Ian and I had the same interests and values and to top it off, we were both involved in the Twelve Steps of A.A. and AL-Anon (See Index B, p. 311), which keeps one attuned to his/her own actions and feelings. The Twelve-Step programs are places where one is encouraged to talk to others in the program when having trouble and doubts. Ian and I were both practicing our respective programs and committed to continue working the Twelve Steps for the rest of our lives. Unbeknown to us, however; mental illness was lurking just under the surface, ready to play havoc with our plans and our future.

After the wedding, Ian and I left to go to Kauai, Hawaii for our honeymoon. We were there for a day or two, when Ian started to get antsy and seemed to want to spend time alone. He became critical of me and started saying that maybe we could have a "different kind" of marriage when we got home. He told me he needed a lot of alone time and was worried that if Christina and I moved into his house, like the plan called for as soon as we got home from the honeymoon, he would feel stifled and anxious. So, he started throwing out ideas, like he could buy us our own condo and all of us could live together on weekends at one of the houses. Or, we could still move into Ian's house, but he would expect Christina and me to go out every Saturday, so he could have the house to himself. I told him that I wanted to live under one roof, like most married people.

My new husband got restless and left the luxury resort we were staying at. Ian took the car and was gone for the whole day and I did not even know where he went. I was alone on my honeymoon, with no transportation and having a pity party. I felt desperate, so I called Bonnie F. at home to tell her what was going on and to get her advice. She happened to be in the middle of having a party at her house and had to take the call in another room. Bonnie said later that she will never forget that call and could not believe it was happening to me. I asked her to help me because I was on my honeymoon alone and did not know what to do. Moreover, Ian said he might go home early to Berkeley and leave me in Hawaii until the original week he had already paid for was done. I was not sure if he had left Hawaii already, but I couldn't stay in the room by myself.

Later, Ian came back with the car and left the room again, leaving me alone. Since I now had the rental car, I researched where the Twelve-Step meetings were held nearby and found my way there. When it came my turn to talk, I said to the group, "Help me, I am on Honeymoon from Hell!" That sure got their attention and they listened carefully to my story. Going to a meeting helped me not to have to go through this crisis alone, but obviously it did not fix my problem. I spent the week mostly alone in Kauai, which was heartbreaking, when looking at other honeymooning couples holding hands and kissing, while I was by myself.

I hardly saw Ian for the rest of the week we were in Hawaii because he stayed away. I asked God, why this relationship drama kept happening to me. I had gotten a lot of help where I thought I had understood what went wrong in my other marriages. Then I wondered if somehow, I was not worthy of having someone treat me well and love me for life like the relationship my parents and grandparents had. Needless to say, I wasn't feeling like the love-sick honeymooner, as Ian and I boarded the plane to come home.

For about a month, I went into a deep depression, living back on the base without my new husband. Sadly, the depression lasted a few years, but the worst part was during the first month after our trip. My staff was perplexed with my behavior and indicated later, when looking at me before I finally told them what had happened, it seemed that the lights were out and nobody was home. I was afraid to talk about it because not only was I humiliated, but I knew if I talked about it, I would start crying and was afraid I would never stop. I did not tell my staff or bosses anything at first because I was hoping Ian and I would still be able to work it out. The only time I cried in front of my staff or other Officers, was a few years later when my Admiral's wife died at the end of my career.

Ian and I agreed to meet with his therapist together to talk it out. During the session, when I told him that I wanted a real marriage, not one where we lived separately, he started to go into a catatonic-like state and fell into a fetal position on the floor. That is when his therapist called the ambulance. I visited him on the psych ward at the hospital for about a week, but nothing was settled yet. I was never told his exact diagnosis, but I surmised he had a break with reality. My therapist, Mark, warned me about trying to have a relationship with Ian after what happened, and our shared lawyer tried to get us back together again because she heard us both talking separately about how much we still loved each other. Even so, there was too much unhealthiness to weed through our problems.

After he got out of the hospital, Ian and I agreed that although we both still loved each other, the marriage was not going to work. I had not even moved all my stuff into his house yet and was still staying at my townhouse on the base. In addition, I didn't want to bring Christina, who was now four, into a relationship colored with mental illness that could affect her negatively for the rest of her life. I could have asked for an annulment because we never even lived together as a married couple, but that would mean I had to divulge Ian's mental breakdown and I could not do that to him. If it had become public it would have hurt his business and I would not do that. Ultimately, we had to go through a divorce.

Later, I learned that it was not uncommon for recovering alcoholics to have an underlying mental illness that doesn't show its ugly head until later, when a special stressor is present (like getting married, going to the psych ward or through a divorce). Since I had to get the few things I still had at Ian's house, Bonnie, brought her truck to help me move. Then, Ian and I awaited our divorce.

Consequently, for the next month, I went through the humiliation of giving back all the wedding presents, telling my colleagues and my family and everyone was sad for me, but very supportive. Thank God I had good colleagues, friends and family to keep me busy and give me emotional support. When Ian was stable enough after he got out of the hospital, we arranged to meet at the shopping mall parking garage by Macy's because I needed to give him back the wedding and engagement rings.

Ironically, on that very sad give-back-the-rings-day for me in 1991, it turned out to be a beautiful, warm, sunny, dry, mid-October day with a little breeze, when I hugged him goodbye and went back home to my duplex on the base. After having a sleepless night, the next morning I decided to clean out my drawers to keep me occupied, so I would not think about it so much. As I was cleaning, I turned on the radio around noon. I became concerned when I heard the announcer say that a fire had started near the Caldecott Tunnel on a ridge near Berkeley Hills, close to where Ian's house was located.

At first, there was a small fire, but because of the dry and breezy conditions, the fire spread rapidly. That fire was creeping so close to Ian's house, I was getting worried, so I started calling him to see if he was OK. There was no answer, so I talked to some of his friends, who said they did not know where he was and couldn't get a hold of him either. His friends said they would keep trying and would let me know if he was safe, when they finally contacted him. As the fire roared out of control all day and even jumped the Highway Twenty-four Freeway, spreading into Oakland, we were all very concerned.

Knowing Ian, I worried that he was trying to fight the fire himself by hosing down his roof, like many were doing to save their houses. Finally, by the end of the day, his friends had gotten a hold of him on his car phone. He had gone for a mindless long drive to clear his head and didn't even know about the fire, so they broke the news to him that his beloved house was destroyed. Indeed, he was now homeless and he would have to live in a hotel for the time being.

Here, I was trying to put our broken marriage behind me, but due to the T.V. and radio coverage, I could not get it off my mind. I called his secretary for news a few times, but Ian told her that if she still kept talking to me, he would fire her, so we broke off contact. Since I lost contact with Ian's secretary, I did not know what was happening with him regarding the fire. Sadly, I thought that my valuable engagement ring, still in its ornate box that I had given back to him the day before the fire, had probably burned up in the intense heat of the conflagration.

Indeed, Ian's whole street was destroyed and looked like a burned-out war zone, with only black-singed trees and chimneys still standing. I found out later that when Ian went to survey the damage, the only articles he found in the rubble of his home were a Buddha statue and my ring box, with the ring unharmed inside. Later, it was reported that three-thousand homes were lost and twenty-five people were killed during what was starting to be called, "The Firestorm" of 1991. It was the worse fire in California's modern history to date.

As a result of all the trauma, my therapist, Mark, suggested I go to this treatment program for depression that he put together with several of his therapist colleagues. These six or seven therapists designed the treatment to look like a vacation because it was set in Cabo San Lucas, Mexico at a resort. The advantage to the patient was that they could get the treatment they needed without having to check into the psychiatric ward of a hospital, which could have been a stigma on the patient's record. In the Navy, it would have been the final nail in the coffin of my career if they knew about it. I did not get diagnosed with ADHD until after I retired.

My Commanding Officer (CO) approved my leave papers for ten days of vacation time and I put down Cabo San Lucas as my destination, which was true, but he did not know I was going there for mental health reasons. It wasn't cheap, so I took all the money I had and paid for it out-of-pocket to keep from getting the Navy involved.

The treatment was held at a hotel, but consisted of mostly intense psychotherapeutic treatment, with therapists conducting daily group therapy in different hotel rooms and big group meetings where we participated in psychodrama and arranging other patients in sculpture-like formations that reflected relationships in our own families. Believe it or not, the ten-day intensive therapy was helpful in gaining insight, but obviously, I needed much more to help me come out of the abyss. The ten-day intensive therapy, along with my close relationship with Bonnie, helped me on the road to recovery.

Of course, as a supportive friend, I still had Karen, who lived in San Diego. In fact, she had come to San Francisco and Mare Island to be my maid-of-honor when I married Ian and she then took Christina back to San Diego to stay with Christina's grandmother, Antoinette, while I was on my honeymoon. Karen and Bonnie were also my faithful friends when things didn't work out with Ian and me.

Thank God for friends like Karen and Bonnie to be supportive and hold me up when I fall. I will never forget their love and kindness when all these horrible things happened in my life and I am grateful that they are still my close friends today, even though they both live in California and I now live across the country in Florida. Marriage in general seemed out of reach for me after three failed ones. Believe it or not, for the time being, I was OK with that and focused on raising Christina, and on my career to keep me going.

Christina, age 4,
Pre-school.

Kathleen and Christina in
Berkley, CA in 1991

Bonnie looking at the ruins from the 1991 Berkeley Hills Fire Storm, where Ian's house was destroyed in 1991.

Kathleen with friend, Karen Perry

(B) Kathleen standing in front of Bldg. H-1, on the left is her SMS Hdqrs. Bldg., Mare Island.

Christina 4 years old in Berkeley Hills, CA

Kathleen about to be dunked by one of her sailors at Mare Island Navy Relief Fundraiser, (see page 231, next chapter)

Bonnie F. visiting Kathleen in Chicago, IL

Chapter 25: *Back to the Midwest, Tally-Ho!*

Love is a fruit in season at all times,
and within reach of every hand.
— Mother Teresa[84]

In March, 1993 I was on Lake Shore Drive going north, having just driven through Chicago city proper, on my way home to the northern suburbs where I grew up. It was so gratifying to be coming home to the Chicago area after sixteen years away in the military. Coincidentally, the 1971 song "Lake Shore Drive," (where Oprah Winfrey lived in a penthouse for about twenty-five-years) by the group Aliotta Haynes and Jeremiah, was on the radio. I enjoyed singing along to the catchy lyrics.[85]

About forty-six miles farther north of Chicago's Lake Shore Drive, in Grayslake, IL was where I would eventually end up after leaving California five days earlier. I had already bought a new house when I came to the area a few months back on a house-hunting trip, allowed by the Navy when you have to change duty stations that require a move.

Grayslake was close to my new duty station, Naval Training Center (NTC), Great Lakes, IL, near Chicago.

Photo of Chicago Lake Shore Dr. https://en.wikipedia.org/wiki/Lake_ Shore Drive[86]

There, I would be taking over a large department to include a big Navy technical school called Combat Systems with eight-hundred people. As schools were added, I had as many as two thousand five hundred individuals under my authority. Again, it was an all-male operation, except for me and a female Navy Chaplain. I was told that I was the first woman to take the Officer-in-Charge job at Combat Systems School that anyone remembered in recent history.

The ratings (occupations) most prevalent in the school were Fire Controlmen, Electronics Technicians and Gunner's Mates consisting of several buildings with radar and launchers mounted on top. Their mission was similar to my last school and set up in a comparable way, but it was much bigger than the Surface Missile Systems School I had back in Mare Island.

My headquarters building was located on the bluffs along Lake Michigan, where we had a stunning view of the water. In the old days, sailors used to practice firing big ship's guns out into Lake Michigan, so that is why we were located so close to the water. The base at Great Lakes, had been around since 1911 and the construction bill for the training center was signed by none other than Teddy Roosevelt. At that time, there were three NTCs and I had been stationed on all of them during my career.

The first leader of the Navy Band stationed here was the renowned John Philip Sousa, so there was quite a lot of history on this base too. Sousa wrote many famous marches like "Stars and Stripes Forever." Wikipedia describes him as follows: "John Philip Sousa (/ˈsuːsə/; November 6, 1854 – March 6, 1932)[87] was an American and conductor of the late Romantic era known primarily for American military marches. Upon the outbreak of War World I, Sousa was awarded a wartime commission of lieutenant commander to lead the Naval Reserve Band in Illinois."

Most of the buildings in NTC Great Lakes[88] were attractive large red brick two-story rectangular structures. They lined a huge parade ground where I am sure Lieutenant Commander Sousa's group of sailors got a lot of practice playing instruments, while he drilled the Navy Band up and down Ross Field. My boss, Captain Chad Hickey was the Commanding Officer of Service School Command (SSC), and resided in a large semi-mansion there given to him for his three-year tour at Great Lakes.

All these senior officer houses were built not too long after the base was constructed in the early Twentieth Century and a lot of interesting history could be found in each one. Every senior officer's house came with a book describing who had lived there before. Some of them were well-known and I was really looking forward to getting my hands on a piece of that history, when I received an invitation for a soiree at Captain Hickey's residence.

At the party in Captain Hickey's house, I was able to thumb through the small book which told of Wallis Simpson living in that home with her first husband, a Naval officer in the early decades of the Twentieth Century. She had lived there way before she met the future King of England, who in 1936 abdicated the throne to marry her. Being a history buff and exploring both Mare Island and Great Lakes was such a treat. Finding these kinds of historical treasures were thrilling to me.

Built in 1854, Mare Island was the oldest Naval base on the West Coast and we were blessed to have a small Chapel there with windows designed by Tiffany. I was always uncovering interesting historical facts while stationed at those two duty stations. One interesting tidbit was that Naval Training Center (NTC), Great Lakes, built in 1911, was the first Naval base that accepted African-Americans for both enlisted and officer training.

One great history-making event I had as a staff member there in 1994, was when we celebrated the fiftieth anniversary of the graduation of the first African-American Officer Candidates called the "Golden Thirteen." They arrived at Great Lakes in 1944 and when they were tested at the end of their training, they had the highest scores ever achieved on the final comprehensive test, something that had never been seen before. By the time of this celebration, only eight out of the thirteen were still living. They attended, some with crutches or wheelchairs. One of the people that benefited from their pioneering Navy careers, was Admiral Mack Gaston, as guest speaker (see picture p. 210)[89]. He was the first black Commander of the Naval Training Center (CDR, NTC) and my boss.

The Navy was starting to change, by allowing women officers to be in charge of these technical schools, especially if they had a related sub-specialty (Management, Education, and Training) like I had. There are some comical incidents that happened at both Mare Island and Great Lakes, where I was the first woman the men who worked for me had ever had as a boss. Some of the funny things that came up due to my gender were priceless and I chuckle to myself about them, even to this day.

One time I was all hot under the collar about something and my most senior enlisted person, Master Chief Banning, who ran the school at Great Lakes as my right-hand person, wanted to calm me down away from the others in the office. So, he said, "Commander, put your cover on and follow me." In the Navy, we must wear our covers (hats) outside, so I put mine on and followed him out the front door.

When we got outside, Master Chief Banning, pointing to several parts of the structure our offices were in, said, "Now

Commander, do you see any mooring lines attached to this building?"

I shook my head, "No."

He asked, "Are we getting underway tomorrow?"

I replied, "No, Master Chief."

Then he looked at me smiling and said, "Then I think it would be a good idea for you to calm down."

At the end of our conversation, I could not help but calm down and then laughed at how he was playing me so well. That was so great about our working relationship. I had told him that I didn't want "Yes Men" working for me. I wanted to know the score, even if I had to make a different decision than what was suggested. He knew I respected his wise counsel, born of twenty-five plus years of experience as a Gunner's Mate, part of it on a gun boat in Vietnam, for which he was given a hard-won Purple Heart.

Another time, at Mare Island, the Chiefs challenged the Officers to a baseball game. Well, I am not athletic in that way. In my day, most of us women did not learn how to play ball games or at least play them well, so I told my assistant, Master Chief Pacelli that I didn't know what to do. I had enough Officers working for me, Lieutenants and Warrant Officers, to make a team, but I never really played softball much at all. So, what did the Master Chief do? He came over at lunch time a week before the game and asked me to go out on the field so he could teach me how to play better. I said, "Master Chief, I will be on the opposing team, why are you helping me?"

He said, with a chuckle, "Well, I don't want to be embarrassed in front of the other Chiefs (meaning embarrassed by my bad playing) because you are my boss."

He had a point, so I went along with it, but I knew my being on the team was going to embarrass both of us. In good fun, I let him train me, but it wasn't enough for me to look like I knew what I was doing. Of course, the Chiefs won the game and I was relieved it was over. I was thoroughly amazed when a few days later, the Officers and Chiefs that worked for me came to my office and presented me with a funny looking bat that was short and not regulation. They had engraved a brass nameplate with the date of the game and my name on it for being a good sport.

Once, when we had a fundraiser for the Mare Island Morale, Welfare and Recreation Fund, they asked me to participate. I laughed when I saw what they wanted me to do. The Chiefs had a mechanical contraption delivered that was called a "dunking machine" (see drawing on page 228) to be set up near the other game booths that they had gotten together for a small "fair" to raise money in our parking lot. I had to sit on the seat on top of a tank of water and the sailors who paid money for this "game" would be given a few tries to throw a ball to hit the backboard, which then would release the seat I was sitting on and I would tumble into the full-size tank of water, soaking me clean through.

This dunking activity raised a lot of money for the Morale, Welfare, and Recreation (MWR) Fund and was indeed popular because many sailors wanted the chance to "dunk" the Commander. Even though, I was technically a Lieutenant Commander (the rank just below full Commander—see page 308) it was proper to just call me "Commander," like a Rear Admiral is called just "Admiral," when being addressed in person. I must admit that being dunked in the water was fun and it did raise money and solidified my reputation as a team player and good sport and helped to develop respect for me as the boss.

Since these Chiefs rotate every two-to-three-years like I do, my assistants would be changed at least once during my tour. At Mare Island, I first had Master Chief Pacelli and then I had a Senior Chief Dietrick as my assistants, who oversaw the staff and the training mission. At Great Lakes, running the staff as my assistant was Master Chief Banning, who I mentioned above.

All three of them gave me the same speech (separately, in two different locations, Mare Island and then, Great Lakes) after they each had worked for me for at least a year. All three men told me separately, that they had changed their minds about working for a woman after having me as their boss. I asked, "How so?" All their answers were similar, so I will put it into one sentence.

"Well, Commander, you listen to us and you let us do our jobs."

They also told me that many of the officers they had before as their bosses were "ship drivers" (also called "black shoes"—Commissioned Officers stationed on surface ships). These ship drivers were described to me as micro-managers, who hovered over them and "...didn't let us do our jobs."

At Mare Island, there had been a Senior Chief Tucker working for me for six months when I first got there, who was not really cut out for the job of running the school, so I was getting a lot of side complaints from the Chiefs and the other Enlisted, who worked for him. However, I knew he had a love and affinity for work with computers. So, I asked him if he would like to transfer to the computer area on our base in a different building and he was delighted. It gave him a chance to shine in the area of his interest and expertise.

Trying to find creative solutions to difficult problems was a winning leadership strategy for me. I was not surprised that Senior Chief Tucker did very well at the new computer job I sent him to. That situation and how I handled it was mentioned by my Master and Senior Chief assistants, as one of the reasons they liked working for me better than a male ship driver. Both the Master and Senior Chiefs said that their old ship driver bosses would have just fired a guy, who wasn't up to snuff and sent him to any old job, whether he was good at it or not. I was delighted that a sticky situation like that could be handled without hard feelings. Who knew that my artistic background would be helpful in these types of jobs? I firmly believe my success was a direct result of finding creative solutions to difficult problems.

Other creative solutions were available, at Great Lakes, as well as, at Mare Island. In both places, there was not a woman's head (restroom) to be found close to my office, since previously they were all male operations. The woman's head was either way up on the second deck (floor), or way down at the end or somewhere else remote in my building. This is where I had to be inventive.

Women's facilities were not needed, since few women worked in a technical school that trained combatant sailors (unless they were the Director/Administrator or the Chaplain, which was rare) until after 1994. That is when Congress enacted the repeal of the Combat

Exclusion Law. I happened to have two back-to-back jobs training the same type of combatant ratings (jobs), so I encountered working mostly with men at the end of my career in both schools before the Combat Exclusion Law was repealed.

At Mare Island, I worked with about three-hundred men and at Great Lakes, at its peak, I had about two-thousand-five-hundred males under my purview. Being inventive at both schools, I created a woman's bathroom out of other men's bathrooms. I did this by having the Seabees from the Construction Battalion retrofit the men's head closest to my office. By building a separating wall, without taking away the men's facility, I had a place to go to the restroom close by.

Another story illustrates the mindset I was dealing with at Great Lakes. I was the first woman Office-in-Charge (OIC) of Combat Systems School, which also included the Gun School and the Armory (see p. 245). Gunner's Mates were trained there. They were responsible for operating and maintaining gun launchers and the small arms and rifles for the whole training center. Since I was the new OIC, I was required to take inventory of the many small arms and rifles for accountability purposes. Gun School was one of the five divisions of my Department, so I often spent time there. For other branches of the U.S. Military, like the Army, a Division is larger than a Department, but in the Navy it is usually smaller.

One time, I had to inspect this building that we called the Gun School. When I arrived for the inspection, I asked to go to the Women's Head. They in fact had one, so they escorted me to it and when I got there, I saw two signs. One said, "Officers" and the other said, "Women's Lounge." I decided to have some fun with them, since they seemed so proud of being able to show me to a proper restroom just for women (when usually there was not one). But I saw the one that said "Officers" first.

Trying to hide the smile on my face, I told them that since I was an officer, I should be able to use the one that said "Officers" and I started to open the door. Several of them got very nervous and led me to the second one that said, "Women's Lounge." Looking extremely perplexed, I said, "What is this 'Women's Lounge?' In the Navy it is called a 'Women's Head.'"

Stammering, they replied, "But Ma'am, this bathroom has a couch, so it is a lounge."

Rolling my eyes, I remarked, "Uh huh."

The next time I came to the Gun School, they excitedly commented, "Commander, you have to see our new sign for the Women's Head." I went to see it and this is what it said: "Women's Head, With Couch." I graciously chuckled and thanked them for changing the sign because I did not want to burst their bubble. After all, they were serious and so proud of what they had come up with.

Those kinds of little interactions with my staff throughout my time in the service, allowed the humor and the camaraderie to show through and increased our teamwork. I think because of these types of agreeable or humorous incidents, the sailors went over and above to do a great job, especially, when I needed them to come through for me. And they didn't disappoint.

After about two years as Officer-in-Charge of Combat Systems at Great Lakes, a person I knew who worked for the base Admiral as a Civil Servant named Don, was retiring. He asked if I wanted to transfer over to replace him in his job in Building One as the base Total Quality Leadership (TQL)[90] Coordinator. Building One (see page 264), where the Commander of the base's office is located, has three floors and a clock tower and is constructed of red brick, like most of the buildings lining the rectangular-shaped Ross Field. These red brick buildings were built in 1911 when the base was constructed on the bluffs of Lake Michigan. During this time, the base contained thirty-thousand military and civilian workers.

The NTC Commander's building stands at the top of the Ross Field parade ground rectangle toward the lake, with the base main entrance located at the bottom of the rectangle. With three floors and a clock tower, Building One is iconic in the area for its beauty and it smacks of the power residing there. The back of the building overlooks Lake Michigan, with a beautiful view and has a door conveniently leading to the base Commander's house, a one-star Admiral. In addition to the Admiral and his staff offices being located in that building, there are the courtrooms for the base Courts Martial system and a few other related units.

Admiral Gaston seemed to like me because I knew a lot about the new (at the time) Navy initiative called Total Quality Leadership (TQL), a program that he was required to launch throughout the training center. It is similar to civilian programs like Six Sigma at Motorola or the Total Quality Management (TQM)[90] system being used in corporations. Its purpose is to improve the quality of organizational products and processes (both commercial and systemic) by using flow charts and statistical tools to monitor their main processes.

Designed to enhance the performance of the organizations, who use this system, Quality Management doesn't just complete the mission, it improves the quality of the products delivered to their customers. It was an offshoot of leadership training I had had in accordance with getting my Master's Degree in Human Resources Management (HRM). In addition, I read voraciously and had taken many Navy TQL classes, so that is why I learned a lot about it before and after the Navy launched this new initiative.

One good practice as a leader can be illustrated here. Even though I didn't always welcome change, like the TQL program purported to be, I jumped on board early learning about it because I saw it coming down the pike in the larger Navy. When you jump on board early to learn about a new program, it makes you the expert, therefore, indispensable to your boss. It also increases your own enthusiasm and buy-in. That has always been a successful leadership strategy for me.

The TQL system is based on the teachings of W. Edwards Deming, a statistician who helped the Japanese improve their automotive sector after WWII, when Americans would only drive big cars then; they would not listen to his teachings. And we all know how Japanese cars were considered junk in the sixties and then twenty years later, they were thought of as THE highest quality cars in the eighties because they used the TQL system.

American car dealers were late to the party, but now we can see that they have improved also, because they use a similar quality management system. An example is Ford Motor Company, which started a campaign called "Ford is Quality One" that has been touted on T.V., since the late eighties and early nineties.

You might be thinking, "What products or processes does a training center have to improve itself, using the tools I mentioned above?" Well, the process to put a student through a technical school in a timely manner comes to mind, so they can go out on deployment as soon as possible, to fulfill the Navy's mission at sea. The product would be the newly well-trained sailor and the process would be all the steps it took for the sailor to get prepared to go to the deploying ship ready to begin work.

Or, consider the need for a document that must be edited and approved at different employee levels like: those who prepare attachments to go with it, those who have to sign off on it and finally those who prepare the cover letter for the Commanding Officer of the organization to sign. This is when flow charts come in handy, so wasteful duplications can be found and deleted. The flow chart ensures it goes to the right people quickly; therefore, it can be rapidly processed in support of the mission of the organization.

As evidenced by my enthusiasm for the subject, I loved this stuff, so I agreed to taking Don's place and spending my last year at NTC in Building One as the TQL Coordinator working directly for the Admiral, who was an enthusiastic supporter of the program. I became responsible for training up instructors, scheduling and executing the base TQL classes. The purpose of the TQL training was so sailors and civilians on NTC could start using these tools to improve the quality of their particular workplace systems on base.

Moreover, as facilitator of the TQL Executive Steering Committee (ESC), Rear Admiral (RDML) Gaston asked me to get to the bottom of base-wide issues that the leaders felt needed to be addressed, using TQL principles. The ESC was made up of the larger base command Captains (0-6) and Commanders (0-5), who would be writing a strategic plan and using TQL strategies with their own subordinates.

These base Commanders, who also worked for bosses in their specialty fields, oversaw their own areas (called tenant commands). Examples would be: Dental, Medical, the Navy Exchange (like the Army PX, similar to a department store), the base hospital, the Corpsman School (like a school for nursing assistants), the Naval Reserve Center, Recruit Training Command (Boot Camp) and several others. Remember, our whole NTC mission was to get our product (trained sailors) out to the fleet in a timely manner.

I started by doing individual interviews with the ESC members to collect data about problems which might hinder the mission of NTC, including their relationship with the Admiral. Then I consolidated the 0-5 and 0-6s information to present to the Admiral. In order to preserve anonymity, no individual Captain/Commander that I interviewed for their candid assessments of how the base processes were working, would be named. I would analyze the data and sanitize it before I presented it to Mack individually and then with the whole committee present. After discussion, they all could decide by consensus and prioritize what would be the best courses of action to improve base processes.

This ESC data collection process was a little tricky for me because I was only a Lieutenant Commander (LCDR/0-4), asking higher-ups to tell me about problems on the base that my boss,

RDML Gaston was responsible for, who out-ranked all of the committee members. Leadership ability is the highest value of all sailors, who must continually get promoted or leave the Navy. I had to figure out how to couch some of my negative findings in a language that would not directly offend Mack Gaston, but at the same time would give him valuable feedback on how he was doing as the highest- ranking-leader at NTC, according to his ESC members.

During my briefing to Mack on the results of the ESC interviews, I never mentioned the word "leadership", but treated the data as problems to be solved together as a committee. My boss was smart enough to connect the dots, but I left a little room for his dignity to stay intact. All in all, it looked like a successful approach and he asked me, "Kathleen, what should I do next?" I told him that the Executive Steering Committee needed to hear that he had read my sanitized report, without knowing who said what because of the confidentiality of the interviews I had conducted.

Also, Gaston needed to tell them that he had taken their feedback seriously and that he trusted in their ability to solve the problems that had come up in the report. Furthermore, I reiterated how important it was to let the Committee get to work as a team to fix the main problems they had highlighted, without too much interference and direction from Mack. After all, they were all high-ranking officers themselves and were used to taking on complicated problems daily.

RDML Gaston went into the next meeting and did what I asked him to do without getting defensive, but stayed open to their suggestions. I was there to facilitate the problem-solving process the ESC then tackled to very productive outcomes. For me, it was one of the most satisfying jobs I had done in the Navy. Mack Gaston was great to work for because he really wanted to use TQL practices for a high-performance-outcome of the commands located on his base.

Moreover, Mack gave me a lot of room as a leader to help him the best way I knew how. Fortunately, I used the skills I learned in Bldg. One and they proved to be paramount to my future success as a management consultant and teacher after leaving the Navy. Facilitating groups is one of my favorite things to do, something I studied as part of my Master's degree, as well as, my counselor courses and all the TQL training I had received in the military. I enjoy helping groups collect and analyze information and come to solutions and consensus toward improving workplace systems.

An interesting situation happened the first week I was in my new job as TQL Coordinator in Building One at NTC Great Lakes. RDML Gaston happened to know the Chief of Naval Operations (CNO), Admiral Jeremy "Mike" (0-10) Boorda[91] (see picture p. 210) well from their sea-going days and Admiral Boorda had become a good personal friend. RDML Gaston, a one-star Admiral, invited the CNO, a four-star Admiral and the highest-ranking member of the U.S. Navy to visit the base. The purpose of the visit was for the CNO to observe training operations and to serve as the Reviewing Officer for the up-coming week's graduation of recruits (Boot Camp).

Amazingly, the CNO, Admiral Boorda had graduated from our recruit training in 1956 and made it to the top officer in the Navy (CNO) and was the first to do so starting from the lowest enlisted rank. During his time, usually, Admirals had come from the Naval Academy and very few other officer programs, but Admiral Boorda went from Seaman Recruit (SR/E-1) the lowest in the enlisted ranks, all the way up to the top job in the Navy, (See Navy Rank Charts in INDEX A, pp. 307-308). I think that is why today they have a shiny newer enlisted barracks at NTC Great Lakes with his name on the front: Admiral Mike Boorda Hall, to honor his legacy as the only one to enter the Navy as a Seaman Recruit (SR) at NTC Great Lakes and make it all the way up to the CNO position.

During my first week working for Admiral Gaston, he told me I would have to present to the CNO in one week's time about what we were doing with TQL. I had just started the job and didn't have a lot of knowledge of what had gone on before. Don, the guy I replaced was retiring, so I was on my own. Very few get to present to the CNO and usually they are Captains (0-6) or Admirals (0-7 through 0-10). As a nervous wreck with a faltering voice, I barely squeaked by. I noticed that the other presenters, who were all the highest-ranking-officers on the base were just as visibly nervous as I was, which made me feel better as a lowly Lieutenant Commander (0-4).

The CNO was also invited to return to Great Lakes to be a part of Admiral Gaston's retirement ceremony, of which I was in charge. Responsible for designing and executing Plan A and Plan B for the ceremony, I was allowed to pick other base personnel to be on my committee to help me with this important task. If we went to Plan

A, the ceremony would be held outside on Ross Field, the parade ground, which was how it was usually done.

On the other hand, if we had to go to Plan B (inclement weather would be a reason), the ceremony would be held inside a large building, usually one of our huge hanger-like drill halls. Whichever plan was used, it had to include set-up, movement by formation and marching of recruits, photography, ceremony staging and script, award-giving, speeches, guest invitations and seating, military protocol, Navy Band procedures, VIP seating, the sound system, fire department plan, police plan, guest parking, and the reception afterwards. There were other plans, but I can't remember them all.

On the morning of Admiral Gaston's retirement ceremony at 6:00 a.m. because it was raining, and we needed to be under cover, we made the decision to go to Plan B. This indoor set-up is a little trickier than the outdoor Plan A, especially with marching troops. But all went well and I sighed with relief. The biggest surprise was that a few weeks later, I got an informal call from one of the CNO's assistants, which I cherish until this day. He explained to me that Admiral Boorda wanted him to tell me that I did a great job on organizing and producing the Change-of-Command/Retirement Ceremony for his friend, RDML Gaston.

Admiral Boorda, known for being sailor-friendly, noticed how the Retirement Ceremony/Change-of-Command was organized and executed and made a special effort to tell me I did a great job. That is what I call great leadership – to take the time to recognize the performance of sailors' way down in the chain of command like me, from the Navy's top dog, who also is a member of the Joint Chiefs of Staff for the WHOLE Military! I was truly honored to be singled out by him.

About a year later, in May of 1996, I was stunned and saddened to find out Admiral Boorda had committed suicide.[92] We were told that some Newsweek reporters were coming to ask him about a scandal involving the medals he wore on his uniform that some said he didn't deserve. His ship had been in Vietnam combat operations during the war and a citation was written up for his service here, so he mistakenly thought that he could wear the Combat V for valor on his ribbons. His actual citation was missing some crucial wording pertaining to the Combat V.

The reporters coming to interview him were investigating the error and he was so humiliated, he indicated around that time that he didn't want to contribute to hurting the reputation of his beloved Navy, even though his mistake had been unintentional. The Navy had recently been under fire for incidents of sexual harassment and the Tailhook fiasco, so everyone was being extremely sensitive to any wrongs done by someone wearing the Navy uniform.

I hope that if anyone from Admiral Boorda's family reads this book, that they understand how much his encouragement meant to me, especially because I knew I'd never be promoted again due to my indiscretion with John a few years before. His support reminded me that I served the Navy that I loved so well, regardless of my affair, in that it did not characterize my total performance of my Navy career. Just like the Admiral's mistake of wearing the Combat V does not characterize his whole wonderful career, the mistake I made does not characterize mine. If I could talk to him now, I would say in Navy tradition when someone is going away, "'Fair winds and following seas' on your journey, Admiral Boorda, wherever that may be because you were respected and loved by this one sailor, as well as, all the others whom you commanded."

For most of my Navy career, there was a law that if you had eighteen years of service and were already a Lieutenant Commander (LCDR/0-4), you were allowed to stay in until you had twenty years in service, so you could get a retirement. But just a month before I had eighteen years in and I thought I was home free for another two years until I was eligible for a twenty-year full retirement, an electronic message came out and was delivered to all the bases. The powers that be in Washington D.C., knowing that my class at Officer Candidate School (September 1979) was one of the largest classes at the time to graduate (including the largest class of women), realized they had to take action before time ran out to warn us of a new system coming soon.

The Navy was starting to downsize after the first Gulf War, but they had to give people at least six months' notice. So, a few weeks before I was to hit eighteen years in May of 1995, the Navy-wide electronic message that was put out in April of 1995 said they were changing the statutory law about the eighteen-year minimum for Lieutenant Commanders who wanted to get a twenty-year retirement. The new law said that if we had fifteen years or more in service by the message date of April 1995, we were required to retire and get out of the military by November 1, 1995.

Now under the new system being announced, if you retired before twenty years of service, your retirement pay would be prorated according to how many years (fifteen or above) you had in the Navy. That meant I would lose one and a half years' worth of service inserted into the retirement formula because I would not make twenty years, being forced by the new April 1995 electronic message to get out of the Service in November of that same year. Under the old law, I would have been guaranteed to be able to stay in to reach the normal twenty-year retirement because I had made LCDR (0-4) before I had eighteen years in. Now, with this new ruling, we had to be a CDR (O-5) at present, when the April electronic message came out, to be able to remain at least twenty years.

When that message arrived, telling of how the Navy was downsizing and what the new rules were, I was in a panic because I was going to be short of about three weeks of being able to stay in the Navy for the full twenty-year retirement. In addition, I was a single parent and my separation from the Navy would be at least a year and a half earlier than I had expected. In seven months, I would be out on the street and would need a new job. I had not saved enough money for this or done a resume since I came in the Navy in 1977, so I was frightened.

If you recall, I had had that affair with my boss, John, several years earlier (that kept me from being promoted to 0-5—full Commander). This April message changed everything, so I was only guaranteed to stay twenty years if I had at least eighteen years of service in and was a Lieutenant Commander (LCDR/0-4) on the date of the April message, but I wouldn't make eighteen years in service until May 19, 1995. I was a few weeks short of the April deadline, so that stupid mistake I made in the late eighties would cost me, besides my promotion, money in retirement.

The April message put me in a tailspin, but after thinking it over, I knew it could have been worse and I could have been kicked out without retirement pay, due to the affair. I am grateful that I have a retirement at all. Luckily, because of cost-of-living raises, that paycheck has grown over the years since I retired. Most people could not live very well on it, but now added to my public-school teaching retirement check and Social Security, it is better than I expected and I am not complaining. Actually, I am very grateful.

The only shame it periodically causes me is when someone, who knows how retirement in the service works, (usually you must have a minimum of twenty years to get one) asks me how long I was in the Navy. I just say I received an early out, due to downsizing and leave it at that. I try to focus on my good performance and how much I loved being in the service for my country and don't dwell on the mistakes I made, otherwise I would go nuts.

Having to leave my beloved Navy early was soul-crushing for me. I have dealt with a lot of the pain it caused me in therapy and try to move on, since it can't be changed. Normally, I can forget about it until someone in the know asks me directly if I received a twenty-year retirement. It then comes up again, but after all these years my soul has hardened to the hurt and I try to dwell on the wonderful experiences I had in the service. Those great Navy experiences add up to many more years than those four months that I unwisely had the affair with my boss in the late eighties.

It was bittersweet when I had my retirement ceremony on September 15, 1995, which was held at the Gun School of "Women's Lounge" lore. A big green glass edifice that housed the launchers and the base Armory, being proposed by the community to be put on the list of historical treasures, was eventually scheduled for demolition. It was a glorious September day and my command went all-out for me, putting together a grand ceremony. The 95,000 square feet building, covered with unique green glass rectangular panels, had been designed by architect Bruce Graham, who famously designed both the Sears Tower (now Willis Tower) and the John Hancock buildings in Chicago."[93]

Unfortunately, the distinctive Gun School building (see photo p. 245) was demolished around 2012, but I have fond memories of it being the site of my Navy Retirement Ceremony and the place where the Gunner's Mates made a new sign for the women's bathroom: "Women's Head with Couch." Being the first full-time woman Officer-in-Charge of Combat Systems School, I wish I had known ahead of time about the demolition. If that were the case, I would have requested to have the unusual women's restroom sign that the Gunner's Mates had made for me. To me, it was priceless!

My staff sent out beautiful, formal retirement invitations to relatives, co-workers and friends of mine and they set up a stage in the Gun School. The Navy Band was placed up high on a platform that contained a launcher, decorated with American Flag-themed bunting. The Great Lakes Navy Band Leader (the latest title descendent of John Phillips Sousa) sang one of my requests, called "God Bless the U.S.A." by Lee Greenwood[94].

Every one of my Navy peers and staff, who participated in the ceremony, was dressed in their "Dress White" uniforms with medals and swords, looking very impressive. Admiral Gaston, now retired for only a few months, came back to conduct the ceremony in his civilian suit and to award me the Navy Commendation Medal for outstanding performance in my job.

Since many of my relatives were nearby, due to NTC Great Lakes being near my original hometown of Glenview, IL (in the Chicago area), many of them attended the ceremony. Before this, cousins had never participated in any Navy ceremonies of mine because I lived in other states, so it was doubly special to have so many of them there. My cousin Dennis O'Brien (see picture, p. 302) also sang a song that reminds me of my father, called "Leader of the Band"[95] by Dan Fogelberg, who wrote it about his own father.

My sibling, Terry had first asked Dennis to sing it at our father's funeral in 1987. Later, for big events in my life, like retiring from the Navy and when I got married, Dennis kindly indulged us by expressively singing "Leader of the Band." His gorgeous and soulful voice gives me the feeling that Dad is standing there in the worst and most important events of my life, trying to comfort and teach me, like he always did in life.

During other turning points in my life, I almost see Thomas Joseph O'Brien standing in heaven with God and St. Peter and shaking his head when I have messed up, saying, "Honey, I am so sad you have to go through something like this again, but you haven't learned your lesson. Keep trying. Understand that I am so proud of what you have accomplished and I love you very much. You know I am always here for you, whatever you are going through."

Dad was the only one in my life, except for my husband Bill, who has ever given me such long-lasting unconditional love and it is what has sustained me during hard times. Also, that unwavering unconditional love helped me to appreciate the awesome times too, even though I was sad he was not physically there to celebrate them with me. Dan Fogelberg's song, "Leader of the Band" spoke to my heart about my father's edifying attention to his three children and his strong character that inspired us all.

Fogelberg uses poetic words to describe his father's perfect balance of discipline and love. That was so poignant and described my father's style as a dad so well that I still cherish it today. He depicted his father as having a soft, yet strict approach. My dad was like that, strong in his convictions, which he never was wont to express when needed, but also, he handled us with so much wisdom and care that you never wanted to make a mistake or to cross him again, for fear of disappointing him.

One time a few years after Dad died, my two brothers, Michael and Terry and I sat down to plan an intervention we wanted to have for Mom to confront her about her drinking. With my experience as a drug and alcohol counselor, I read up on the subject beforehand and we used that information as a guide. Just as we were planning it, the radio was on and we heard, "The Leader of the Band," which gave us confidence of Dad's blessing about what we were doing. Mom didn't end up stopping drinking for good, but it put her on notice that we were concerned and let her know that as long as she was still drinking, she wouldn't be allowed to be alone with her grandchildren.

After my retirement ceremony, where my eight-year-old daughter Christina had been given a bouquet of red roses and a letter from the Navy thanking her for her sacrifice during my Naval service, there was a reception in the Great Lakes Officer's Club, where they served delicious food. Since I was not married then, I chose to have Christina act in place of the usual role of a Navy spouse. That is why she was given the letter and the bouquet of roses. In addition, my young daughter was escorted up close to the stage to watch the ceremony in a special chair covered in white linen, usually the place of honor, reserved for the Navy spouse. As my final ceremonial act as a Naval Officer, Christina and I walked arm in arm through the gauntlet of six of my peers, dressed like me in their dress whites.

To create the traditional retirement gauntlet, they were standing in two rows facing each other as the Boatswain (a Navy ship rating), piped me (with the traditional whistle) "over the side" for the last time. Every time I attend a retirement ceremony for others, I usually tear up at the moment the Boatswain plays the haunting pipes, and this brought me to tears also, because it was now for me. As I saluted for the last time at the end of the gauntlet, I wondered if a new satisfying career, as I had had in the Navy, was going to be out of reach for me during this new phase of my life.

Even though I retired ceremonially in September, I asked to work until the last day of active duty before my official retirement, November first because I needed the money. I did not have a job yet and the holidays were almost upon us. Just like I did when I first entered the Navy, I had a photo taken in a studio documenting my retirement. As I was in the dressing room taking off my uniform for the very last time, I cried because I really was at the end of my Navy career; however, I dried my eyes, straightened up because I had a child to raise and was excited, if not scared, about the new phase of life that was soon to begin.

(Above) The Gun School and Armory at NTC Great Lakes
https://wikipedia.com[96]
(Below)
Kathleen handling a 45

(Below) Kathleen wears her uniform for the last time for her retirement photo.

(Below) Kathleen's family at her retirement reception, 1995

(Above) Christina receives a plaque from CDR McCullom for supporting her mother.in the service of her country.

(Below) Admiral Gaston, retired, guest speaker (On right) at Kathleen's Retirement Ceremony

{Above) Kathleen's retirement cake

(Right) Christina, Kathleen and Karen at Kathleen's Navy retirement

(Below) Kathleen giving out a plaque to one of her Sailors.

(Above) The Great Lakes Navy band playing at Kathleen's retirement

(Left) Kathleen visiting Karen P., Leslie M., Pete S. and Pam at DAPMA, 1990

(Below) Kathleen taking the oath while being promoted to Lieutenant Commander,

(Above) Kathleen (R) and her staff for Division 4 return a salute to one of their recruit companies Passing-in-Review (Boot Camp graduation), 1988.

Chapter 26: *Undergoing Radical Change For the Better*

Failure gave me strength. Pain was my motivation.

— **Michael Jordan**[97]

A few weeks before my retirement, the officers of NTC held what is called a "Hail and Farewell" gathering, a tradition to honor people coming to and leaving the command, in this case NTC Great Lakes. Since I was planning on settling in the area, I was looking for activities and organizations to round out my life near Chicago. At this function, I sat next to two Chaplains who were also leaving the Navy.

I asked them if they knew of a good church in the area, since they had a lot of connections locally from working at the base. They mentioned a big church they knew about because it had a large singles ministry that had events like dances and other fun outings. The two Chaplains said it was an Evangelical church called Willow Creek Community Church (WCCC) and I asked what type of church "Evangelical" was. They said it was Bible-based.

I wasn't sure I liked that it was Bible-based because I was afraid it was a church that leaned toward "fire and brimstone" teaching, but I said I would look into it. My background was mostly Catholic and in later years, mainstream Protestant with a little of Unity thrown in.

I longed for a spiritual life in church, but I didn't know how to find one that was right for Christina and me. Due to my membership in both Al-Anon and Overeaters Anonymous, I wanted my new church to be compatible with these Twelve-Step programs (see Appendix B) that included relying on a Higher Power, which I chose to call God. Christina and I had tried different churches everywhere we had been stationed in the Navy, but we both did not feel comfortable with any of them.

One of the first positive things I did after I retired from the Navy was to try the church that the two Chaplains told me about in South Barrington, IL, called Willow Creek. We lived in Grayslake, a northern suburb of Chicago, close to the southern border of Wisconsin. South Barrington was forty-five minutes southwest of

Grayslake, so it was a long haul, but I like to go by recommendations of people who have been to the place or know the person I am interested in seeing, so I was willing to try it.

Even though I could have just started going to churches myself, I had already tried a few that weren't for me, when I was still at Great Lakes. At this point, I was now ready to try a referral, not far from where I wanted to live, somewhere closer to my family near Glenview, where I grew up. To do this, I would have to move about half an hour south of Grayslake, which would be in the ballpark if I started going to the recommended church in South Barrington. The first time Christina, who was nine and I drove into the WCCC entrance she remarked, "Wow, Mom, this looks like the mall."

Indeed, this church was huge, laid out like a college campus with beautiful trees and a pretty lake, visible as you come onto the property from Algonquin Road. The church had just celebrated their twenty-year anniversary the week before we pulled onto the long driveway and into the parking lot on a quiet Sunday in October of 1995. I had heard from those two Chaplains about Friday night dances Willow Creek held at the restaurant down the street called the Barn of Barrington. I had gone to one of the dances the Friday before and talked to a lot of nice people there about Willow. One thing that impressed me right away was that they did not smoke and drink in the room rented to the church. Moreover, for a nominal entrance fee of about five dollars, we could have soft drinks and light hors d'oeuvres and dance the night away.

Christina got involved in the wonderful children's ministry called Promised Land and I joined the thirty-to-forty-something ministry for singles called Focus. I was impressed with the teaching and the wonderful community activities arranged for us, like: camping trips, roller skating, Praise and Sing Nights, volleyball, picnics and other church events. The men and women in our ministries, who had children, included Christina in Bible studies and learning about God.

Even though the church was considered huge by most standards, it felt small and intimate to us because of the closeness that was developed in the small groups in the Promised Land and Focus ministries. I also noticed that there were other single parents like me, including attractive guys around my age, who were serious about God and spiritual things. I did not smoke or drink, so I didn't want to meet men in a bar or some place that would encourage those things. I had never thought of meeting someone at church before because when I was young and being raised in the Catholic Church, we did not have a lot of events to meet singles like they have instituted in the last twenty-to-thirty years or like the singles activities regularly held in the Evangelical and Protestant churches.

On that first Friday night dance, at the Barn of Barrington, the people I met gave me directions to WCCC for services and the following Sunday, Christina and I drove there for the first time. I will admit that it scared me at first because I had never seen anything like it. Also, their contemporary music was great and in those days, they had a drama piece to go along with the theme of the service and the pastor's message. I was hooked and could not wait to come back, especially when I picked Christina up from the Children's Ministry and she told me she loved it. She said, "Mom, this is our church!" That cinched it in my eyes and we started going to it regularly.

What I loved about Willow were all the activities for the singles. As a single going to church, I usually felt like a third wheel because all the events struck me as being geared to married people. Not so at this church – it was rich in activities for singles, divided roughly by age and that is why I went to Focus, because I was in my early forties. For the next six months, we went to many activities with people I was introduced to, starting with a Focus Christmas Party, where I met Connie Jean Catalano, who was the volunteer leader for a medium-sized group called Synergy. Synergy was a group of about three-hundred people divided into thirty groups with volunteer leaders for each one.

One of Connie's best talks for this large group was about sex and the single Christian. Using scripture and examples, Connie simply addresses how Christians should handle the question of sex, like what is appropriate for the Christian outside of marriage. When Connie first told me the subject of her talk, I felt sorry for her, thinking that not many people would show up, especially the men we knew. So, I was determined to go to the lecture because (in my mind) she would need support, when not many others would show up. At least I, and the rest of the small group she led would be there.

The evening of Connie's speech, I arrived early to help set up the chairs and tables. As we were preparing the room, I noticed big groups of people walking in and taking a seat. By the end of the setting up period, I was amazed at the crowds pouring into the large space. About three-hundred people showed up for Connie's talk, both men and women.

As I watched people pour into the room, I thought back to when I was talking to Connie earlier, and she told me that even though we were older singles and had probably been married before or had experience, the Bible said that there is not to be intercourse outside of marriage. I couldn't believe it and said, "Connie, I don't believe this, show it to me in the Bible!" and she sure did.

Because of that conversation, I was sure that no one would show up for this event. I was so wrong – there were a lot of singles that were hungry for this information. All in all, three-hundred people showed up. It took me a few months of other scripture reading, praying, etc. and discussions for me to start to see the wisdom of this teaching, but I am getting ahead of my story.

A few months before, I had been studying a Christian book and filling out a workbook to go along with the Bible study assignment in Connie's all women's small group. We were talking about being a Christian. Of course, I knew I was a Christian because I had been a Catholic all my life. Or so I thought I knew. Someone asked if I had ever prayed the "Prayer of Salvation." Not knowing what that was, I answered "No."

They explained that to know for sure that one is a Christian, we have to repent to Christ of our sins first, and ask Him for forgiveness. Then we need to tell Him that we receive Him as our Lord and Savior, asking Him to come into our heart for all time. I told the group, "I am already a Christian and have been all my life."

They were not questioning my *belief* in Christ, but it was the first time I was told you need to be in a *relationship* with Christ. Saying the "Prayer of Salvation" is the first step. So, in order to humor Connie a few days later, I said the prayer as we knelt down together. I thought, "What harm could it do?"

That night everyone in the group was congratulating me for what they call, "Coming to Christ" (officially becoming one of His children by saying the prayer above). I told Connie, "Yeah, yeah. If this makes you feel like I am now officially a Christian, so be it," and I played it down. They told me that people who do what I did by saying the "Prayer of Salvation" with Connie, often experience some kind of spiritual experience, but it is not required.

Since I felt that I had been one of Christ's own most of my life as a Catholic, I did not feel the necessity to have a spiritual experience or so I thought. I was just humoring the group because I thought I knew what was what. The other reason I did what Connie asked me to do was because I knew she was a Catholic for most of her life until she started coming to Willow Creek Church seventeen years before, so I thought that following her suggestions might be a good idea. I then went on with my life and two weeks went by.

One day, on a Sunday afternoon, when I had some time to kill because Christina was visiting her father in California and I wasn't supposed to pick her up from the airport until evening, I decided to take in a movie. It wasn't exactly a movie that I was dying to see, but it had great actors in it and was called "Dead Man Walking."[98] In the film, Sean Penn played a felon on death row for killing the boy and raping the girl in a teenage couple he randomly came across, just for the heck of it. Since Sean's character was written as a composite of two real-life killers, I will continue to use Penn's real name when referring to the character he plays. Susan Sarandon played a real-life Catholic nun named Sister Prejean who had started visiting the inmates on death row.

After visiting him for a few months, she tried to talk to Penn about salvation in Christ, which he didn't seem interested in at first. He wanted to know why Christ would save him if he had done so many horrific things; he did not believe he could be saved at this late date. Much of the movie was Sister Prejean at the prison talking to Sean Penn about how it does not matter the extent to which one has fallen, no one is barred from the love of Christ. Finally, it was almost midnight, the hour of the planned lethal injection on the day of his execution. She had told him to admit what he had done, which he was reluctant to do.

Sarandon explained that by admitting his crime, it would give peace and closure to the families of the victims, something that was truly good. Sister Prejean further explained to him that maybe he did not have such a great life on earth, but he would have an amazing life in the next one with Christ if he would just admit, repent and ask Christ to come into his heart as Lord and Savior, thereby receiving the grace that passes all understanding: a free gift. Free gift means one doesn't have to keep doing things to get the grace of God; it is given to us freely if we repent and ask Him to be our Savior.

251

By following her suggestions about what to do in the last few minutes of his earthly life, Sister had him recognize that he could die in peace and ensure that the families knew who killed their loved ones. Watching the movie, I could see that by admitting to his sin of killing the victims, this would be a way to pay forward to the families, the gift of knowing for sure what happened. And, in turn, the free gift of salvation through Christ would be Penn's, if he decided to repent and ask for forgiveness. So, unbelievably, Penn acquiesced and did as the good Sister asked. She told him that she would be right there with him, holding his hand as he received the lethal injection, until he would see the eyes of Jesus on the other side.

I had said almost the same words as Penn two weeks earlier, as I had kneeled with Connie to ask God to come into my heart because I was so sorry for things I had done in life. In the last scene where Penn repents and is given the lethal injection, I recognized my own story and why I needed Jesus in my life because I sure hadn't made a lot of great decisions all along by myself. Watching the scene of Sean's admission of guilt, repentance and reaching out for God's forgiveness, I actually felt Christ come off the screen as I sat stunned with His forgiveness and love. What irony—it took a real-life Catholic nun and a convicted felon to teach me the lesson of God's mercy and grace!

At forty-three years old, I could not stop the tears as I sat in the theatre watching the credits for the film run. I knew in that moment that I would never be the same. I could not stop sobbing because I could not believe Christ forgave me. When you know that whatever happens, Christ has your back and nothing can separate you from the love of Christ, it instills a deep conviction to follow the Savior and to try and live up to His ways.

We know we are human and can never be perfect, but Christ's forgiveness of our mistakes and being in relationship with Him make up for our imperfections. In reality, I came to believe that Christ is the Lamb, who was sacrificed, so I don't have to be, to make me righteous before God the Father, the first part of the Trinity. His son, Jesus, the second part of the Trinity, sacrificed his life on the cross and gave us salvation, our free gift, undeserved, but given because the God of the universe loves us and wants to be in relationship with His children. It makes sense according, to the Old Testament, where there needed to be sacrifices (usually animals) in order to be righteous. In the New Testament, God had made it easier to be right with God because His Son was sacrificed for us once and for all, making it possible to have a more personal relationship with us.

It was then that I knew I would never be alone again, He would always be with me, not an unreachable far-away god, but always near, so I could talk to Him and pour out my heart, whenever I wanted. All I had to do was listen, be quiet and open, so I could sense His guidance through His Holy Spirit, the third part of the Trinity, whom He sent for that purpose. One God in three persons, forming the Trinity and having a job to do to keep us righteous so we can spend eternity with Him. And since that day I knelt with Connie, March 22, 1996, and subsequent spiritual awakening at the end of "Dead Man Walking." Two weeks later, a feeling of awesome peace and serenity came over me and it has kept my faith strong. At Willow Creek Church, I also learned that humans are meant not only to have a personal relationship with God, but to also be in fellowship, and to do life together. I have embraced that wisdom ever since.

Moreover, I always feel Him near, especially since I prayed with Connie and have been able to call on His Grace and peace whenever I need to. What a huge free gift! In reality, it wasn't such a stretch to believe in the miracle of salvation, because as the reader will remember there have been several miracles encountered by me that I have already described in my story.

A couple of years ago, my husband Bill and I moved to Parrish, Florida and have found another great church, just like Willow Creek, only smaller and have begun to make friends easily because of the strong community we found in Bayside Community Church, Bradenton, Florida. It proves to me that the Holy Spirit resides wherever people are gathered to praise God the Father, Christ His Son and the Holy Spirit (the Holy Trinity). God gave us the Holy Spirit to help us with our faith, pointing us to acts that only a Supreme Being can do, thus I have seen many contemporary miracles, some small and some large, but miracles nevertheless.

I believe that God shows us miracles before we ever pray the "Prayer of Salvation" as a way of reminding us that He is there and showing us what He can do in our lives if we let Him. There was one miracle I witnessed before I became a true Christian by asking Christ into my life. It shows Christ was knocking on my door before I ever recognized it. In the following miracle story, His purpose was to warn me about something that was about to happen, to give me time to make things right with the person in question. No other explanation makes sense to me.

In early July of 1987, I came home on leave to go to a family reunion with my husband Sal and my almost seven-month-old baby, Christina. Christina was the first grandchild for my parents, even though my dad, at sixty-eight years old (my present age) was a bit elderly to be a first-time grandpa. Mom was only fifty-seven, so she was still in the ballpark to be a new grandparent (My daughter recently married and I hope to be a grandma soon).

Even though I had a lot of issues with my mom, watching her with my daughter, baby Christina, swelled and softened my heart toward her. As I reflected on how she loved that baby, it made me realize that Mom probably treated me with similar loving care, when I was a new baby, and it made me happy; from this, I garnered a more mature and balanced view of her as my mom.

Dad was extremely delighted with his new granddaughter and enjoyed holding the nine-pound-two-ounce baby, Christina Marie. At our family reunion picnic, held in Lake Geneva, Wisconsin, I noticed my dad was slowing down, having to sit down and rest if he walked any distance. Dad showed me a medicine patch his doctor had attached to his chest to deliver the needed medicine to his heart. He had caught a cold that appeared to go into his heart, making it weaker and the medicine was supposed to make it stronger. This family reunion was on Dad's side, the O'Brien clan, where he was the head honcho, the wise dad of three and uncle of ten nephews and their families; sadly, it was his last family reunion.

My cousin Casey told me later that he had a great talk with my dad sitting on a bench by Geneva Lake as they watched the boat pull away from the dock, carrying the rest of the family on a scenic evening cruise. My dad asked Casey what he wanted to do with his life. He was trying to fill in the gap that my dad's older sibling, Uncle Ray had left since he died when Casey was only fifteen years old.

Dad had a gift for encouraging others and he used it with Casey, the youngest of the ten. He told Dad that he had a dream of opening a little hot dog stand. My dad, the ultimate entrepreneur himself, listened, made suggestions and encouraged Casey to go for it. He told him to follow his dreams. Casey never forgot that advice and has since owned his own restaurant.

Anyway, after the reunion, Sal and I, along with baby Christina, went back to my parents' apartment near Chicago to prepare for our flight the next day back to San Diego, California where we then lived. As Sal was taking suitcases down the elevator to the rental car, my dad was dressed in these crazy, goofy yellow golf shorts and matching polo shirt, standing by the window watching Sal load the rental car. Just as I was supposed to go out the door, I got this strong urge (I now call the Holy Spirit's prompting) to run back; I fell into my dad's arms, giving him a big hug, and I am so glad because I didn't know that that would be the last time I would ever see him alive.

I truly believe it was the Holy Spirit's prompting that I felt. My wonderful daddy with the funny yellow shorts standing in front of the window and our subsequent impromptu hug is a memory I still hold close to my heart. Imprinted on my brain, as I closed the door to leave, was his radiant smile, Celtic blue eyes, light tan and his impish Irish face. So, handsome at six feet one, I remembered how much he loved me and what wisdom he would always bestow on his children.

Poignant memories flood my brain and heart when I think of that picture of him standing by the window as I saw him for the last time. Memories like the devastation I felt when I lost my first teaching job at a Catholic all girl's school and Dad was there for me. Inconsolable, I called up my parents and told them what happened. After staying inside all weekend in my dark apartment crying, I heard a knock on the door. Typical of my sensitive father, he was standing there in his light trench coat. As soon as I let him in, I burst out crying, as he took me in his arms and let me grieve. Tears still come to my eyes when I think of it.

Related to losing some of my classes to an unexpectedly returned "retired" nun and my lack of political savvy with some of the other nuns, my contract for the next year was not renewed in the spring of 1976. This was my first teaching job, something I strived for my whole life and I felt like such a failure.

Another time, when I was having a hard time in Officer Candidate School, I called my parents up to tell them how hard the course was getting due to ever-building pressure laid on us by our leaders and instructors. That sixteen-week school was designed to weed out the officer candidates by gauging our reactions to extreme stress, like officers often experience in the Navy, especially out at sea. My father collected notes of encouragement on a cocktail napkin from my cousins at a family gathering he attended and then sent it to me, which really lifted me up. That was Thomas J. O'Brien's M.O. He was sensitive to others' problems and feelings and that is when his encouragement gift expressed itself.

In addition to having the gift of encouragement, Dad was fair-minded, had integrity and a wonderful impish sense of humor. When he laughed, he sounded just like T.V. star Jim Backus' character, Mr. Magoo. Even though Dad was a tall guy, I truly believed that if you looked up the word "Leprechaun" in the dictionary, his picture would be there instead. And that thought always brought a smile to my lips. Until I was in my late teens, my dad's touch of the blarney was not always apparent until he finally confessed that his full name was only Thomas Joseph O'Brien, NOT what he had me believing my whole life until then: that his full name was Thomas Joseph Peter Aloysius Kevin Barry O'Brien.

In late July 1987, when Sal and I left to fly home to California from the Chicago family reunion, I did not realize it would be the last time that I would see my father. A few months later, the unthinkable happened. One Thursday night in mid-September, Terry called me to say that Dad had gone into the hospital for tests. All that sticky summer, Dad had been having trouble walking because he was often out of breath and Mom would have to pull the car up to the door with the car air conditioning blasting, so he could catch his breath. With that in mind, Terry said he felt relief that Dad was in the hospital, so maybe they could do something to alleviate the weakness in his heart.

I now know the Holy Spirit was working on me earlier that week because he touched me through a dream that was miraculous. My dream was so vivid and disturbing, that I tried to put it out of my mind. In that dream that I had during the week of September 14th - 16th in 1987, I saw my father's funeral and above the casket a date was flashing. It said: "September 22nd."

Consequently, I was so disturbed by what appeared to be a premonition dream that I told my sibling, Terry, who still lived close to my parents near Chicago, about the dream. I told him to not let Dad have any surgical procedures or operations on that date, the upcoming Tuesday. After talking to Terry on Thursday, September 17th, I called my dad on Saturday, September 19, 1987 at the hospital to see how he was doing and tell him that I loved him. We had had some disagreement recently, which was rare and I wanted to clear everything up with him and say I was sorry.

Thank God for the dream because it spurred me to take action by quickly making amends to Dad on the phone. I've read that Muslims have been known to have dreams that change the course of their lives, but I had never had one that vivid before or since. I don't remember at all what the disagreement with my dad was about, but my mom told me later that my father had remarked to her that he was so encouraged by my call and he seemed so happy that I had made it.

The same day I called my dad to make amends, back in San Diego, Sal and I made plans to go out to a party to which I wore peach slacks and a peach top, a flattering and fairly new outfit. Rarely did I ever wear it again after that because it brought to mind the event that would rock my world. A little before 11:00 p.m. PDT (Pacific Daylight Savings Time) Sal and I returned home from the party. We were staying at Antoinette and Frank's house because we were having a house built and it would not be done for a few more months.

Still decked out in my peach outfit, I was talking with Sal and my in-laws in the kitchen when the phone rang. It was late on a Saturday, a time I hardly ever got calls, so my heart dropped as I was told it was for me. It was around 1:00 a.m. in Chicago and Terry was on the phone, hysterical and upset. When he calmed himself down, I was finally able to take in his message: Our beloved father, was dead; he died peacefully in his sleep at 1:00 a.m. CDT (Central Daylight Savings Time), Sunday, September 20, 1987. Terry was home in Chicago, where due to the time difference, it was actually two hours later than California time and into the next day (Sunday).

After the call, I immediately started packing for a flight to Chicago. I noticed Sal was not doing anything and my mother-in-law took me aside, telling me that Sal had not gone to any funerals since he was twelve and his favorite uncle, Joe had died. With a heavy heart, I went back into the living room where Sal was sitting and said, "Why aren't you packing? We need to get going."

Sal reiterated what his mother warned me about, that he wasn't going to go with me. Given that he had loved my dad a lot and knew how close I was to my father, I could not believe that my husband of four years could be so selfish. I wondered how Sal could let me go alone to the funeral, when I needed my husband with me more than ever, to comfort me and my family? He could see that I was a mess, knew how big a loss this was for me because I was such a card-carrying "Daddy's Girl" and understood that I really needed him to accompany me. *Isn't that a husband's job? Why wasn't he there emotionally when I needed him most?*

Finally, I looked at Sal and told him that if he did not go with me, he could expect divorce papers in the mail. I told him that I would not put up with such a lack of understanding about how to be there for his wife and her family at their greatest hour of need. Needless to say, Sal accompanied me to my father's funeral, but looking back, that instance was a defining moment in our marriage and the beginning of the end for me. Our marriage only lasted three more years, as we were divorced in 1990. *I wondered, who would be in my corner now?*

At the funeral, Sal cried hard and was inconsolable because he really loved my father, who was very encouraging to him. I don't think even his own father, Frank, had had that kind of effect on him. It seems to me that my dad was the first man besides Sal's beloved Uncle Joe, who openly cared for him and showed it. For the funeral, I wore my dress blue uniform because my dad was always asking me to wear it when I came home. He had always been so proud to see me in it, so of course I had to honor Thomas J. O'Brien by wearing it to his funeral.

An honor I was glad to bestow upon my dad during the funeral, was a snappy salute as I looked at the casket passing me by at the church. Like you taught me long ago Dad, I hope it was snappy enough and up to your standards, not a sloppy salute, but really sharp. When my brother, Terry and I compared notes after the funeral, he said, "Well I guess your dream was off a few days because Dad died on the twentieth and in your dream, the date September twenty-second was flashing.

I said, "No Terry, my dream was accurate. It showed his funeral only, with the right date according to my dream: September twenty-second, as the date flashing over his casket and that was the day of his funeral." If my premonition is not a miracle, I don't know what is. There was no way I could have known that date ahead of time. I had the dream even before Dad went to the hospital for tests.

After Dad passed away on early Sunday morning, (CDT) the twentieth, my mom and Terry were still living in the Chicago suburbs, so they planned the funeral. I had not taken part because I was still in California preparing to come to Glenview, IL for the Catholic service at Our Lady of Perpetual Help, so I did not yet know when it would be held. Once I realized it was set for the following Tuesday, September 22, 1987, I knew God had given me the gift of an amazing one-time premonition, allowing me to call up my dad and make amends right before he died. A vivid dream like this had never happened to me before in such detail, and I have not had any other dream with such clarity happen to me since then.

Another miracle story I remember, was something my husband, Bill and I and our Willow Creek Community Church (WCCC) small group witnessed starting in 2003. One of the couples in that church small group, the Nelsons, had a twenty-three-year-old daughter, who was very sick with a rare cancer. The right way to treat this disease was unknown, even by the Mayo Clinic, where their daughter, Emily was going for diagnosis and treatment.

The members of our small group, all living in the Chicago suburbs, began praying fervently for this girl's healing. Also, as she was living in Washington D.C., her parents were not able to be closely involved in her health issues and they were very worried. To complicate matters, Emily had a boyfriend there that her parents were not sure about, especially since he was not a Christian.

Emily and her brother, Tyler had been raised at Willow Creek Church and the family hoped Emily would be able to have someone by her side who would turn to God, as she was dealing with this insidious illness. Furthermore, they had always hoped that when they were gone, Emily would be there to help her autistic younger brother, Tyler. Now they worried about both of them for the future.

This seemingly hopeless situation was going to need a lot of prayer from all of those who loved them. As a church small group, we also needed to help the family wade through these terrible times until they could be assured that Emily would recover. Small groups can help by praying, but also by being the hands and feet of Jesus to help the members that are in crisis. This is the purpose of community as outlined in the Bible.

One day, Karol Nelson and her husband Dale came to our church couples' small group and told us about a new pastor intern at Willow Creek. Karol worked in accounting there and the new intern, Jacques Didier, often walked by her cubicle. One time he stopped when he noticed Emily's picture pinned up near Karol's desk. Emily is a gorgeous girl with long brown hair, lithe body and a fashion model's beautiful face. In fact, she looks a lot like her mom and both had been models at one time or another.

Anyway, when Jacques, as a native French Canadian who spoke both French and English fluently saw Emily's picture, he stopped dead short and asked Karol, "Who is that beautiful girl?" Karol proudly informed him that it was her daughter, Emily.

In addition, Karol sadly said to him that Emily had a boyfriend back where she lived in D.C. "And, oh by the way," she told Jacques, "Emily has cancer."

Jacques, tall and very good-looking himself was not deterred. Karol told him that Emily would be coming to the Chicago area soon to visit and maybe he could meet her then. Karol liked Jacques right away and knew that he must have talent to be able to intern as a pastor at Willow Creek, so she said she would let him know when Emily was coming to town.

Well, the following Thursday evening, when we had mid-week services at Willow, most of the members of our small group led by Patty and Dan, (who I talked about in an earlier chapter), were there together to worship, as we usually did. My husband Bill did not attend the service because he was working, so he did not meet Jacques who was sitting with our small group at church that evening. Everyone seemed to like him.

Later, Karol asked us to pray that Jacques and Emily would get together. I thought, *OK, Karol, I'll pray for them,* but in my mind, it appeared to be a long shot. After all, Emily still had her Washington D.C. boyfriend and was still very sick, with no cure for her rare illness. Although Emily was still working in her chosen field of Crime Scene Investigations (CSI), and really loved her demanding career, none of us knew how long she would be able to keep it up due to her cancer, much less start a new relationship.

In the meantime, all was arranged for Emily to come home to the Chicago suburbs on a family visit. Aunts, uncles, and cousins were invited to Karol and Dale's house for a get-together during the time that Emily was to be home. Karol also invited Jacques to come over and gave him a party flyer with the directions to her house. As Jacques was riding north on Quentin Road toward Palatine on his motorcycle, a wind came up and the flyer flew off and it was lost.

Jacques tried to remember the directions, but he got them wrong. Instead of turning left at Northwest Highway, he turned right. Jacques was looking for a townhouse complex, which he found a few streets down and turned right thinking he saw a car like Karol usually drove parked in the driveway of the third townhouse on the right. So, he pulled into the spur street and then left into the driveway where the car he saw was parked. Jacques got off his motorcycle and walked up to the townhouse door and knocked.

My husband, Bill was just about to leave for the evening shift where he worked at Federal Express, so he had already changed into his uniform. Answering the door to Jacques's knock, Bill asked him what he wanted. As soon as Jacques did not see anyone he recognized in the house, (he hadn't met Bill yet like the rest of our group did). So, Jacques said to Bill, "I think I am at the wrong house."

Bill asked, "Whose house are you looking for?"

Jacques replied, "The Nelson's house, Dale and Karol."

Bill then said, "When you came up to the door, I was just hanging up the phone from talking to Dale. They are our dear friends from church. I can take you over there myself. Follow me."

So, Bill climbed into his truck and Jacques got on his motorcycle to follow Bill to the Nelson house. As they drove, it was apparent to Jacques that he had turned right when he should have turned left on Northwest Highway from Quentin. It was just a fluke that he turned into our complex instead. Or was it?

Once Bill got to the Nelson house, he knocked on their door, still in his FedEx uniform, with Jacques hiding around the corner. He announced, "I came here to deliver a package to you." Jacques popped out and everyone was amazed at the story they told the guests at Karol's house. Well, Jacques and Emily met that day, started talking in the living room and were still talking there at five in the morning, when Jacques finally left Karol's house. The rest is history.

Emily went back to Washington and immediately broke up with her boyfriend. Jacques and Emily started dating and after about a year they got engaged. Emily's doctor told her that when she got married, she should not get pregnant because her life-threatening disease was hormonal and they did not know what pregnancy hormones would do because her disease was so rare. They suspected that pregnancy would make it worse because of the expected increase in hormones that babies always bring.

261

Well, shortly after their wedding, of course, Emily got pregnant. It scared the daylights out of her friends and family, but the couple's calm faith seemed to carry them along and Emily didn't get sick during her pregnancy at all. In fact, the pregnancy seemed to put her into cancer remission.

We all consider it a miracle and so do Emily's doctors because since 2004, when she married and got pregnant, she has had no recurring symptoms of her rare cancer, even though she had two healthy pregnancies since then. The doctors determined that instead of the increase of hormones of the pregnancy making Emily sicker, it somehow made her go into remission. When tested, her doctors could find no evidence of the disease at all and it has never come back.

Today, Emily and Jacques live happily together in Virginia with their seven kids (several of them adopted from overseas). Emily now teaches CSI-related subjects at a local university and Jacques is a church pastor, just like both of them had dreamed their lives would turn out. Their inspiring story shows how God can work to restore wholeness in what even seems like a hopeless situation.

There have been a lot of what I and my friends call, "God Stories" in my life, which need to be told in addition to the real miracles already described. These stories are a way of reminding myself that God is always with us, even if we cannot always see or hear Him. Because I have had enough wrong turns and bad decisions in my life to fill up an ark like Noah's, talking about all the good that God has done in my life, mitigates the negatives that I could dwell on. God Stories are ways to remind us there is a Higher Power who is never out of our reach and always in control. Moreover, God Stories do not always include miracles like those I told, but there are always people in them who really touch our lives in a spiritual way. The following are a few that I'd like to recount.

One of the most rewarding, but unpleasant duties I had in the Navy was serving as a Casualty Assistance Calls Officer (CACO). It is the dreaded doorbell ring that every Navy wife is afraid of when her husband is on deployment. Seeing the Chaplain and another officer in their dress blues coming up the front walkway will stop any Navy spouse's heart. A CACO's job, like I had, was to accompany the Chaplain to the spouse's or next of kin's house to tell the family that their loved one had died. About three years before my father died, I had duty as a CACO, and it was my turn to go in my dress blue uniform with the Chaplain one time when we got the call.

The widow lived in a large house that also included her five young children and her parents in Mira Mesa, a suburb of San Diego. We will call them the Logan family. I hated to tell Mrs. Logan that her husband was reportedly missing after he had hitched a ride on a Navy transport airplane to San Diego from northern Washington State, where he was working. He had planned to come home for the weekend to see his family.

A few days later, the plane was found, crashed onto Mount McKinley. Because of the freezing conditions, the bodies were mostly intact. My job was not only to deliver the horrible news, but also to make arrangements for V.A. and Social Security benefits, help Mrs. Logan to complete the paperwork for insurance, assist with funeral arrangements, and other duties as needed. I spent a lot of time at the family's house and got to know them. The widow and her Naval Officer husband were only in their early thirties, with their five children and the wife's parents depending on them for support.

The Navy expects us to go above and beyond for the family of a sailor, especially if they are killed on duty. We other sailors would not want it any other way because we know our families could need it someday ourselves. As the CACO for the Logan family, I went above and beyond. "Above and beyond" was demonstrated by me by being at the funeral home directing the combing of the deceased's hair into the style that he usually wore. Because the mortician had combed it in an odd fashion in order to cover a cut on his head, I was asked to go to the room the casket was in before his wake and try to make him look more like he did, when his family last saw him.

It was fortunate that only one cut on his head was visible, so the problem was fixable, even though we expected worse because he was in an airplane crash. In the end, assisting the Logans through that tragedy was an important experience in empathy for me. I could not believe how well the family treated me, like one of their own and they were very gracious and kind. I thought, *How can they even look at me, since I'm the one who brought them the bad news?*

Even though, I was grateful for the Logan family's comportment around me, I did not get it, until a few years later, when my father died. Upon coming back to San Diego after Dad's funeral, I drove straight from the airport to their house. I had not seen the family in a couple of years, yet I had this burning need to see them. I felt compelled to tell them that I understood why at such a terrible time in their lives they could be so kind to me. I explained that my father had just passed away and that I would never forget who was there for me at the worst time of my life, so I finally understood why they were grateful to have me around in the worst time in their lives. Five years after I was a CACO for this family, I was happy to attend another ceremony at their house. You see, the widow was getting remarried and they invited me to share in their happiness instead of the sorrow I had experienced with them five years earlier. What a delightful contrast to see the family so happy! This showed me that life goes through its full circle due to the plans God has for us. I don't think we can really experience full joy unless we have already experienced deep sorrow; hard-won lessons that stay with me. From these experiences as a CACO (I had other cases too after the Logans) I learned the lesson that where there is sorrow, hope is not lost because the tremendous love of God will always help us find a way to be happy again, as seen in the rest of my story. I started to see that maybe I may have had and will have pain, but I also can trust in God that love and joy will not be out of reach for me in the future.

(Above) Tom and Elaine with Christina, at six months, July, 1987. Last time Kathleen saw her dad before he passed away.

(L) Admiral Gaston's Headquarters Bldg. 1 at NTC Great Lakes, 1994 wikipedia.org

(L) Tom & (R) Elaine with first grandchild, Christina, San Diego, 1987

Chapter 27: *Chain of Sorrow*

*"So, it's true, when all is said and done,
grief is the price we pay for love."*

— *E.A. Bucchianeri, Brushstrokes of a Gadfly*[100]

As I sat listening to Bozoma St. John[101] speaking, at first, I thought that this girl has a lot of serious sass and is not afraid to say what she thinks. She was very attractive, impeccably dressed and presented her thoughts succinctly. Bozoma seemed to be strong and an "in-your-face" person, someone I won't forget easily. Thus, I was not prepared for my eyes tearing up and identifying with her experiences so much.

First of all, Bozama was a high-powered leader, fitting in well with all the other leaders who have spoken at this transforming conference that I go to every year. Called the Global Leadership Summit, there is world-class training from leaders all over the planet at my church of twenty-two years, Willow Creek Community Church, in South Barrington, IL. Although fifteen to twenty years younger than me, it appeared that Bozama was like me in several ways. We were most alike in our desire to be constantly growing, learning and using our leadership skills, so I identified with her exponentially.

Second, as soon as she started her self-assured talk, I thought that I would not have that much in common with her; she seemed way more confident than I felt. I have struggled with low self-esteem all my life, but writing this memoir has helped me realize that I have done good things as a leader and as a person, as she had done. Also, I teared up because Ms. St. John showed her vulnerable side and I truly identified with her story. Her recounting of her life, both good and bad, made Bozoma so much more human in my eyes.

Third, as a marketing powerhouse at several of the biggest American companies, she seemed to exude professionalism. Very successful as a marketing executive at top tier companies like, Apple, Uber, Pepsi and currently, Netflix, she reminded me why I loved having leadership skills. Standing next to this tall, stately and smart Ghanaian-American beauty would make anyone feel like grandma's leftovers. But instead, her talk lifted me up and enabled me to see that there is always hope in even the darkest times, like losing someone you love.

Fourth, I didn't think I would like her because some of the friends she mentioned were on the opposite side politically from me; however, her story equalized us in humanity because we both had experienced debilitating sorrow. I too have felt the kind of pain she was talking about when she lost her husband to cancer because I lost a serious boyfriend to suicide. Being consoled by her work colleagues when her husband died was so unexpected for her. She had no idea that they cared so much and it was a great comfort. Her story resonated with me because I also had a similar experience of being consoled by my co-workers when I lost someone I loved.

That someone was Clark Camden Peterson, who sadly took his own life in 1997, at the age of forty-two. Also, like Bozoma, I too had a young daughter at home when I lost my significant other. My daughter, Christina was only nine years old when Clark passed away. His death affected both of us very strongly, as well as devastating his only daughter, who was then twelve years old. Clark was really good with kids and they were drawn to him because of his curiosity, tenderness and sense of fun.

One of Clark's favorite singer-songwriters was John Prine. John, like Clark, was born in the Chicago area and some of Mr. Prine's songs reflected that too. Clark liked him because his songs were very insightful and his lyrics contained creative, funny words, as well as, sad ones. How much John understood the emotions of love and pain as part of the human condition, was not lost on Clark.

John Prine also appeared to understand people who don't feel like they fit in, like Clark often felt. Due to Clark's Bipolar Disorder and as a result of my ADHD, we each at times felt like misfits, stuck and frustrated, so John's lyrics spoke to me too, especially the song "Bruised Orange (Chain of Sorrow)."[102]

Clark loved music and it gave him a lot of comfort. Also, it lifted him up, especially in the late summer or early fall before he usually had to deal with his manic tendencies. Thus, the most fun we had as a couple was to go see concerts. Together, we went to see John Prine play and Gloria Estephan sing, one of Clark's favorite chanteuses. I think he loved Gloria's enthusiasm, as well as her gorgeous voice. Music can be a great healer for the anxieties and depression that bother those of us with mental illness.

In the summer of 1996, Christina and I got a little purebred black miniature schnauzer puppy and we named him Chance Uva Lifetime, Chance for short. Clark was not only good with kids, but with dogs also, including his big golden retriever named Bubba. We would bring Chance over to play with Bubba and it was hilarious to see that Chance thought he was the "Alpha Dog" because he tried to play rough, slightly biting Bubba and chasing him. Bubba seemed to just humor Chance and let him think that he was in charge of the much bigger golden retriever. Dogs are really simple, but at the same time so smart. Also, their love for their owners is very genuine.

Comically, Clark's huge golden retriever would sleep with him, taking up more than half the bed and wherever he went, he shed, so Clark was always vacuuming him and everything else the dog touched. Christina, my daughter, Clark and I were a little family for a while and we were not complete without the two dogs, Bubba and Chance. As dogs are known to do, those fun-loving canines gave us unconditional love and many playful times together. We may have become a real family if it were not for one thing, Clark's Bipolar Disorder, which unfortunately, had gone on for many years without being properly treated.

According to an article on the website "Very Well" written by Kimberly Read on August 19, 2019 "… It is estimated that nearly thirty percent of those diagnosed with Bipolar disorder will attempt suicide at least once in their lives. The suicide rate for people with bipolar disorder is twenty times that of the general population."[103]

A doctor explained to me that when a Bipolar is not properly medicated for a long time, new bad pathways form in the brain and take over, causing severe anxiety, depression or both. Then suddenly, often in the summer, like others with Bipolar, Clark experienced manic periods where he felt superhuman, like he could do anything. This grandiosity would cause Clark to be impulsive, like when he bought two new cars in the same week, even though he didn't have a job and he already had a perfectly good car in his garage.

When I met him in June of 1996, Clark was in his early forties, cute, had light brown thinning hair, a medium build and a Mediterranean appearance from his mother, Joan's side. He was intelligent and appeared to be fine, even though he was just about to start a manic episode. When he told me about having Bipolar, he looked like he was handling his disorder well with therapy and medication. Since I had to take medication for ADHD and it worked well for me, I wasn't put off by his having Bipolar because his disorder was new to me. He took several medicines, including some for depression. Since I also took medication for depression, I thought he could get and stay better like I had.

What I did not know was that it was common during a manic episode, when a patient felt more than better, for the bipolar person to stop taking his medication. Additionally, I still didn't in fact understand how his disease affected him yet. However, Clark's disorder was more serious than regular depression because it also had a manic side. During the late summer and early fall after I met him, Clark started to go into a manic phase. It was only later when I read books about the insidious part of the disease and how it is like a madness, that I started to see how serious this illness really is.

As is frequently my custom, when I do not know about a subject, I read a lot about it. Hence, I dove into books Clark gave me, like the excellent 1995 autobiography by Dr. Kay Redfield Jamison, a professor of psychiatry at Johns Hopkins University School of Medicine, called: *An Unquiet Mind: A Memoir of Moods and Madness.*[104] The book was about Jamison's horror and ultimate healing, when she was diagnosed with Bipolar Disorder while in medical school.

Another good memoir I read about the illness was written by the late Patty Duke in 1988 called: *Call Me Anna*.[105] She describes a terrible childhood of abuse at the hands of a couple whom she stayed with while she was underage, who took charge of her career. Later, Manic Depression (the older term for Bipolar) took hold of her and her memoir describes the devastation of it and then later, good health, when she finally was properly diagnosed and medicated.

Reading these books taught me a lesson: You should read about something you are unfamiliar with to make it less scary to confront. I learned also that pouring into relevant books gives good information about any illness you don't understand, so you can help your loved ones make wise decisions about treatment. When Clark went into his depressive state, usually in late fall or the winter, he just wanted to lay on the couch and not participate in activities or even play with Christina or his daughter like he usually did. This prompted nine-year old Christina to say, "Clark, didn't you take your medicine? I take medicine too and it really helps."

Jack Peterson, Clark's father, was a believer in Christ and was thrilled to find out that I had gone with Clark to see the WCCC prayer team, who prayed with him to receive Jesus. At least Jack and Clark knew that they both were going to heaven. Jack was ecstatic because of his son's new repentance and relationship with the Lord. Even so, though he loved all of us, Clark saw suicide as the only way out of his pain. For him, it was like a debilitating physical agony in the brain.

Later, Clark told me that after his earlier attempts to end his life, he kept looking at our pictures and those of the rest of his family, so he wouldn't kill himself. Clark said to me that he didn't want to take his own life, but he had recently told us that the new medication he had started, like all the others he had tried over the years, wasn't working anymore and he felt, "…like the whole weight of the world was on my shoulders…" and like, "a knife was sticking in my head."

In 1996, as the fall and winter set in, Clark was despondent and hopeless, and especially troubled because he could not work as an engineer anymore and that is why he was on disability. His sister Judy and her husband, Roger tried to help him, but it was difficult with four kids of their own to worry about. Several times that winter, he attempted suicide and was sent to the hospital in an ambulance.

The Peterson family told me he was at a genius level before Bipolar took over his mind, causing him to be frustrated because he couldn't complete his work successfully. After college, for a time, he had been able to support his family with an engineering job before he was divorced and lost it all, due to the ravages of his condition.

Of course, we could tell he was extremely intelligent because he could answer in detail about any complicated scientific or engineering question that Christina, or anybody else had. Clark had loved being an engineer and it was a source of pride, but after trying many different medications and psychotherapy and nothing worked, he lost all hope.

In desperation and hoping their son would snap out of it, his parents came to live with him. To give him a much-needed sense of purpose, they stayed at his house for months, encouraging him to work on home projects, chores which he used to love. He would work as much as he could to feel like his life mattered. During the days he felt better, he applied to engineering jobs. Unfortunately, when he did get an interview or a short temporary job with Sears as a garage door installer, he couldn't keep up, due to his depressive state, which included an unsettling anxious phase.

It wasn't all his Bipolar Disorder that affected his mental state. Years before, he had hit his head when he fell off a bicycle and his doctors thought that could have been a reason that the medications he tried didn't seem to work for a long period. He also admitted, maybe he did not stay on a particular medication long enough for the doctors to adjust it correctly for his body size and his particular issues. After all, treatment for this disease is both an art (talk therapy) and a science (medication) and it can take a long time to get it right.

Toward the end, Clark acknowledged to me that when he was in a manic state, he felt overly good and wouldn't take his medication at all, typical of bipolar behavior. During those periods, he felt he didn't need a doctor anymore and that he was cured, but invariably he would cycle back to depression and/or anxiety, often during the winter when it was cold and dark, negatively affecting his mood.

The doctor told me that if Clark had been medicated properly and given the right psychotherapy since he first got symptoms in his early twenties, he could have had a more normal life. Due to his manic phases, which sometimes caused delusions, Clark felt he didn't need help anymore. He cycled through these phases, about once a year and then those debilitating up and down periods got closer together as he got older.

Clark's head injury could have caused a comorbid condition with his already difficult Bipolar Disorder, which made it even harder to treat. It became more serious and frightening for all of us when he attempted suicide a couple of times, but was found just in time by his sister, Judy, laying on the floor of his garage before he could asphyxiate himself with his car exhaust. Each time, Clark was brought to the hospital in an ambulance.

Nothing seemed to work, even though Judy and her husband, Roger did everything they could to help Clark, to include going to support meetings for Bipolar at the hospital with him. Clark was such a kind soul, very intelligent, and fun loving, with a quirky sense of humor, so that he was loved by many, especially those family and friends in his life. Accordingly, it was sad for all of us close to him to watch this progression of his disease take him in a downward spiral and we all felt so helpless.

Ultimately, a few months after Clark's last attempt and ambulance ride, he actually was successful committing suicide in his garage on April 21, 1997. Being the creative engineer that he was, he found a way to hook up a hose to his car's exhaust, turned on the automobile, put his head on a pillow on the floor and laid with his nose and mouth right near the hose to await his death. He left us a note saying he was sorry, but that he could not take it anymore, it was just too painful. Although I was deeply saddened by this turn of events, there was a part of me that understood because he was in so much psychic pain.

His death happened the morning his parents left to travel home to another state. To make it worse, I was not picking up the phone because the day before, Clark and I had decided to take a break in our relationship. We took a break so he could take the time to get better without worrying about maintaining a relationship just then; therefore, I didn't answer my home phone because I was afraid that if I talked to Clark or listened to his messages, I would cave and enable him to continue on without trying to get more help. That is why his sister, Judy tried to get a hold of me at work because I wasn't picking up my phone messages at home.

Also, when we had last seen each other, I wasn't worried about Clark attempting to hurt himself; I thought his parents were still staying with him, trying to help him get back on track. Unfortunately, I did not know then that his parents had left to go back home two days after I last saw him. Later, I learned from Judy that the family found a Willow Creek Church Sunday service program on the front seat of his car, dated for the day before he died. It gave us comfort to know that he tried to turn to God the day before his suicide.

After Judy found Clark deceased in the garage the same morning that his parents left to go home, she listened to his phone messages. Ironically, Clark had several messages from companies calling in response to his earlier applications for engineering jobs and asking him to come in for an interview. It is so sad to think of Clark lying already dead on his garage floor a few hours after his parents had left to drive home, while those calls came in.

Clark and I had dated for almost a year and much of that time he inspired me with his strong work ethic, even being as sick as he was. During that time, Clark was always trying to become an engineer again or even do less stressful jobs related to gadgets, cars and anything electrical. He truly didn't want to be a burden on anyone and he liked to work to keep busy.

In the end, when Judy finally got a hold of me at work at the Bradford Group (a collectibles company where I worked after retiring from the Navy) the day after his death to tell me about it, I started wailing in my semi-open cubicle, which my boss, Tammie, the HR director and many around me could hear. After a few minutes, Tammie and others came into my cubicle to see what happened and ask how they could help.

Ultimately, my co-workers decided I was too distraught to drive myself home forty-five minutes away. Thus, two of the employees drove me home, one in my car and the other in his own car, so I did not have to come back for mine later. Tammie gave me five days of Bereavement Leave and I had not even worked for the company for very long (only three months there as the Manager of Organizational Performance). That meant, technically, I hadn't yet earned all those days they were giving me off, but they did it anyway, for which I will always be grateful.

Just like Bozoma St. John's experience with her co-workers when her husband died, I was royally cared for by those who worked around me. The leadership lesson I learned from that experience at the Bradford Group was monumental: it is to always take care of your people, especially in times of crisis. Employees will then be very loyal to the company and give you that extra amount of excellent performance, which I did after my bereavement period was over.

Thankfully, my church small group all showed up at my house the night I found out Clark died to console me and I lived pretty far away from most of those women because I hadn't yet moved closer to church, like I was planning to do in a few months. You can see why I identified with Bozoma because I was so touched that these people from work that I hardly knew, as well as my church small group, really cared. And even though Bozoma and I were from different ethnic environments (my family being Irish and her family being originally from Ghana), I knew we would understand each other, due to our similar experiences.

WCCC, where I worshipped for twenty-two years before moving to Florida in 2017, was essential in helping me recover from Clark's suicide. They had a weekend workshop for the family and friends of people who died, which was so helpful. There we learned we are not alone in our sorrow. The table I was assigned was made up of all significant others of suicides. Just like Bozoma felt when she lost her husband, the people at my table were going through similar stages of grief as was I. Like Clark, most of our suicides had Bipolar Disorder too. The workshop leaders told us that ten percent of all Bipolars kill themselves.

Another commonality between Bozoma and I was contending with young daughters at home while grieving our significant others. Our compassion, empathy and humanity bonds us together because of our common experiences, however painful, no matter what our backgrounds are. Hearing Ms. St. John's story convinced me of the fact that human understanding ties us together in a crisis, without respect to our differences.

After Clark's death, the kindness shown to me by my co-workers, church family and others touched me deeply and reinforced my conviction that God always has our backs and we don't have to ever be alone; we just have to ask Him for help. When Jesus died on the cross, he did not abandon us. He left an important part of His Trinity nearby to guide us with wise counsel called the Holy Spirit, so we are never alone. Sometimes we don't realize it, but even when going through a crisis, He really is never out of reach for us.

(R) Kathleen with church friends, Jeanette T. & Bill K.

(A) Kathleen's church group and (L) Bradford Group coworkers, who all helped her through Clark's death.

(L) Christina, 9 years. old with cousins, Mackenzie and baby Madison

Bozoma St. John at WCCC, 2019 Wikimedia commons photo by Maya A Darasaw

Kathleen re-enlisting one of her sailors, 1990s

(L) Kathleen's dog, Chance, (Above Right) Photo by Gabriel Lerma [107]

(R) Gloria Estephan, singer that Clark loved. Photo from Wikimedia [108]

(L) Clark P. with daughter, Mandy, and dog, Bubba

(R) John Prine, singer that Clark and Kathleen saw together. Photo by R. Baker, Wikimediacommons [109]

Chapter 28: *The Guy in the Glass*

For it isn't your father or mother or wife
Whom judgment on you must pass,
The fellow whose verdict counts most in your life
Is the one staring back from the glass.

— Peter "Dale" Wimbrow Sr., 1934[110]

In March of 2001, my younger sibling, Mike O'Brien of "Mike's Venom Sauce" fame, came down with a bad cold, for which he was given standard cold medicine. Instead of it improving his symptoms, he steadily got worse; his skin was taking on a yellow cast. About twenty years before, Michael had contracted Hepatitis C, which was still an incurable disease at that time. He was not sure how he contracted it, although he had been a drug and alcohol abuser but not into needles, which would have been one of the most common ways to get it – by sharing dirty needles. It is possible that Michael was in a black-out and didn't remember an episode where he shared needles with someone. Black-outs are common occurrences for addicts, where they do not remember an hour, a day, a week or even more while using their substance of choice. When I talk about drugs in this memoir, I also mean alcohol, since it is a mind-altering chemical too.

In the eighties and the early nineties, substances usually associated with needles like heroin or other opioids were not as commonly used as they have become today, so I am not sure how Michael got Hepatitis C (Hep C for short). The disease is contracted by an exchange of bodily fluids, similar to how people contract AIDS. By the time Mike found out he had Hep C, he was forty-one years old and had been clean and sober for four years. Before that, he had been abusing drugs and alcohol since he was fourteen years old, when he went away to a boarding high school called St. Thomas Military Academy in Minnesota.

Mike later told me that he felt so bad that my parents sent him away in 1968, that that was when he started using drugs. Our parents thought the new school discipline would help him academically because like me, he had problems paying attention and was doing poorly in school. I am sure they had had no idea that their action in sending him away to school would be the very catalyst for him to begin using drugs. It would have broken their hearts to know how he felt because they thought they were helping him.

Some of Michael's friends had had liver transplants due to their livers being adversely affected by substance abuse, leading to serious diseases, like cirrhosis and Hepatitis C. Usually, Hep C stays dormant for many years before the symptoms show up, and they can go a long time before the liver shuts down, even after the addict stops using drugs; therefore, it is difficult to pinpoint exactly when the disease starts in an individual.

It became a life-threatening issue in March of 2001, because Michael's liver could not process the medicine that his doctor prescribed to alleviate his cold symptoms. At forty-seven years old, Michael was at peace with both his life-threatening disease and his probable death sentence because he knew he had God on his side.

Unfortunately, Michael's liver was failing and in May of 2001, Terry and I rushed to Indianapolis to see Mike before he went into liver transplant surgery to save his life. I noticed that he had lost a lot of weight and that his skin had turned a deep yellow color. As he was wheeled into the operating room for this serious surgery, we were confident it would work because it had worked well for some of his friends and we were hoping he would get to live another twenty years with a new liver.

We knew the Hep C virus would attack his liver again because the virus was still present in his body, but we hoped he could live with it a long time before the virus caused his new liver to fail, just like had happened with his original liver. Surgery would buy him time before a cure could be found, which appeared to be just over the horizon, with all the research going on. As it turns out, scientists did come up with a cure, eleven years later, in 2012, but that is getting ahead of my story and too late for Michael.

After the surgery, the fifty-thousand-dollar operation gave us the appearance of being successful and Mike was started on the anti-rejection drug therapy that he would have to take for the rest of his life. In addition, his normal color came back, (freckles and all) and he seemed more energetic and in good spirits. The whole family rejoiced at the marvels of medicine that allowed a liver to be transplanted to save Michael's life.

At forty-seven, Mike was a very handsome man, taking after our gorgeous mom. He had jet black straight hair, almond shaped crystal blue Irish eyes, small ears, freckles and adorable dimples under his high cheekbones, displaying an impish grin when he smiled. Although different from my mom's brownish-yellow eyes, Mike's expressive eyes were the same deep blue color as our dad's, completing the perfect picture of a man sired by just the right combination of the best traits of both his parents.

As the summer wore on, reports from Michael's wife, Karen, that he was gaining strength and looking more like himself each day, energized our hope for a strong long-term recovery. Furthermore, Karen and Mike were happy to settle back into their normal lives, after all the disruption of the last year of doctor's visits, medicines and transplant surgery. Buying their new house and taking care of two cats named Snowball and Pudding, as well as Karen's demanding job, kept them busy.

Since he felt better, Michael started going back to his Twelve-Step recovery meetings, which is something he could still manage while taking care to rest enough during his extended convalescence. Karen went back to work as the Supervisor of Parking for U. of Indiana Hospital, the same hospital where Michael's surgery took place. Fortunately, since Karen was an employee of that hospital, the enormous costs of his transplant surgery were covered by insurance, which was a godsend. Life seemed to fall into place and it seemed Mike was on his way to a full recovery, with many good years left ahead of him.

I had planned to go see Mike in August, just three months after his surgery, when he felt well enough to have visitors at the new house he and Karen had recently bought in Indianapolis. Those plans were changed, however, because I was offered a job teaching French at a high school and classes were beginning in August. Due to my stopping work to go back to school to update my teaching credentials, I was relieved to find this last-minute teaching job. So, we rearranged our plans to be able to visit Mike in November, during my school break.

Moreover, my organizational leadership consulting jobs had dried up and I wanted something more regular with benefits that I could count on, like teaching. Although I had been consulting for five years after leaving the Navy and it paid lucratively, getting this type of work was hit or miss and I needed something with a regular paycheck and work that did not require me to scramble for my next contract, so I could put food on the table and pay the mortgage.

I like to think my "Higher Power (HP)" upstairs was looking out for me and my family. Michael also believed in a "Higher Power," something he was introduced to through his Twelve-Step recovery programs: Alcoholics Anonymous (A.A) and Narcotics Anonymous (N.A.). The tenants of A.A./N.A. posit that one cannot recover through his/her own power, but with the help of a "Higher Power." Usually, many of the Twelve Steppers (Index B, pg. 309) come to call their H.P., God, Jesus, Yahweh, Allah or whomever was the God they have been taught about in childhood. In our case, we were raised in Christianity, so our H.P. was one God in three persons: God the Father, His Son Jesus, and the Holy Spirit.

During one phone call after Michael had been in Twelve-Step programs for some time, I asked him if he knew his Higher Power's name. He didn't answer, so I reminded him that it was Jesus, as part of the Trinity we learned about in childhood as Catholics. Just to solidify Mike's personal relationship with his Higher Power, we recited together the "Prayer of Salvation" asking Jesus to come into his heart, take away his sins and forgive him for those sins.

Now we had a shared understanding of our Higher Power, which made our sibling connection even stronger. Furthermore, for the last eleven years, Mike and I had also grown closer with our shared understanding of the importance of working our recovery programs, Mike in A.A. and N.A. and me in Al-Anon, for friends and loved ones of Alcoholics and Overeaters Anonymous (O.A.). Because we both worked our programs diligently, we slowly began to speak the same language of recovery and Christianity and how they had brought us peace and continually improved our lives.

Michael told me about a poem he loved that someone in A.A. had written and how it summed up his struggle with his addictions. The poem is called, "The Guy in the Glass" and it impressed me so much that I named this chapter after the poem and I have included a verse under the title. Written by Peter "Dale" Wimbrow Sr. in 1934, if you want to read more, it can be found on the internet, at: https://www.theguyintheglass.com/gig.htm,[110] which gives blanket permission to use it.

For many years, people thought the writer of the "Guy in the Glass" was anonymous, but in 2002, the name of the author of this popular A.A.-loved poem was discovered. The theme of the poem is that one has to look at him/herself to see where things went wrong in one's life, instead of blaming other things and other people and once the person gets that right, he/she can recover. It puts the onus back on the alcoholic and addict to understand and fix their own problems by taking responsibility for their own actions.

I think the "The Guy in the Glass" resonated with Michael because just like the Twelve-Steps, it challenges the recovering alcoholic/addict to reflect on the negative thoughts and actions that affected all spheres of his/her life which contributed to this disease. People cannot change or improve what they don't understand and Michael was hungry to understand how he had become an addict and what he should do to recover from it.

"Guy in the Glass" perfectly captures the idea that the alcoholic needs to take a hard, long, painful look at him/herself to be able to recover and the Twelve Steps are designed to do just that for addicts of food, alcohol and drugs, as well as other substances. The poem resonated with me as well, which caused the two of us, Michael and me, to discuss our foolish actions in the past that contributed to the disease of substance abuse or unhealthy behaviors.

For Al-Anon members like me, unhealthy behaviors develop around trying to control another person's substance problems. Discussing how our wrong thinking and unhealthy living had destroyed our past relationships, compounded our problems, and jeopardized our work situations and was crucial to recovery. Our discourse helped us to discover why many things had gone wrong in our lives, and in my case why previous marriages broke up. I used to think that Mike and I were so different, but through these discussions over the eleven years of his sobriety, I began to see the commonalities in our lives.

Finally, I had someone in my immediate family who understood these things and I began to feel comforted that I was alone no more with these types of struggles. Even today, I miss Michael when I want to ask how he would see other family members or situations I don't understand. Over those years, Mike became a trusted confidant. Moreover, while working our respective recovery programs, we both became aware of some of the unhealthy behaviors of our alcoholic parents that contributed to our inability to create real healthy intimacy with others or even be as successful at our jobs as we had dreamed of being. Getting to know Michael on such an intimate basis, through our mutual love of Christ, as well as, the Twelve-Step programs, really for the first time, made me feel that I had an ally in discovering the extent of dysfunction in our family of origin.

For a long time before Mike got clean and sober, I had felt so alone, while trying to be honest about the "elephant" in the living room of our family home in Glenview and beyond. When I say "elephant," I mean in classic recovery lingo that there was something in our house, visible or understood by every member of the family, but ignored and denied, so, this large beast was not confronted openly. Trying to discuss or address it felt like walking on eggshells, if truth be told. The elephant in the room was, of course, addiction.

I had been getting help for several years before Michael joined the ranks of alcoholics, addicts or Al-Anons, trying to recover through the Twelve-Step programs. What a relief to have Mike by my side. Whenever I tried to talk about the elephant in our house, family members, cousins and close friends of the family would shut me down, saying things like I was exaggerating or dismissing my concerns like my mom did, by calling me, "so dramatic." One of Mom's favorite sayings.

Early on during my teens, the only one among my aunts and uncles that really took me seriously about this was my mom's older sister, Aunt Lois. She believed me and understood what I was going through. Most importantly, she validated my concerns because she noticed unhealthy behaviors going on in my house too. This all happened one time when Lois and her family came to stay at our house for a few days, as they lived out of town.

During their stay, my parents had a particularly vicious argument that had me crying and confiding to my aunt. In the past, whenever Aunt Lois told me something about our family that was true, but uncomfortable, my mom used to remark, (again, as a way of dismissing it), "That Lois, she is so dramatic." It was taboo to tell Mom what others said about her drinking; however, not long after this, I noticed her imbibing more and more. In order to disguise the contents, she carried around a large glass of what looked like water with ice cubes.

Unfortunately, Mom's ever-present glass was filled, not with water, but it contained straight vodka—first with a "splash of vermouth, then as the years piled up, she drank it with no vermouth at all, which either way looked like water. This became her drink, "du jour" and was placed next to her every day that I came home from school and work when I was a teenager. I tell this story to explain how a family with the elephant in the room can make you feel crazy until a trusted confidant validates your perceptions with their own, like my brother Mike or my Aunt Lois did for me.

During the time Michael and I were both in recovery at the same time, we each became different people for the better than we had been before. Less selfish, more introspective and compassionate towards others, we both facilitated this growth in each other. He would share with me helpful audio tapes from good A.A. speakers that he had heard. In addition, we also both discovered a mutual love for God, whom we both saw as our "Higher Power" (HP), Jesus.

Dad never got to see Michael recover, but we felt him cheering us on anyway. When our father died in 1987, I believe Michael did not handle the grief as well as Terry and I did because he had not been able to say goodbye. Mike knew our dad was sick, but he was still drinking and drugging; therefore, Michael did not get to see Dad and apologize for his behavior or make peace with our father before he died. Without good closure with a loved one, grief is compounded ten-fold and I believe my Michael really suffered. This is another lesson I took from my father's death: do not wait to clear things up. Make amends or apologize to someone because you may never get the chance again. I would need this lesson again, sooner than I thought.

In January, 2002, Mike's wife, Karen called to tell us that Michael had taken a turn for the worse and that we had better come to Indianapolis to see him. He was back in the hospital. Terry and I drove there together to see Mike. Again, he had that yellow tint to his skin. Unfortunately, Michael had contracted the virus again in his new liver. Mike had told Karen that this time he did not want to wait for another liver for a new transplant which was his only alternative, since his new liver was failing. In fact, he did not want to go through the transplant process again. He was done! So, the family was all on their way to say goodbye.

The day before, while Mike was still awake and conscious, I watched with tears streaming down my face as a line of young men that he was sponsoring in A.A. each came in to see him for the last time. Sponsors are like mentors to the newer A.A. members, helping them navigate the pitfalls of trying to keep sober in a drinking world. One guy who Mike was sponsoring came in crying, and laid his head on Michael's lap. He said, "Mike, I got another sponsor like you told me to."

Another one said, looking directly at us, "I am his bad boy. I keep going back out there to drink."

I looked at the last guy and said, "You will not do that anymore because you are going to go out there to help someone else stop drinking because that is how the program works! You know you can't keep sobriety for yourself if you don't give it away."

At that moment, Mike who couldn't talk anymore, but could weakly move his arms and legs, pumped his fist and made a noise that sounded like, "You tell him, Kath!" His action seemed to take every ounce of strength he had left.

Mike was still conscious on the third day of our vigil, but as the day wore on, he started to go in and out of consciousness. At the beginning of that day, Karen had told us that she had just received the paperwork for Mike to sign for some benefits he was supposed to get. Mike was half sitting up and so we brought the paperwork over for him to sign on his tray table. Since he seemed too fragile to even hold the pen, I decided that I would try and take a stab at helping him sign by putting the pen in his hand and cheering him on to write. I knew Karen needed the money, so I didn't want to let the benefits go to waste if they did not get a signature before he died. I tried everything to increase his adrenaline with the purpose of getting him to sign, including encouraging him and when that did not work, later saying nasty things he did in the past to get his adrenaline up for doing it.

Regretfully, I could have cried because of the things I said, but it did seem to get his adrenaline and his will going because he started to write, but it was very shaky and he could not finish it. I told him I was very sorry for the things I said and he seemed to understand that I was trying to help Karen. I guess I will never know for sure if he really was able to forgive me for saying those nasty things because soon, he was unconscious.

I pray to God he truly knew that I was so sorry. Hearing is the last sense to go, so I am pretty sure he could still hear. Karen and Mike had had a code they had practiced the last time he was in the hospital where he would blink once for "no" and twice for "yes."

While we were present, she asked Mike if he was still hanging on because he was waiting for my mom to get there from Florida. He blinked twice, so we knew he had heard her question, and that told us his answer was "yes."

My cousin Patrick O'Brien and his wife Rosalie were kind enough to fly down from Chicago to be with the family as we waited by Mike's bedside for the inevitable. When there was friction between Terry and me, due to some decisions that needed to be made, Pat talked to each of us separately to calm down the tension in the room. I am so grateful for his support and love during one of the worst days in our lives.

Pat died five years ago, so I cannot talk to him again about it, but I believe he is up there in heaven clowning around with Michael and having a good laugh; however, I will never forget Pat and Rosalie's kindness by being with us during such a difficult time. The pastor who married my brother and sister-in-law twenty-one years before also arrived. His presence there was very comforting, especially when he started to read "Psalm Twenty-Three" out of the Bible. We could tell Michael was responding to it because he was mouthing the words as he listened with his eyes closed:

23 The Lord is my shepherd; I shall not want.
[2] He maketh me to lie down in green pastures:
he leadeth me beside the still waters.
[3] He restoreth my soul: he leadeth me in the paths of
righteousness for his name's sake.
[4] Yea, though I walk through the valley of the shadow of death,
I will fear no evil: for thou art with me;
thy rod and thy staff they comfort me.
[5] Thou preparest a table before me in the presence of mine enemies: thou
anointest my head with oil; my cup runneth over.
[6] Surely goodness and mercy shall follow me all the days of my life: and I
will dwell in the house of the Lord forever.

— King James Version (KJV) Psalm 23:1-6

It broke my heart to see Karen, the love of Mike's life sitting on a cooler, next to his bed with her head on his chest. It was the only seat there that she could pull up right next to the head of the hospital bed, so she could be as close to him as possible. Although exhausted, she never left his side. What a great example of a loving marriage to us! Karen demonstrated to all of us what dedication and great love of a spouse looked like throughout the highs and lows of an intimate relationship. To this day, when faced with trouble in my own marriage, I remind myself of Karen's selfless devotion to her spouse.

The flight coming from Florida bringing my mom, Elaine and her younger sister, Nancy to Indianapolis was delayed. That resulted in them just missing Michael's last breath, but I believe he knew that they got there to see him because I count on there being an afterlife. I don't understand how people can go through tragedies without holding on to something greater than themselves to help them through.

Since I believe that there is a Creator, I refuse to accept that we are just dust when we die, so it makes sense to me to give credence to there being an afterlife with the One who made us in His image. This idea of us not becoming just dust when we die has been proven to me time and time again through many of the unexplainable coincidences and spiritual events which I have already outlined in this book, but I have one more that I like to believe was Michael's doing because it has to do with his favorite relative, Aunt Nancy.

On January 14, 2002, my sweet brother took his last breath, devastating Terry and me and the rest of the family. During Mike's funeral in Indianapolis, there was the same country preacher speaking at the service as the one who prayed the "Twenty-Third Psalm" with him at the hospital. The Preacher really nailed how one can get to heaven in a simple way, by telling us that all we need to do is ask Jesus to forgive our sins and to come into our hearts. I was surprised how many people at the funeral commented to us how great that old preacher did in explaining the gospel to the attendees.

With that in mind, we left for the burial service in one of the limousines. My mom was riding towards the front and my Aunt Nancy was sitting next to me in the back as we drove to the cemetery. I was really grieving Michael's death and quietly crying as I spoke to God in my heart as to why Michael had to be taken so soon. I knew it was a rhetorical question, but I kept asking it, even though Mike told me when he was still conscious that he was at peace about it. He told me that he should have died by the age of thirty or thirty-five with all the chemicals he had put into his body.

As I was pondering this in the funeral car, my Aunt Nancy was talking about how great the preacher had delivered his sermon. Then she turned to me and said, "Kathleen, the preacher said if we asked Jesus into our heart, we could become a Christian. What do you have to do exactly to truly become a Christian?"

At this point, I am thinking, "Oh no, Lord, I am in grief here. Do you REALLY want me to do this now?" But I knew the Lord expected us to do what He required of us as soon as possible. I also knew that Aunt Nancy was Mike's favorite aunt and that he would want her to be in heaven with him. I asked my mom if she wanted to pray with us, but she looked at me and said, "Get away from me!" which was hurtful, but I also knew she was not truly all there because a few years before she had been diagnosed with Alzheimer's; therefore, I concentrated on my aunt, taking her hand and looking into her eyes. To start, I took a deep breath, dried my tears and replied to Nancy with these words,

"Well, you just say a certain prayer after me and you will be a Christian. Some people call it the 'Sinner's Prayer' (aka the "Prayer of Salvation') and there are no exact words, except you must repent for your sins and ask the Lord to come into your heart."

My aunt closed her eyes and said something like the following prayer after me: "Lord, I ask you to come into my heart. I am so sorry for what I have done. Please forgive me of my sins, so I can become a part of Your family of believers, and follow You as my Lord and Savior. Amen."

I congratulated and hugged her and told her that she was now a Christian. I felt my sibling, Mike's presence in that car and felt sure that through Jesus, he was guiding me to help my aunt become a Christian, so Michael could be assured of her salvation.

Not long after, when my mom, Elaine was placed in a memory care facility, I went to visit her one day and she became lucid for about five minutes. I took the opportunity to have her repeat the "Sinner's Prayer" after me and she did it! I asked everyone I knew if they thought it counted to ensure her salvation and everyone agreed that it did, so we are now assured that Elaine will be there in heaven with our family. I believe my father had prayed like that at church before he died, so I expect to see my parents together up there with

Michael when I pass away. What a gift salvation is! I don't have to run a treadmill of doing works and wonder if I am going to heaven in the future—what a relief! Thank God, Salvation is within our reach.

How can any family do without the support of our Creator when in crisis? I once heard the first President George Bush being interviewed about sending the troops into the first Gulf War. The interviewer asked him how he made the difficult decision to send those young men and women into harm's way. I am paraphrasing him, but I remember that Mr. Bush said words to this effect, "I get on my knees and pray. I do not know how any president can make this decision without doing that." It impressed me that even our Commander-in-Chief knew that he needed God to do his job effectively.

My husband and I moved to the Sarasota/Bradenton area of Florida in 2017. Coincidentally, Mike and Karen once lived nearby in St. Petersburg for a year and we visited them there. Next to the huge Sunshine Skyway Bridge, built in 1987, Mike loved to fish on the remnant ends of the old bridge, which were turned into fishing piers for both serious anglers and hobby fishermen. Every time I cross that huge, high bridge to go into St. Petersburg, it comforts me to look over the railing and see my brother there in my imagination, doing his favorite thing, catching a large fish. I sigh and I say, "Hi, Mike. Hope you are having fun out there."

Kathleen (8) and brother, Michael (6)

(Above) Mike's Funeral Reception, January, 2002
His widow, Karen, is on the far right next to Aunt Nancy and cousins Mike and Shelly. Terry and Stacy are seated near her relatives. Bill and Kathleen are standing in the left back.

286

(Below) Terry O'Brien holding
his newborn daughter,
Mackenzie in 1994

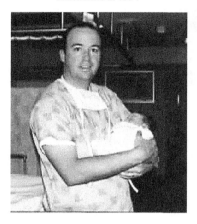

(Above) Elaine, Kathleen, Mike, and Karen
O'Brien at Terry and Stacy's wedding, 1992

(Below) Kathleen's cousin, Patrick
O'Brien, with wife, Rosalie, 2015

(Above) Sister-in-law, Karen O'Brien, visiting
Kathleen at her house in Grayslake, IL.

(Right)
(L-R) Terry holding
Mackenzie, Stacy
holding Madison,
Kathleen with
Christina holding
Chance, Mike and
Karen, 1990s

(Below) Aunt Nancy Hodges in
Largo, FL. in early 1990s

(Above) Michael and Kathleen in
Grayslake, IL. 1990s

(Above) Siblings, Kathleen and Mike,
godparents to Mackenzie O'Brien, Sept.,

(Above) Mike with niece, Christina
wearing his Chef's hat, about 1992

(Above) Photo of the Kathleen's first cousins, the ten O'Brien brothers,
just before Pat (first row, second from left) died, July, 2017

Chapter 29: *The Greatest of These is Love*

But now faith, hope, and love remain—these three.
The greatest of these is love.

1 Corinthians 13:13, WEB

When Mom moved to Florida to be near her sister Nancy in 1994, it affected me a lot because I had just come back home to the Chicago area and was looking forward to spending much needed time with my family. After being gone for sixteen years in the Navy, I was transferred to nearby Great Lakes, Illinois for my last tour until I was to retire sometime in the mid-to-late nineties. I thought I would get to be closer to my mom and Terry in Chicago and Mike in Indianapolis, by moving back to the Midwest in 1993 to finish out my career.

Not only did Mom's move affect me, but because of it, she didn't see Christina much, who was born in 1987. Also, her heavy drinking problem and the early onset of Alzheimer's ensured a sporadic connection with her first grandchild, at that time. Elaine moved to Florida, in part because Terry, Michael and I had confronted her about her drinking with an intervention, but she refused to go to treatment. As a result, we told her that she could not see the grandchildren alone. Shortly after that is when she moved to Largo to be with her sister, Nancy. This was not long before the onset of Mom's Alzheimer's disease.

In early 1998, I was sorry to find out that Antoinette Causarano, Sal's mom, died. About a year before, we had gone through the death of Sal's dad, Frank Causarano. Again, I had to be the one to break it to Christina, which is one of the hardest things I think a parent has to do: tell kids about the deaths of their loved ones. Christina and I had traveled to San Diego from Chicago, where we were then living, to both Frank's and then Antoinette's funerals. At sixteen years old, I had endured my first death of a close family member, my grandpa Dewey Robinson, my mom's dad, in 1968. "Christina Pastina," as Christina's dad lovingly called her, was only nine when she lost her grandfather. Then, a little over a year later, her beloved grandma passed away. Even though we moved to Illinois, these beloved paternal grandparents in California were always involved in her life, not like the absent Elaine, due to her drinking.

Moreover, Mom moved away from Illinois to Florida, only a year after Christina and I transferred to Illinois to be near her and Terry.

Due to all the losses in Christina's life and my divorce from her dad, Sal, we both had been coping by going to psychotherapy. During a counseling session with Steven, my therapist, I was complaining about these "Christian guys that I'd meet, who never asked me out." Steven told me to be patient, that there were plenty of good Christian guys out there. After all, he was one of them, albeit now married, and that I had to wait for God's timing, not my own. I shook my head and told him how doubtful that that was the case, but I was actually OK if I never got married again, the reason being that I was content in my busy single life at the church and by being the parent of Christina.

Steven saw that I wasn't totally convinced by his little speech about all the good single Christian men around my age still out there that wanted to find a single woman, like me, with a child. That was when he finally looked at me, smiled and said, "Kathleen, someday I am going to DANCE at your wedding, you'll see!"

Chuckling, I thought to myself, *Yeah! That'll happen when pigs fly!*

Down the hall from Steven's office, Christina was with her own counselor, Kerry, who had helped her through so many things in her life. On top of my problems with being a single parent with ADHD, for which I had been diagnosed a few years before, Christina was dealing with her grandmother Causarano's death, which occurred less than a year before and my divorce from her dad, Sal, eight years before that. My heart broke those times that I sat in Kerry's therapy sessions with my daughter, crying about her losses, especially about how much she missed her grandmother.

Kerry was a very tender-hearted therapist, focused on Christina's well-being. There were times that she and I had tears running down our faces as we were listening to the anxiety and pain endured by young Christina. After getting my own help, I was able to talk to my daughter about all these things and tell her how sorry I was for my part in causing her more anguish, due to my divorce from her father. Christina and I both had done a lot of work on ourselves individually and in our relationship to get healthy and it was starting to pay off, just prior to meeting my future husband, Bill.

Unfortunately, Mom's move to Florida in 1994 and Michael dying not many years later, wreaked havoc with my plans to become closer to my family, except for Terry, who was still living in Glenview then. As a result, I used this opportunity to get to know my little brother better as an adult. Terry was married to a pretty blonde Sales Representative, named Stacy Biederman in 1992 and by 1994 their first child, my goddaughter, Mackenzie Rose O'Brien was born. This wonderful event was overshadowed because it was connected to the first incident that pointed to the discovery of Mom's early onset Alzheimer's disease.

Of course, one of the first people Terry told of his wife's pregnancy was his mother, Elaine. Not long after, when my cousin Michael O'Brien heard about it, he told my mother that he was thrilled for her to become a grandmother again. The sad part is that Mom didn't remember Terry telling her his first baby was coming, so Terry had to explain that in reality, he had already told our mom his most important news. Of course, everyone knew that a grandmother would not forget something as important as a new grandchild's upcoming birth, unless something was wrong.

Sadly, the "something wrong" was the onset in Mom's early sixties of the vicious disease of Alzheimer's, which was eventually diagnosed by a doctor. This was followed by a symptom progression that was slow at first, but definitely noticeable. Incidents like her stopping at her favorite liquor store to ask where she lived, not attending my Navy retirement ceremony in 1995 or my wedding to Bill in 1999 because she said she "…had a cold," were not really in keeping with her normally sharp mind and love of attending big family events.

Because of Mom's slowly deteriorating brain, (we surmise now, but in truth didn't know then) that she really didn't want to go out of the house, probably because she was afraid of making mistakes or losing her way in unfamiliar places. Sadly, her illness was undeniable and we knew the time was coming when Elaine would have to be admitted to a treatment facility.

For several years from 1994 until Elaine was formally diagnosed around 1999, she lived with her sister, my Aunt Nancy in Florida, who took great care of her. We had thought Elaine's memory problems were due only to her advancing age, coupled with her high alcohol consumption, resulting in the later stages of addiction.

Mom's entire problem became clearer when I visited the two sisters there one time, due to me observing some unusual behaviors that Mom was exhibiting. For example, Elaine was not interested in her normal favorite pastimes anymore, like reading, after having been a prodigious reader all her life. In addition, she could barely pay attention to a television program or engage in wide-ranging conversation.

Another time, I really got worried early one evening because I found Mom face down, out cold and strewn across her queen bed, with all her clothes still on. Moreover, when we talked to Elaine about something, she would nod and give simple answers, but it seemed like the lights were on and no one was home.

Not long after that, I visited Florida again and observed that she wasn't drinking alcohol or smoking cigarettes while I was there. I asked about it and my aunt said that one day, Mom was looking for her cigarettes and her glass of straight vodka. Nancy reported that she told Elaine to look in her own bedroom and a few minutes later, Elaine came back empty-handed because Mom had forgotten what she was looking for. From that time on, she never again asked for or remembered to smoke cigarettes and drink alcohol.

What a blessing that she forgot to drink or smoke! Although, we were not happy that she had to acquire such a serious disease to do it! This event happened after a more than fifty-year, hard-core, non-filtered Chesterfield cigarette habit and at least a thirty-year alcohol dependency. To me, that was a divine intervention that my mom stopped or "forgot" to drink and smoke for the rest of her life, combined with a little of God's ironic sense of humor mixed in.

Still, until the incident with Mom forgetting about Terry having already told her that he and Stacy were going to have their first baby, we didn't realize that her memory symptoms were mostly due to Alzheimer's, coupled with her alcohol problem. Alzheimer's did not seem to be a disease prevalent in the family, either because those afflicted didn't talk about it or they had died before the disease was properly diagnosed. Much later, we found out that her older siblings, brother, Dewey and sister, Lois, showed many symptoms of memory loss before they died.

My Aunt Nancy needed to take Elaine for a medical evaluation. My aunt's heart was broken with the idea of having to put her sister in a facility, but taking care of Elaine at home for about six years had exacted a huge toll on Nancy's health. Aunt Nancy, at only four feet eleven inches had to have back surgery from trying to lift up my five-feet-four-inches-tall mom. She could not go anywhere without worrying about Mom's safety in the house or outside if Elaine wandered off. It took a while to get Elaine to agree to go to the doctor, but she only consented because Nancy told her they both needed to get their physicals done, purposely not mentioning Mom's memory problems.

I don't know what our family would have done if Nancy hadn't been available each day for her sister because Mike, Terry and I still lived in the Midwest and had full-time jobs and families to tend to. Even so, when my aunt finally took her sister to the long-term care facility, she cried. I had to reassure Nancy that she was doing the right thing by putting Elaine in a home. There is a special place in heaven set for Nancy, I strongly believe because of her kindness and self-sacrifice regarding her sister, Elaine.

When Mom finally went into a long-term care facility, which was across the street from their apartment complex. Nancy was there almost every day, bringing Elaine a milkshake, painting her nails, putting make-up on her and giving Mom a much-needed emotional boost. Nancy was also like a "Mama Bear," ensuring Mom got the best medical and emotional care as possible and that her sister was treated with the utmost respect. Nancy was Mom's advocate until the end, when Elaine died in 2006 at seventy-five years old. Mom was so blessed to have such a loving sibling with her throughout her Alzheimers ordeal. That is what I call sisterly love! Sadly, Mom's passing away meant that having a closer relationship with her on this earth would be forever out of reach for me. But, maybe in the next life in eternity…

Unfortunately, as I have been writing this chapter, Nancy just entered the hospital again to unclog her feeding tube, so I am really worried and praying for her. Nancy has lived the longest of any of my relatives on my mom's side and much longer than anyone on my dad's side of the family. She is the only one left of my parents' generation of both the Robinson and the O'Brien sides of my family.

True to my sister-in-law, Karen's loving character, she has been here in Florida at Nancy's side in the hospital and at home, helping my cousins, Danny, Shelly, Mike and Pat cope with the feeding tube clogs and giving them moral support as they go through this phase of my aunt's treatment for cancer. I am sure that if Mike can see us from his preferred fishing spot in heaven, he is proud that his wife is helping out his favorite aunt and her family at this difficult time. In crisis, families often grow closer and when Aunt Nancy died, we knew that Heaven was in her reach because she believed in Jesus Christ as Lord and Savior, since she prayed with me to receive Christ at my brother Mike's funeral in 2002.

(Update: I am sad to say that my beloved Aunt Nancy died right after her 87th birthday (April 8, 2020). Au revoir, my precious aunt, whom we love so dearly.

(Below) Mike O'Brien fishing off St. Pete. Pier, 1998

(Above) Elaine and Tom O'Brien's 25th Anniversary, 1976

(Below) Antoinette Causarano (Right) with her sister, Mary

(Above) Sisters, Nancy Hodges (Left) and Elaine O'Brien living in Largo, FL.,

Chapter 30: *Farther Than Your Grace Can Reach*

"The reality of loving God is loving him like he's a Superhero who actually saved you from stuff rather than a Santa Claus who merely gave you some stuff."

— *Criss Jami, Killosophy* [111]

February 27, 1999 was the happiest day of my life. I was walking down the aisle, on my brother Terry's arm, to my favorite song, "Farther Than Your Grace Can Reach"[112] in the Chapel at Willow Creek Community Church in South Barrington, Illinois. Most of our preferred people were in attendance, including our family and friends. Dressed in a flowing off-white satin gown, with pearls at the neckline and a short veil, my favorite worship singers were around the piano singing this song by Jonathan Pierce. The song talks about *not ever* going so far that God's love and forgiveness cannot reach us. The song expresses how I felt after meeting Christ two years before, when He came out of the movie screen as I watched the film, "Dead Man Walking". I could not believe that God had accepted me into His Kingdom after all I had done. And now to find the love of my life, Bill Iverson at church and that all these blessings were finally in reach for me at this time of my life; it was beyond a most poignant moment.

The wedding worship team was made up of regular singers at Willow Creek Community Church (WCCC), to include lead singer/pianist Joe Horness, accompanied by singers, Barb Olita and Harry Neuman, popular Christian musical performers around our church. This group wowed the guests in the Willow Creek Chapel with more than the usual amount of wedding songs, so much so, that the team jokingly called our wedding; "The Concert." That is just how Bill and I had planned it because the words in these songs painted a picture of two flawed people who not only found God, but found each other through Willow Creek.

As I walked down the aisle, I thought my heart would burst with love and happiness. Unsurprisingly, at that moment, I felt "...the peace of God, which surpasses all understanding..." from Philippians 4:7 (WEB), of which Jesus speaks in the New Testament. Moreover, in Ephesians 2:8-9 (WEB), the Lord tells us more about the miracle of grace: "...for by grace you have been saved through faith, and that not of yourselves; it is the gift of God, [9] not of works, that no one would boast."

Wikipedia defines grace like this: (Christian theology) - "...spontaneous gift from God to people, generous, free and totally unexpected and undeserved."[113] Knowing that by God's grace, not on a treadmill, I have been saved from my own sin to be part of God's family. What a way to start a marriage!

My daughter, Christina was my junior bridesmaid and dressed in an off-white satin dress similar to mine. At twelve years old, Christina was radiant and beautiful as she stepped down the aisle. Bill and I surprised her with an addition to the ceremony that solidified our new relationship as an unbreakable unit of three, including a special blessing for our new blended family. The minister, Rick Mink called Christina up to stand right next to Bill and me for the blessing, so we stood all together on the dais and she was totally surprised during the blessing part: Bill put a special gold Claddagh ring (a traditional Irish wedding ring) on her finger because in a way, she was marrying Bill too.

The Claddagh-style ring, which I also gave to Bill to wear as his wedding ring, consists of three symbols depicted on it: the hands symbolize friendship, the crown symbolizes loyalty and the heart symbolizes love. Knowing I was proud of my Irish heritage, and loved the symbolism of that ring, my Maid of Honor, Bonnie, had started it all by giving me a Claddagh ring to wear on my pinky several years ago.

The description of our wedding is a tender picture painted of our story, but the real tale began exactly a year before to the day on February 27, 1998. I was standing in line for dinner on the cruise ship called the "Sovereign of the Seas" (Notice the ship's name — God has a real sense of humor, never letting us forget "Who" is in charge of whom"). I was with some of my small group girl friends from church and suddenly, I felt a tap on my shoulder. I turned around and a good-looking man smiled and said, "Hi, Kathleen, do you remember me?"

He looked familiar, but I could not place him right away. He saw my puzzled look and said, "I'm Bill Iverson. We spoke at the Willow Creek Church Singles Picnic last Labor Day." He proceeded to tell me all these things about myself that I had talked to him about at that picnic. At first, I guess I did not recognize him because when I met him at the gathering, he was wearing a ball cap, so I did not know he was bald.

When I finally remembered who he was, I did recall his gorgeous blue-green eyes and handsome smile. Moreover, I started to think back to the picnic and was reminded that we had had about a forty-five-minute conversation about what Bill did for a living and my time as a Naval Officer among other subjects. During our talk, I thought maybe we had something going on there until my daughter, Christina, who was about ten years old skated up. Out of the blue, Bill quickly said his goodbyes and was gone. I remember some of the girls I knew that were standing close by then asked what happened to him. I told them that I wasn't sure and we proceeded to talk about, "...these guys at church and how fickle some of them could be."

After that picnic, I proceeded to forget about Bill, but I couldn't help but wonder why he walked away so suddenly and never asked for my phone number. Later, I told Bill that I suspected that he left the picnic so quickly because he did not like that I was a single mom, which he found out when Christina skated up to us earlier. At first, Bill denied this, but later he recalled that he WAS looking for a single woman without children because he had never been married before.

My so-called desires in a new man were different. Looking for someone, who had been married before and had had children already, was what I thought I wanted. I was thinking it would be easier to relate to my situation for a guy in those circumstances. But God, Whom I think has an ironic sense of humor that just keeps going like the energizer bunny, had other plans for us.

Five months later, after meeting him again on the ship, we were sitting on his couch when he suddenly took my hand and asked me to dance to the CD he had just put on called "He'll Find A Way"[114] sung by Bill and Sarah Gaines. I think Bill put this song on because he knew I was embarrassed about having been already married three times. He played this song to reassure me that everything was in God's Hands, before asking me to marry him. While we were dancing, I noticed that Bill's hands were sweaty, which was unusual. I asked him if he was nervous. Suddenly he blurted out, "I love you very much. Will you please marry me?"

Taken by surprise. I said, right away, "Yes, I will." This was how our engagement began.

Getting back to my tale of meeting my husband Bill and our wedding day, I remember the happiness on everyone's faces, even though I had been worried that when I walked down the aisle for the fourth time (but only the first time as a "Born Again" Christian) those present, who knew my history would say in their heads, "*Oh, here she goes again.*" They did not really understand how I had changed and what I had done to prepare myself for this moment of a committed Christian marriage. Besides many years of therapy to understand why I had to go through so many marriages and to consider my part in all these catastrophes, I went to relationship courses, classes and groups to grow my spiritual life further.

As Bill and I had been planning the wedding, I, in fact, told Bill I was thinking that we should just go to Las Vegas and elope. I was embarrassed to walk down the aisle again in front of friends and family in a long off-white wedding dress with a veil. Bill, who had never been married before and was forty-one years old said, "Don't you think because you have repented and asked the Lord to be the leader and savior of your life that your sins "…shall be as white as snow" (Isaiah 1:18 KJV)? Also, that he has taken away our sins "…as far as the east is from the west" (Psalm 103:12 GNT)?"

I replied, "I agree that the Lord did those things for me, but I do not think other people will see it that way." Then Bill said that he thought I should walk down the aisle in the white dress and veil and that we should have the whole big wedding because I was now a child of God as a "Born Again" Christian. Bill added that I was his own "emotional and spiritual virgin" due to accepting Christ into my heart. He made me accept the fact that it was okay to come down the aisle as any new bride would in traditional wedding garb.

That was all I needed to hear to be convinced that I was a new person in the Lord, and that I should not worry about what others thought about me being married in a white dress. Bill was reminding me of the free gift of grace from Christ, which we don't really deserve on our own merits, and not to worry because we are forgiven by Him.

As my wedding march song by Jonathan Pierce expressed: the Lord's grace can touch us, no matter what anyone has done because He has saved us from the consequences of our own sins, through His death on the cross. As one of my old pastors used to say, "It's a done deal." Knowing that, I walked down the aisle in my beautiful off-white dress and veil with my head held high. Jesus is the God of second chances and in my case: third, fourth and probably more chances, but I know this marriage is sticking due to our faith, commitment and love of the Lord. Not only because I am "Born Again" but because we have been married now for many years and I don't think we could have done it on our own without divine intervention.

When Bill and I were talking about what songs to include in our wedding service, Bill, who had been single and never married until then, really wanted to include a song by Stevie Wonder. He wanted the song, "For Once in My Life," as we happily walked back (or should I say danced) down the aisle to the back of the Willow Creek Community Church chapel, shaking hands and smiling at our guests. This song talked about it finally being his turn to have true love.

The song depicts the fervent desire Bill has had to be married and have a family and our wedding was the start of that dream. He had been in so many of his friends' weddings and had always wondered if and when it was to be his turn. His close friends, the Paul and Janet Inserra family prayed for him to realize this desire of his heart for two whole years. That's what I call dedication!

Paul had previously been Bill's Bible Study Men's Small Group Leader and knew about Bill's background, his commitment to practicing his faith with integrity and Bill's desire to be married. My Bible Study Women's Small Group Leader had been Connie Catalano, the one who shepherded me and held my hand through my decision to follow Christ, praying with me to receive Him into my heart as my Lord and Savior. Because of Paul and Connie's close relationship to both of us, Bill and I asked them to each say a few words at our wedding ceremony.

We saw their prepared talks, as a way to communicate to the wedding guests at church, the extensive preparation and commitment we undertook to be ready to enter into our serious decision to marry. Paul had married into a blended family, as had the pastor and his wife, Rick and Joanne Mink. These couples showed us that blended families could have happy endings. That is why we had asked the

Minks to be the ones to conduct premarital counseling for us and then had asked Rick to perform the wedding rites.

During the ceremony, Paul and Connie each talked about the steps Bill and I had taken to prepare for marriage, consisting of not only counseling by Rick and Joanne, but also taking the church marriage preparation course called "Fit to be Tied" that was all-encompassing towards our learning about each other, as well as, how to start our marriage on a good footing, with Christ at the center. This course also included financial counseling, preparing a joint spending plan, understanding how to handle our differences, why it was important to always keep Christ at the center of our marriage and in our case, how to handle a blended family.

During their prepared wedding talks, Paul and Connie also told the wedding attendees of our commitment to abstain from sex until our wedding night, which is something the church encouraged. I am sure my brother and some of our cousins raised their eyebrows at that. After all, we were both in our forties and I had already had had a child.

A few years later, Connie wrote and published a book called, *Love Life of a Single Christian* by Connie Jean Catalano (pp. 121-122)[115] in which she wrote about Bill's and my courtship and marriage as an example of staying sexually abstinent before the wedding and how it fulfills God's plan for marriage. This was still true for people like me getting remarried in my forties. Many people may not agree with this decision, but my Christian therapist, Steven explained to me why it was so necessary for me, especially.

He said to me, "Let's say you were engaged to be married, and you came in here for counseling before you were a Christian. Putting the Bible aside for a moment, I think, Kathleen, you still should wait to have sex until the wedding night because of your history in choosing men and getting divorced. When sex is involved, you do not seem to take the rose-colored glasses off and consequently, you haven't made good decisions in the past."

It was hard to hear, but I knew that if I wanted my new marriage to last, I would need to not do things the same way I always did. In Twelve-Step programs they refer to that as the "definition of insanity" — doing things the same way, expecting different results. I made up my mind to follow Steven's advice and wait until the wedding night to have sex with Bill.

Several weeks before our wedding, I was in Steven's office again. I asked him if he remembered what he told me before I met Bill. He chuckled and knew exactly what I was talking about. I told him, "I did not believe you a year and a half ago, when you said I would find a good Christian man to marry. So, to prove how strong you felt, you said you would dance with me at my wedding. Well, the time has come to pay up. The wedding is on February 27, 1999 and I expect you to be there with your dancing shoes on!" (No, I did not see any pigs flying!)

Sure enough, Steven, accompanied by Christina's counselor, Kerry, were there to see Bill and I get married and watch Christina walk down the aisle with me towards her new step-dad. At the end of the ceremony, as we walked and skipped and danced towards the lobby, I caught their eyes as Stevie Wonder's song was playing, "For Once in My Life"[116] on the CD. It seemed like such a happy day for the two therapists too, to see their hard work helping us, pay off in such a beautiful way.

Incidentally, Bill turned out to be a wonderful step-dad and to this day, Christina looks to him for love and advice at thirty-three years old. In fact, when she recently got married in July, 2020 Bill was the one who walked her down the aisle toward her new husband Thomas Pepperz. She is now a step-mother to Thomas's eight-year-old son, August, and on February 11, 2022, she became a mom herself, having a baby they named Selah Noelle.

And as for me? The decision to wait to have sex until the wedding night to consummate our marriage was the absolute right one for us. I was able to keep a good head on my shoulders during the courtship and engagement period. Before marrying Bill, keeping my head on straight through abstinence was the right decision for me.

Feelings come and go, but a Christ-centered marriage has been more intimate and fulfilling than I ever thought possible, making all the difference in my ability to be a good partner. Through Christ, and His amazing grace, this new healthy union, as opposed to my other marriages, was finally within reach for me. And oh, by the way, as I put this book to bed, Bill and I have been married twenty-four years. How is that for making this marriage stick?

(Left) Kathleen seated (Front) and Bill standing behind her on the Sovereign of the Seas ship, when they met in Feb., 1998

(Right) Kathleen with small group on the ship, Sovereign of the Seas (Left Side Front at banister) Kathleen, Connie, Carol, Sylvia, Debbie, Bill is standing third row up by wall.

(Above L-R) Chris and Jim K. with Kathleen and Bill at a wedding, 1998

(Above) Kathleen and Bill at a wedding, 1998

(Above) Chris and Jim K. giving out programs at the Iverson wedding

(Above) Karen and George Foster

Cousin, Dennis O'Brien singing as he has done for all Kathleen's big events.

(Below)Terry walking Kathleen down the aisle at Willow Creek, 1999

(Above) Connie C. and Paul I. speaking at Kathleen and Bill's wedding

(Below) Bill and Kathleen, February 27, 1999

(Below) Iver and Iggy Iverson, Bill's parents

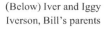

(Below) Iver and Iggy Iverson, Bill's parents

(Above) Bill's brother, Bruce with wife, Kathy and son, Eric.

(Above) Kathleen with Maid-of- Honor, Bonnie F.

(Above) Iver and Iggy Iverson (Bill's parents) with Bill at his wedding, 1999

(Above) Bill, Kathleen and Christina

(Above) Terry and Stacy with kids, Meckenzie, 4 and Madi, 2

1) Bill K., Janet & Paul I. & Jeanette T.
2) Siblings: Lisa, Christina & Josef Causarano
3) Joyce & Dave B., Kathleen & Bill
4) Christina's Graduation, 2009
5) Randy & Lorraine B., 2016
6) Kathleen & Connie C., 2014
7) Jerry & Sandy W. & Kathleen
8) Karen & George Foster, 2020
9) John & Linda T. & Bill & Kathleen, 2019
10) Bill & Kathleen with cousin, Danny Austin, 2020
11) Kathleen, Aunt Nancy & cousin, Shelly, 2019
12) Cousin Pat Austin with dog, Laverne, 2020

(Above Left) Thomas, Christina, Kathleen & Bill, 2019
(Above Right) Cousin Mike Austin and Kathleen, 2020
Note: Cousin Mike Austin sadly died not long after this picture was taken.

About The Author

Kathleen O'Brien Iverson lives on the west coast of sunny Florida with her husband, Bill. She has always loved writing and did a lot of it in all her jobs, but this is her first book. In her free time, she enjoys reading, genealogy, painting, going out for dinner with her husband and friends, loves traveling and being a new grandma to Selah Noelle and August Pepperz.

She's a retired Naval Officer, French and Art High School Teacher, Organizational Performance and Human Resources. Consultant. Kathleen is a proud supporter of the U.S. Military and likes to promote awareness of Attention Deficit Hyperactivity Disorder (ADHD) and substance abuse issues.

Christina, Kathleen & Bill with their dog, Chance (2004)

Christina and Thomas' Wedding, July 10, 2020 with her brother, Josef (Far Left) and sister, Lisa (Far Right) and parents, Kathleen and Bill

Some of Kathleen's Favorite Scriptures...

Philippians 4:6-7, *6Be anxious for nothing, but in everything by prayer and supplication, with thanksgiving, let your requests be made known to God; 7 and the peace of God, which surpasses all understanding, will guard your hearts and minds through Christ Jesus. - NKJV*

Jeremiah 29:11, *"For I know the thoughts that I think toward you, says the Lord, thoughts of peace and not of evil, to give you a future and a hope."- NKJV*

Romans 8:28, *And we know that God causes everything to work together for the good of those who love God and are called according to his purpose for them. - NLT*

1 Corinthians 13: 4-7, *4Love is patient and kind. Love is not jealous or boastful or proud 5or rude. It does not demand its own way. It is not irritable, and it keeps no record of being wronged. 6 It does not rejoice about injustice but rejoices whenever the truth wins out. 7Love never gives up, never loses faith, is always hopeful, and endures through every circumstance. - NLT*

John 3:16, *For God so loved the world that he gave his one and only Son, that whoever believes in him shall not perish but have eternal life. - NKJV*

John 14:1-3, *1"Let not your heart be troubled; you believe in God, believe also in Me. 2 In My Father's house are many [a]mansions; if it were not so, [b]I would have told you. I go to prepare a place for you. 3 And if I go and prepare a place for you, I will come again and receive you to Myself; that where I am, there you may be also. - NKJV*

Ephesians 4:29-31, *29Watch your talk! No bad words should be coming from your mouth. Say what is good. Your words should help others grow as Christians. 30Do not make God's Holy Spirit have sorrow for the way you live. The Holy Spirit has put a mark on you for the day you will be set free. 31Put out of your life all these things: bad feelings about other people, anger, temper, loud talk, bad talk which hurts other people, and bad feelings which hurt other people. - NLT*

INDEX A
Navy Ranks from the Lowest to the Highest

The table below lists all the standard ranks in the U.S. Navy and their respective pay grades, abbreviations, and classifications and 2020 pay range.

PAYGRADE	RANK	ABBREVIATION	CLASSIFICATION	PAY RANGE
E-1	Seaman Recruit	SR	Junior Enlisted	$1,733 per mo
E-2	Seaman Apprentice	SA	Junior Enlisted	$1,943 per mo
E-3	Seaman	SN	Junior Enlisted	$24,512 - $27,634 per yr
E-4	Petty Officer 3rd Class	PO3	Noncommissioned Officer	$27,151 - $32,958 per yr
E-5	Petty Officer 2nd Class	PO2	Noncommissioned Officer	$29,610 - $42,023 per yr
E-6	Petty Officer 1st Class	PO1	Noncommissioned Officer	$32,324 - $50,065 per yr
E-7	Chief Petty Officer	CPO	Senior Noncommissioned Officer	$37,372 - $67,169 per yr
E-8	Senior Chief Petty Officer	SCPO	Senior Noncommissioned Officer	$53,762 - $76,676 per yr
E-9	Master Chief Petty Officer	MCPO	Senior Noncommissioned Officer	$65,675 - $101,970 per yr
W-2	Chief Warrant Officer 2	CWO2	Warrant Officer	$43,927 - $73,318 per yr
W-3	Chief Warrant Officer 3	CWO3	Warrant Officer	$49,644 - $87,080 per yr
W-4	Chief Warrant Officer 4	CWO4	Warrant Officer	$54,360 - $101,254 per yr
W-5	Chief Warrant Officer 5	CWO5	Warrant Officer	$96,656 - $126,482 per yr

PAY GRADE	RANK	ABBREVIATION	CLASSIFICATION	PAY RANGE
O-1	Ensign	ENS	Commissioned Officer	$39,445 - $49,637 per yr
O-2	Lieutenant Junior Grade	LTJG	Commissioned Officer	$45,450 - $62,896 per yr
O-3	Lieutenant	LT	Commissioned Officer	$52,600 - $85,576 per yr
O-4	Lieutenant Commander	LCDR	Commissioned Officer	$59,825 - $99,889 per yr
O-5	Commander	CDR	Commissioned Officer	$69,336 - $117,799 per yr
O-6	Captain	CAPT	Commissioned Officer	$83,174 - $147,244 per yr
O-7	Rear Admiral Lower Half	RADM (Lower Half)	Flag Officer	$109,681 - $163,872 per yr
O-8	Rear Admiral Upper Half	RADM (Upper Half)	Flag Officer	$131,994 - $190,289 per yr
O-9	Vice Admiral	VADM	Flag Officer	$186,552 - $197,302 per yr
O-10	Admiral	ADM	Flag Officer	$16,442 per mo
O-11	Fleet Admiral*	FADM	Flag Officer	$ N/A

NOTE: These tables do not include housing allowance or food allowance (if the sailor lives off base), sea pay, hazardous duty pay or special pay for jobs like pilot of Navy Seal. https://www.federalpay.org/military/navy/ranks*[117] Retrieved by Kathleen O. Iverson on 11-9-2020[117]

* There were only four people who achieved Fleet Admiral and that rank has not been used since WWII.

INDEX B

THE TWELVE STEPS OF ALCOHOLICS ANONYMOUS

1. We admitted we were powerless over alcohol—that our lives had become unmanageable.

2. Came to believe that a Power greater than ourselves could restore us to sanity.

3. Made a decision to turn our will and our lives over to the care of God as we understood Him.

4. Made a searching and fearless moral inventory of ourselves.

5. Admitted to God, to ourselves, and to another human being the exact nature of our wrongs.

6. Were entirely ready to have God remove all these defects of character

7. Humbly asked Him to remove our shortcomings.

8. Made a list of all persons we had harmed, and became willing to make amends to them all.

9. Made direct amends to such people wherever possible, except when to do so would injure them or others.

10. Continued to take personal inventory and when we were wrong promptly admitted it.

11. Sought through prayer and meditation to improve our conscious contact with God as we understood Him, praying only for knowledge of His will for us and the power to carry that out.

12. Having had a spiritual awakening as the result of these steps, we tried to carry this message to alcoholics, and to practice these principles in all our affairs.

Special Author's Note and Resources

This book has been about my triumphs and struggles with ADHD and co-dependence and how they have affected me throughout my life. Yes, I have had these afflictions, but dealing with them has made me stronger. Accordingly, I have been able to help others, and even keep a sense of humor. That is what I hope you will take away from reading this book: that it is possible to overcome problems caused by ADHD and/or co-dependence, if you are willing to learn about them and work hard at improving. Positive results will probably never amount to 100 percent, but recovery is doable. And you cannot do it alone. Others are needed to assist in your recovery; it is work, but worth it in the end. Learning to rely on a higher power is also a key ingredient, which for some may be harder to do. Just keep an open mind about what you need to do. It is easier if you take small steps toward overcoming these issues. The important thing is that you get qualified people to diagnose you—ask people you trust for recommendations and go to the library to research doctors, who specialize in ADHD and/or co-dependence.

Below are some resources that might help you get started on your journey to find the answers you need:

Alcoholics Anonymous (AA)/aa.org
General Service Office
475 Riverside Drive at West 120th St.
Eleventh and Eighth Floors
New York, NY 10115 Phone: (212) 870-3400

American Psychiatric Association
Phone: Inside U.S. — 888-357-7924
        Outside U.S — 202-559-3900
https://www.psychiatry.org/about-apa/contact-us

Co-dependents Anonymous (CoDA)
A Twelve-Step Recovery program modeled on Alcoholics
Anonymous— +1 888-444-2359 or CoDA.com

Hallowell, Edward M., M.D. *Driven to Distraction.* Anchor Publishing, 13 September, 2011. Accessed 27 February 2023. (Book about ADHD/ADD which is on Amazon.com, where they have a video too.)

National Resource Center (NRC)/ADHD Helpline Health Information Specialists
866-200-8098, Monday-Friday, 1 p.m. — 5 p.m. ET

Made with emojime

WORKS CITED

1. Brown, Les. "Top 25 Quotes By Les Brown (of 176)." *A To Z Quotes.com*, A to Z Quotes, author/2022-Les_Brown, Par 1. Accessed 21 May 2021.

2. Douglass, Frederick. "A Quote by Frederick Douglass." *Goodreads*, Goodreads, https:// www.goodreads.com/quotes/28899-it-is-easier-to-build-strong-children-than-to-repair. Accessed 27 May 2021.

3. Ovid. "A Quote by Ovid." *Goodreads*, Goodreads, https:// www.goodreads.com/quotes/obdura-dolor-hic-tibi-proderit-olim-be-patient. Accessed 21 May 2021.

4. Kornfield, Jack. "A Quote from Buddha's Little Instruction Book." *Goodreads*, Goodreads, https://www.goodreads.com/quotes/41119-if-your-compassion-does-not-include-yourself-it-is-incomplete. Accessed 21 May 2021.

5. Hubbard, Elbert. "Elbert Hubbard Quote." *Goodreads*, Goodreads, https://www.goodreads.com/quotes/16949-a-friend-is-someone-who-knows-all-about-you-and, Accessed 24 January 2022.

6. Summitt, Pat. "Pat Summitt Quote." *A To Z Quotes.com*, A-Z Quotes, https://www.azquotes.com/ quote/933250. Accessed 25 May 2021.

7. Twain, Mark. "A Quote by Mark Twain." *Goodreads*, Goodreads, www.goodreads.com/quotes/ 26149-a-man-cannot-be-comfortable-without-his-own-approval. Accessed 21 May 2021.

8. Hopper, Grace. "Top 25 Quotes by Grace Hopper." *A-Z Quotes.com,* A-Z Quotes, Par 7, https://www.azquotes.com/author/6894-Grace_Hopper. Accessed 26 May 2021.

9. Hopper, Grace. "Top 25 Quotes by Grace Hopper." *A-Z Quotes.com*, A-Z Quotes, Par 13, https://www.azquotes.com/author/6894-Grace_Hopper. Accessed 26 May 2021.

10. Bradshaw, John. "Bradshaw on the Family: A New Way of Creating Solid Self-Esteem." *Health Communications, Inc.*, Deerfield Beach, FL., 1996, p. 87. Accessed 26 April 2022.

11. Bradshaw, John. "Healing the Shame That Binds You." *Health Communications, Inc.*, Deerfield Beach, FL., 1996, Revised Edition, 2005, E.P., p. 69. Accessed 26 April 2022.

12. Bradshaw, John. "Healing the Shame that Binds You." *Health Communications, Inc.*, Deerfield Beach, FL., 1988, Revised Edition, 2005, E.P., p. 54. Accessed 26 April 2022.

13. "Merry-go-round of Denial—Al-Anon World Service Pamphlet, 1969, 2003." *Al-Anon Family Groups.* Al-Anon World Service Office, https://al-anon.org/reprint-permission/for-use-in-publications-outside-of-al-anon. Accessed 8 November 2021.

14. Bradshaw, John. "Bradshaw on the Family: A New Way of Creating Solid Self-Esteem." *Health Communications Inc.,* Deerfield Beach, FL., 1996, P.35. Accessed 2 March 2022.

15. "Symptoms of the Family Disease—Adult Children of Alcoholics (ACOA). *" Adult Children of Alcoholics World Service Office.* Adult Children, https://adultchildren.org// literature/ problem. Accessed 8 November 2021.

16. Bennett, Roy T. "Roy T. Bennett Quotes." *Goodreads,* Goodreads. 2016, https://www.goodreads.com/work/quotes 49604402-the-light-in-the-heart. Accessed 12 May 2021.

17. "Dysfunctional Family Roles." *Out of the Storm website,* Out of the Storm. *"Scapegoat" section, P.1., Par 1 and "Hero" section, P.1., Par 1.,* https://outofthestorm.website/ website/dysfunctional-family-roles. Accessed 8 June 2021.

18. Goetz, John, LPC. "The Mascot Role as Comedian." Family Roles-Edmond Family Articles, *" Edmond Family.org.* (Based on Dr. Murray Bowen's Family Systems Theory), Edmond Family, https://www.edmondfamily.org/efc-articles/family-roles. P.1, Par 3, Sentence 4. Accessed 8 June 2021

19. Niebuhr, Reinhold. "Serenity Prayer." *Wikipedia, The Free Encyclopedia,* Wikimedia Foundation. https://en.wikipedia.org/ wiki/Reinhold_Niebuhr#Serenity_Prayer , Section 9, Par 2. Accessed 11 April 2021.

20. "Digitally Altered Image of 90-Day A.A. Chip." *Author's Personal A.A. Chip, AA Chip.* photo taken 8 June 2021. Accessed 8 June 2021.

21. Bradshaw, John. "Healing the Shame that Binds You." *Health Communications, Inc.,* Deerfield Beach, FL., 1988, Revised Edition, 2005, E.P., P.100. Accessed 2 March 2022.

22. Wikibooks Contributors. "In+Order+to+Develop+Good+Group+Dynamics." *Wikibooks: Open Books for an Open World,* Wikibooks, https://en.m.wikibooks.org/. Accessed 21 May 2021.

23. West, Mae. "Mae West Quotes." *Goodreads,* Goodreads, https://www.goodreads.com /author/show/259666. Mae West. Accessed 11 May 2021.

24. Wikipedia Contributors. "Close Encounters of the Third Kind." *Wikipedia, The Free Encyclopedia,* Wikimedia Foundation, Columbia Pictures, 1978 (Movie directed by Steven Spielberg and performed by Richard Dreyfuss), https://en. wikipedia.org/wiki/Close_Encounters_of_the_Third_Kind , Accessed 20 May 2021.

25. Wikipedia Contributors. "The UFO Experience: A Scientific Inquiry." *Wikipedia, The Free Encyclopedia,* Wikimedia Foundation, Da Capo Press, 1972 edition, (Based on a book by J.Allen Hynek), https://en.wikipedia.org/wiki/Close_ encounter#Close_Encounters_of_the_Third_Kind. Accessed 21 May 2021.

26. Wikipedia Contributors. "Richard Dreyfuss: The Goodbye Girl." *Wikipedia, The Free Encyclopedia,* Wikipedia, 29 June 2021, https://en.wikipedia.org/wiki/Richard_Dreyfuss. Accessed 11 July 2021.

27. Wikipedia Contributors. "Personal Recollections of Author, Kathleen O. Iverson of Being an Acquaintance of Carrie Snodgress in the 1970s." *Kathleen O. Iverson, 1974-1975.* Accessed/recollected 19 June 2019.

28. Wikipedia Contributors. "Carrie Snodgress." *Wikipedia, The Free Encyclopedia,* Wikipedia, https://en.wikipedia. org/wiki/Carrie_Snodgress. Accessed 30 April 2021.

29. Wikipedia Contributors. "Chicago (band)." *Wikipedia, The Free Encyclopedia,* Wikipedia, 14 June 2021, https://en.wikipedia.org/ w/index.php?title= Chicago_(band)& oldid=1028465823. Accessed 26 June. 2021.

30. Wikipedia Contributors. "Chicago and the Beach Boys Together - Summer of '75 Tour." *Wikipedia, The Free Encyclopedia,* Wikipedia, Chicago Stadium Concerts, produced by James Guercio/Steve Love, June 1-7, 1975, https://en.Wikipedia.org/wiki / The Beach Boys, 1970–1978: Reprise era, Par 8. Accessed 26 June, 2021.

31. "Digitally Altered Image of the Fifth Dimension 1969." *The Fifth Dimension— Wikimedia Commons,* Wikimedia Commons. https://www.commons.wikimedia.org. Accessed 29 March 2021.

32. "Digitally Altered Image of Americana Hotel 1962." *Americana Hotel– Wikimedia Commons, The Free Media Repository,* Wikimedia Commons. https://commons.wikimedia.org/w/index.php?search=Americana+Hotel& title=Special:Media Search&go=Go&type=image. Accessed 29 March 2021.

33. "Digitally Altered Image of Steve Goodman's 45 record." *Buddah Records 1971 /Author, Kathleen O. Iverson's Personal Collection.* Producers: James Guercio /Steve Love, Accessed 30 March 2021.

34. "Digitally Altered Image of Miss North Shore Contestants." *Pioneer Press Newspaper—Northbrook, IL Edition Ad Clipping,* Pioneer Press, 1975. Accessed 29 March 2021.

35. Salt, *Bernard. "Bernard Salt Quotes." Goodreads,* Goodreads, https://www.goodreads.com/aurhor/quotes/393016.Bernard_Salt. Accessed 27 Jun 2021.

36. Wikipedia Contributors. "Robert F. Kennedy's Speech on the Assassination of Martin Luther King Jr." *Wikipedia, The Free Encyclopedia,* Wikipedia, Section 3-Summary of Indianapolis Speech, https://en.wikipedia.org/wiki/Robert_F_Kennedy%27s_ speech_on_the_assassination of Martin_Luther_King_Jr., 4 April 1968. Accessed 14 Jun. 2021.

37. Wikipedia Contributors. "David A. Kennedy." *Wikipedia, The Free Encyclopedia,* Wikipedia, *Paragraphs 1, 3 and 7.*

   https://en.wikipedia.org/w/index.php?title=David_A._Kennedy&oldid=1105 482020. Accessed October 31, 2022.

38. Wikipedia Contributors. "Kent State Shootings." *Wikipedia, The Free Encyclopedia,* Wikipedia, Wikimedia Foundation, 6 May 2021, https://en.wikipedia.org/w/index.php?title=Kent_State_shooting &oldid=1021837843. Accessed 10 May 2021

39. "The Decision to Go to the Moon: President John F. Kennedy's May 25, 1961 Speech before a Joint Session of Congress." *National Aeronautics and Space Administration / NASA History Office / NASA.* https://www.history.nasa.gov/moondec.html. Accessed 27 May 2021.

40. Cloud, Henry. "Henry Cloud Quotes (Author of Boundaries)." *Goodreads,* Goodreads, https://www.goodreads.com/author/quotes/ 1114699.Henry_Cloud. Par 1. Accessed 22 May 21.

41. Keller, Helen. "A Quote by Helen Keller." *Goodreads,* Goodreads, https://www.goodreads.com4811-character-cannot-be-developed-in-ease-and-quiet-only-through#. Accessed 22 May 2021.

42. O' Bon Paris Contributors. "The 5 Best Markets in Paris." *O' Bon Paris.* O' Bon Paris: Easy to Be Parisian - Marché Mouffetard, 20 May 2019, https://www.obonparis.com/en/magazine/best-markets-in-paris. Accessed 21 May 2021.

43. Farnsworth, Clyde H. Special to The New York Times. "Labor Troubles Spread in France." *The New York Times Archives,* The New York Times, 30 October 1974, https://www.nytimes.com/1974/10/30/archives/labor-troubles-spread-in-france-postal-walkout-in-11th-day-unrest.html. Accessed 10 April 2021. (This is a digitized version of an article from The Times' print archive, before the start of online publication in 1996.)

44. "Digitally Altered Image of Hugh Weiss (1995)." *Wikimedia Commons, The Free Media Repository.* Wikimedia Commons, https://commons.wikimedia.org/w/index.php?title=File:Hugh_Weiss_(1995).png&oldid=56600 18993. Accessed 27 June 2021.

45. "Digitally Altered Image of St. Norbert College by Royalbroil, 2 February 2014." *Wikimedia Commons, The Free Media Repository.* Wikimedia Commons, https://commons.wikimedia.org/w/index.php?title=File:Old_Main_Hall_St._Norbert_College.jpg&oldid=506852933. Accessed 27 June 2021.

46. "Digitally Altered Image of Mouffetard Market in Paris, France." *Wikimedia Commons, The Free Media Repository.* Wikimedia Commons. photo by Suvodeb Banerjee, https://commons.wikimedia.org/wiki/File:Market_Mouffetard_Paris_15_October_2009.jpg. Accessed 12 September 2020.

47. Condie, *Ally. "Ally Condie Quotes." Matched, 2010/ Goodreads, Goodreads,* 2021, https://www.goodreads.com /author/show/ 1304470.Ally_Condie. Accessed 27 Jun 2021.

48. Stahl, Michael. "Mike Stahl Recalls: Mixing Chicago in the 1970s: The engineering approach with a seminal fusion group, along with anecdotes and experiences from a unique time…" *ProSoundWeb.* ProSoundWeb, *and Author's Personal Recollections,* 11 July 2014. Republished, 26 July 2019. Accessed 27 June 2021

49. ProSoundWeb (PSW) Staff. "Pro Audio Veteran Mike Stahl Passes Away at 68: Legendary Sound Engineer and Businessman." *ProSoundWeb. ProSoundWeb, and Author's Personal Recollections,* 24 September 2014, https://www.prosoundweb.com/ ?s=Mike+Stahl. Accessed 1 July-2021.

50. "Digitally Altered Image of Mike Stahl at a Clair Bros. console, 'back in the day' as a Sound Engineer in the 1970s." *ProSoundWeb.* ProSoundWeb, 11 July 2014, http://www.prosoundweb.com/ article/article/print/mike_stahl_mixing_chicago. Accessed 5 June 2016.

51. "Digitally Altered Image of "Chicago and the Beach Boys Live at Chicago Stadium—Beachago Tour—3 June 1975." *Barbara Alpert and Author's Ticket Illustration,* Chicago, IL. Created 7 November 2022.

52. Brokaw, Tom. "The Greatest Generation Quotes." *Goodreads.* Goodreads, https://www.goodreads.com/work/com/work/quotes/ 1040051-the-greatest-generation, Par 4. Accessed 20 May 2021.

53. Whiting, William and John Bacchus Dykes. *"Eternal Father Strong to Save/The Navy Hymn—1861." Wikimedia Commons, The Free Media Repository,* Wikimedia Commons, https://commons.wikimedia.org https://commons.wikimedia.org/wiki/File:Eternal_Father__U.S._Navy_ Band.ogg. Accessed 8 July 2021.

54. Wikipedia Contributors. "Situational Leadership Theory." *Wikipedia, the Free Encyclopedia,* Wikipedia, (As mentioned in *Management of Organizational Behavior*, 1982, by Paul Hersey and Ken Blanchard), https://en.wikipedia.org/w/index. php?title=Situational_leadership_ theory&oldid=1012757549, 18 March 2021. Accessed 9 July 2021.

55. Cloud, Henry. "Henry Cloud Quotes (Author of Boundaries)." *Goodreads*, Goodreads, https://www.goodreads.com/author/ quotes/1114699.Henry_Cloud. Par 1. Accessed 22 May 21.

56. "Immigration and Relocation in U.S. History-Irish-Catholic Immigration to America." *Library of Congress,* Library of Congress. https://www.loc.gov/classroom-materials/immigration/irish/irish-catholic-immigration-to-america, Par 3. Accessed 22 May 21.

57. "United States Federal Census-1900." *National Archives and Records Administration.* NARA Microfilm Publication T623. Roger Spillane, Precinct 17 Chicago City Ward 20, Cook, Illinois, United States; Enumeration District (ED) 633, Sheet 13A, Family 246. Accessed 10 July 2021.

58. "Chicago City Directory, 1900." *U.S. Telephone Directory Collection.* Library of Congress, Library of Congress. https://www.loc. gov/item/usteledirec 04765x/. Accessed 10 July 2021.

59. "Chicago Police Department Homicide Record Index. "Victim: Thomas R. Spillane." *Coroner's Inquest Case,* Coroner's Inquest Case, Number 50461 of 10 December 1913 at the 27th Precinct. (Fatally shot at Clinton and Harrison Streets by Archie Carroll, a watchman with whom he had some trouble.) Charge: Manslaughter. Date of Offense:7 December 1913, Chicago, IL. On 7 July 1914, Carroll was sent to Joliet Pen - Judge Brentano, https://homicide.northwestern.edu/search/?s=Spillane/. Accessed 12 July 2021.

60. "United States Federal Census: Fourteenth—1920." *National Archives and Records Administration* (NARA). NARA Microfilm Publications T625 B – C, John O'Brien, Chicago City Ward 13, Cook, Illinois, Enumeration District (ED) 728, Sheet 2B, Family 41. Accessed 13 July 1998.

61. Cloud, Henry. "Henry Cloud Quotes (Author of Boundaries)." *Goodreads*, Goodreads, https://www.goodreads. com/author/quotes/1114699.Henry_Cloud, Par 2. Accessed 22 May 21.

62. Moore, LeCrae. "Top 25 Quotes by LeCrae." *A to Z Quotes*, A to Z Quotes, https://www.azquotes.com/author/_49889-LeCrae. Accessed 12 July 2021.

63. "Digitally Altered Image of 1960s-Like McDonald's Ad." *Created and Drawn by Author, Kathleen O. Iverson to simulate old McDonald's products in 1969.* Accessed 7 November 2022.

64. "Digitally Altered Image of Regina Dominican High School Seal, Wilmette, IL." *Wikimedia Commons, The Free Media Repository,* Wikimedia Commons. https://commons.wikimedia.org/wiki/Category:Willmette,_ Illinois. Accessed 14 July 2021.

65. "Digitally Altered Image of Loyola Academy's Football Game Against Gordon Tech. High School with Tight End Keith on the Right Ramming a Gordon Tech. Player at Chicago Soldier Field, 1969." *Loyola Academy.* Loyola Academy, (Newspaper Clipping of unknown origin, Author, Kathleen O'Brien Iverson's Personal Collection). Accessed 31 March 2021.

66. "Digitally Altered Image of Gillson Park, Wilmette, IL Sign." *Wilmette Park District.* Wilmette Park District, Author, Kathleen O'Brien Iverson's Personal Collection (Unknown origin). Accessed 14 July 2021.

67. Lewis, C. S. "C. S. Lewis Quotes." *Goodreads*, Goodreads, https://www.goodreads.com/quotes/ 257243-the-pain-i-feel-now-is-the-happiness-i-had. Accessed 14 July 2021.

68. Wikipedia Contributors. "Mid-60's Psychedelic Culture, Acid Rock." *Wikipedia, The Free Encyclopedia*, Wikipedia, https://en.wikipedia.org/w/index.php?title=Acid_ rock&oldid=1023323143, Par 1, Accessed 23 September 2019.

69. "Digitally Altered Image of "'The Des Pères' Yearbook Cover." *St. Norbert College (SNC) Yearbook: The Des Pères —1972.* St. Norbert College, Co-Editors: Bob Sklade and Terry Meier, cover art and poem by Author, Kathleen O'Brien Iverson; cover photo by SNC staff photographers. Accessed July 14, 2021.

70. "Digitally Altered Image of "'The Des Pères' Yearbook Cover." *St. Norbert College (SNC) Yearbook: The Des Pères—1973.* St. Norbert College, Editor: David J. Hornung, photo by SNC staff photographers. Accessed July 14, 2021.

71. "Digitally Altered Image of "Kathleen's Theta Phi Sorority Sisters Photo" *St. Norbert College (SNC) Yearbook: The Des Pères—1973.* St. Norbert College, Editor: David J. Hornung, photo by SNC Staff Photographers, P.100. Accessed July 14, 2021.

72. "Digitally Altered Image of the "Gare du Nord (North Train Station) Paris, France." *Wikipedia, the Free Encyclopedia,* Wikipedia. photo by pxhildago, https://en.wikipedia.org/wiki/Gare_du_Nord. Accessed 14 July 2021.

73. "Digitally Altered Image of Nice, France." *Wikipedia, The Free Encyclopedia,* Wikipedia. https://en.wikipedia. org/wiki/ Nice, France. Accessed 4 March 2021.

74. Suzuki, Ranata. *"Quotes By Ranata Suzuki, 2021."* Goodreads, Goodreads, https://www.goodreads.com/author/quotes/ 16288605.Ranata_Suzuki. Accessed 15 Jul 2021.

75. Rumi. "Top 25 Quotes by Rumi (of 1775)." *A-Z Quotes,* A-Z Quotes, https://www.azquotes.com/author/12768-Rumi?p=44. Accessed 23 September 2019.

76. Johnson, Samuel. "Samuel Johnson Quotes." *Goodreads*, Goodreads, https://www.goodreads.com/ quotes/ 1301825-a-second-marriage-is- a-triumph-of-hope-over-experience, Par 1. Accessed 15 July 2021.

77. Wikipedia Contributors. "Divorce and Divorce Demography." *Wikipedia, The Free Encyclopedia,* Wikipedia, https:// en.wikipedia.org › wiki › Divorce_demography and https://en.wikipedia.org › wiki ›Divorce. Accessed 24 October 2022.

78. SparkNotes Contributors. "The Scarlet Letter by Nathaniel Hawthorn—Plot Overview Summary." *SparkNotes,* SparkNotes, https://www.sparknotes.com/lit/scarlet/summary, Par 1. Accessed 22 September 2021.

79. Bradshaw, John. "Healing the Shame that Binds You." *Health Communications, Inc.,* Deerfield Beach, FL., 1988, Revised Edition, 2005, E.P., P.11. Accessed 2 May 2022.

80. "Digitally Altered Image of Rear Admiral Mack Gaston, Commander, Naval Training Center, Great Lakes, IL (1992-1995)." *Naval Historical*

Foundation, U.S. Navy Oral History Project. https://www.navyhistory.org/
oral-history-rear-admiral-mack-gaston. Accessed 17 July 2021.

81. "Digitally Altered Image of Admiral Jeremy 'Mike' Boorda." *Naval History
and Heritage Command.* Navy Department Library, Navy Department
Library,
https://www.history.navy.mil/content/content/history/nhhc/research/histories
/biographies-list/bios-b/boorda-jeremy-m.html. Accessed 19 July 2021.

82. "Digitally Altered Image of US Navy Northrop DT-38A Talon at NAS Miramar
in 1974." *Wikimedia Commons, the Free Media Repository,* Wikimedia.
https://commons.wikimedia.org/ w/index.php? title=File:US_ Northrop_DT-
3 8A_Talon_at_NAS_Miramar_in_1974.jpg&oldid=556104925. Accessed
20 March 2021.

83. Wikipedia Contributors. "Tim Berners-Lee (inventor of the World Wide Web)."
Wikipedia, The Free Encyclopedia, Wikipedia,
https://en.wikipedia.org/w/index.php?title=Tim_Berners- Lee&oldid=
1033422852. Accessed 19 July 2021.

84. Wikipedia Contributors. "Mother Teresa Quote." *Wikipedia, The Free
Encyclopedia.* Wikipedia, https://en. wikipedia.org/ w/index.php?title=
Mother_Teresa&oldid=1036935808. Accessed. 3 Aug. 2021.

85. Von Heitlinger, Eugene. "Lake Shore Drive." *Lake Shore Drive,* (Performed by
Aliotta, Haynes, and Jeremiah)."/*Songtrust Ave., 1971.* Accessed 2 May
2021.

86. "Digitally Altered Image of Lake Shore Drive, Chicago, IL." *Wikipedia, The
Free Encyclopedia.* Wikipedia. https://en.wikipedia.org/wiki/Lake_Shore_
Drive. Accessed 19 July 2021.

87. Wikipedia Contributors. "John Philip Sousa." *Wikipedia, The Free
Encyclopedia,* Wikipedia. https://en.Wikipedia.org/
w/index.php?title=John_Philip_Sousa&oldid=1032199844. Accessed 21
Jul. 2021.

88. Wikipedia Contributors. "Naval Training Station Great Lakes Summary
(Section 1.0) and History1846-1960 (Section 2.4)." *Wikipedia, The Free
Encyclopedia,* Wikipedia. https://en.wikipedia.org/index.php?title=
Naval_Station_Great_ Lakes&oldid=1021020750. (Note: Base also has been
known as NTC, Naval Training Center). Accessed 22 July 2021.

89. "Rear Admiral Mack Gaston, Commander, Naval Training Center (NTC), Great
Lakes, IL (1992-1995)." *Naval Historical Foundation-U.S. Navy Oral*

History Project. Naval Historical Foundation, https://www.navy history.org/oral-history-rear-admiral-mack-gaston. Accessed 17 July 2021.

90. Burton, Dan, et al. "United States, Congress, House of Representatives, Committee on Government Reform and Oversight." *Hearing on Total Quality Management Before the Subcommittee on Government Management, Information, And Technology*. Government Printing Office, 1998, 105th Congress, First Session, June 9, 1997, Serial No. 105-62, https://www.govinfo.gov/content/ pkg/CHRG-105hhrg45403/html/CHRG-105hhrg45403.htm. Accessed 19 July 2021.

91. "Admiral Jeremy M. Boorda." *Naval History and Heritage Command*. Navy Department Library, https://www.history.navy.mil/ content/history/nhhc/search.html?q=Admiral+Boorda. Accessed 19 July 2021.

92. Wikipedia Contributors. "Michael Boorda." *Wikipedia, The Free Encyclopedia,* Wikipedia, and Author, Kathleen O. Iverson's Personal Recollections, 7 Oct. 2022. Accessed 19 July 2022.

93. "Digitally Altered Video of the US Naval Gunnery School, Building 521, Great Lakes SSC, Gunners Mate." *U.S. Navy- Youtube.com.* Naval Station Great Lakes, IL., https://www.youtube.com/watch?v=NYbLQDNZd10. Accessed 31 October, 2022.

94. Greenwood, Lee. "God Bless the USA (I'm Proud to Be an American)." *MAC Nashville,* 1984. Accessed 22 July 2021.

95. Fogelberg, Dan. "Leader of the Band." *Sony/ ATV Music Publishing LLC*, 1991. Accessed 13 May 2021.

96. "Digitally Altered Image of the Gun School, Great Lakes, IL. and Summary (Sections 1 and 2)." *Wikipedia, The Free Encyclopedia.* Wikipedia. https://en Wikipedia.org/wiki/Naval_Station_ Great_Lakes. (Note: Base also has been known as NTC, Naval Training Center). Accessed 1 August 2021.

97. Jordan, Michael. "Failure gave me strength. Pain was my motivation." *A to Z Quotes.com,* A-Z Quotes. https:// www. azquotes.com/quote/644546. Accessed 22 July 2021.

98. Robbins, Tim. *Dead Man Walking*. Director. Gramercy Pictures, December 29, 1995.

99. "Digitally Altered Image of Building One, Naval Training Station, Great Lakes, IL." *Wikipedia, The Free Encyclopedia,* Wikipedia, Section 1.0, https://en.

Wikipedia.org/wiki/Naval_Station_Great_ Lakes. Note: (Base also has been known as NTC, Naval Training Center). Accessed 22 July 2021.

100. Bucchianeri, E.A. "EA. Bucchianeri Quotes." Brushstrokes of a Gadfly, 2011, Batalha Publishers, Goodreads, Goodreads, https://www.goodreads.com/work/quotes/16351434-brushstrokes-of-a-gadfly-gadfly-saga-1. Accessed 24 July 2021.

101. Wikipedia Contributors. "Bozoma Saint John." *Wikipedia, The Free Encyclopedia*, Wikipedia, https:/en.wikipedia.org/w/index.php?title=Bozama_Saint_John&oldid=1031001184. Accessed 24 July 2021.

102. Prine, John. "Bruised Orange (Chain of Sorrow)." *American Recording Studios, 1978.* Accessed 23 May 2021.

103. Read, Kimberly. "Warning Signs to Be Aware of in Suicidal Bipolar Patients." *Very Well, Bipolar Disorder/Very Well Mind*, Very Well, 19 Aug. 2019, https://www.verywellmind.com/red-flags-warning-signs-of- Updated 23 March 2020. Accessed 11 April 2020.

104. Jamison, Dr. Kay Redfield. *An Unquiet Mind: A Memoir of Moods and Madness*. Random House, 1995.

105. Duke, Patty. *Call Me Anna*. Penguin Random House, 1998.

106. "Digitally Altered Image of Bozama St. John." *Wikimedia Commons, The Free Media Repository,* Wikimedia Commons. Mad Works, photo by Maya A. Darasaw, https://wikimedia.org/wikipedia/ commons/2/20/Bozama_ Saint_John_%28Photo_Cred_-_Maya_A_Darasaw%2C_MAD_Works_ Photography%29.jpg. Accessed 16 November 2020.

107. Wikimedia Contributors. "File: Willow Creek Community Church sign.jpg." *Wikimedia Commons, The Free Media Repository,* Wikipedia Commons. photo by Gabriel Lerma, https://commons.wikimedia.org/ww/index. php?title =File:Willow_Creek_ Community_Church_sign.jpg&oldid=530772984. Accessed 6 August 2021.

108. "Digitally Altered Image of Gloria Estefan at the Kennedy Center Honors Ceremony (with Article)." *Wikimedia Commons,* Wikimedia Commons, U.S. State Department, 3 Dec. 2017, https://www.commons.wikimedia.org/w/index.php?search = Gloria+Estefan. Accessed 29 March 2021.

109. "Digitally Altered Image of John Prine at Merlefest (with Article)." *Wikimedia Commons.* Wikimedia Foundation, Inc., 2006. photo by Ron Baker,

https://commons.wikimedia.org/w/index.php? title=File:John_Prine_by_Ron_Bak_er.jpg&oldid=488236210. Accessed 9 September 2020.

110. Wimbrow, Peter Dale, Sr. "The Guy In The Glass" (Also, known as "The Man in the Glass.") 1934, *theguyintheglass.com*, theguyintheglass, 1998, https://www.theguyintheglass.com/gig.htm. Accessed 22 September 2019.

111. Jami, Criss. "Criss Jami Quotes." *CreateSpace*, 2015, *Goodreads*, Goodreads. https://www.goodreads. com/ author/show/4860176.Criss_Jami. Accessed 27 July 2021.

112. Pierce, Jonathan. "Farther Than Your Grace Can Reach." *Mission Album, produced by Bob Parr*, 1997, https:// www.youtube.com/watch?v=Pua4qANuijw. Accessed 27 July 2021.

113. Wikipedia Contributors. "Grace in Christianity." *Wikipedia, The Free Encyclopedia*. Wikipedia, https://en. wikipedia.org/ w/index.php?title= Grace_in_Christianity&oldid=1102022729. Accessed. 24 October 2022

114. Douglas, Donna. "He'll Find a Way." *Lorenz Corporation*, 1988 (Performed by Billy and Sarah Gaines), https://www.youtube.com/watch?7v=C1W94dGLULI. Accessed 30 July 2021.

115. Catalano, Connie Jean. *Love Life of a Single Christian*. XULON Press, 2014, PP. 121-122.

116. Miller, Ronald N. and Orlando Murden. "For Once in My Life." *Motown's Tamla Label / Sony /ATV Music Publishing LLC, 1968* (Performed by Stevie Wonder). Accessed 30 July 2021.

117. "Index A -Table of Navy Standard Ranks from the Lowest to the Highest. Enlisted, Warrant Officer and Commissioned Officer Pay Range, 2020." *United States Navy*, https://federalpay.org/military/navy/ranks. Accessed 9 November 2020.

118. Index B -Wikipedia Contributors. "Twelve-Step Program." *Wikipedia, The Free Encyclopedia,* Wikipedia, Par 5, The Twelve Steps originally produced by members of Alcoholics Anonymous (A.A.) and published by A.A. World Services, Inc., © 1952, 1953, 1981, Rev. 8/16 SMF-121 / General Service Office, https://en.wikipedia.org/wiki/Twelve-step_program. Accessed 10 August 2021.

Made in the USA
Columbia, SC
29 July 2023

21024951R00183